MW00352819

Slipping on Concrete

Slipping on Concrete

❦

A.E. Derban

A.E. DERBAN

CONTENTS

Prelude

<u>Sometime in the sixties</u>

Andrea pushed against the door a little harder to get into the bedroom she shared with her older sister Renee. Upon entering the room, she discovered the wet towel behind the door. Renee raced to close the door before it was wrenched wider than the width of sister's slim frame. She stuffed the wet towel back underneath the door and locked it. Andrea looked at her sister quizzically.

"Girl, what are you doing? It's bad enough we almost got killed last time we tried smoking in the house. Your fast ass gonna get us killed again," exclaimed Andrea.

"Look, this a new kind of cigarette. Mama and Daddy ain't never even heard of it," Renee prodded her younger sister. Renee took a long drag from the cigarette-like substance. It looked like one of the homegrown cigarettes their great Aunt Effie used to smoke, sans the sweet-smelling aroma. This brand was out of the ordinary. "Besides Mama and Daddy at the Lounge on 125th—they won't be back until morning. Uncle Butchie having some kind of party or something." Andrea, still skeptical, walked to the window and checked the driveway.

"Well, let me open a window or something 'cause that shit stink!"

"Don't! Then the neighbors will smell it simple ass. It's natural and you can't die from it and it makes you feel real good. Here take a hit."

"You better not touch me."

"Stupid, I ain't gonna hit you...I mean take a pull, a toke."

"Oh."

"Don't pull on it too hard like a cigarette or it'll go straight to your head." Andrea took the small, tightly rolled white joint hesitantly. She took a long drag against her sister's advice and immediately choked the smoke out through her nostrils and mouth.

"Oooh, now what's this called?" she asked, passing the joint back to Renee.

"I don't know. Solomon passed it to me in the club last night. It's a new kind of cigarette like I said."

"Oh, you saw Solomon last night? He asked for me?"

"Let me tell you 'bout that motha......"

What about your friends?

I grew up with some interesting characters in New York. People I've met in my lifetime have told me that the stories I have told them about my childhood have to be false. Furthermore, the people do not exist. Well, you can make that distinction. Some of the people are real, some aren't; some of the situations are real; some aren't. But I did want to let someone know that we've been there, done that, and there is always a way. I hope you're entertained, educated, and inspired. Most of all, I hope you remember your real friends. They're the ones that God sent you. These stories involve Isa, Kim, and Sage three friends who lose themselves and find themselves again.

1

Book One: Beginning of the Fall

CHAPTER 1: *JULY 1987*
Sage

No one ever taught me how to be a friend. It's something I learned through experiences. I learned what I liked and what I didn't like and then one day I hope to pass those pearls of wisdom on to my children in a purposeful way. I had friends: Isa, Kim, Jewel, and Billie. However, I didn't know how to be a friend or what to expect from one. I was just going through the motions. If it was easier to go along with the crowd then that's what I did. I wasn't different from anybody else in the world, but sometimes I wish I was. It takes courage to be your own person and at twelve, I didn't have one cup. I *did* have a seed and I was going to grow that seed even though I didn't know where to plant it. Finding fertile ground in New York City was impossible.

"You African booty-scratcher! I will punch you right in your mother-fucking mouth! Dummy," hollered Isa, embarrassed.

You know, it wouldn't have been so bad if she hadn't been the one to ask me to do it. Isa asked me to find out if Cream, a very light skinned, skinny boy with a peanut head, mean streak, and a near genius intelligence, liked her. Only *then* was I supposed to say she liked him too. This was a very common scenario in our neighborhood—Concourse Village or as we called it--The Vill located in the heart of the South Bronx. Half of the girls in the neighborhood liked Cream. In fact, he had been a boyfriend to the majority of them as well. Isa was just the latest one to fall under Cream's spell. Somehow the kung-fu grip he had on the other girls held no power over me. It's not that he wasn't cute; he just wasn't my cup of tea.

"Who are you talking to?! Didn't you say you wanted me to tell him you liked him?" I answered back in a voice mixed with fear and agitation. I didn't like confrontations, had never been in a fight, and Isa was supposed to be my friend. It felt like *everyone* in The Vill was watching and listening.

"Not until he said he liked me first stupid! Now he over there laughing with his friends and shit!" Isa said continuing the insults.

With tears in my eyes, which I refused to let drop, I quietly answered.

"That's what I did. He was laughing because one of my braids slipped out in front of them." Isa looked at me as if she were trying to decide if I were lying. She rolled her eyes and started chuckling.

"Girl, I was just playing!" She offered. I just turned and walked toward my building on the Grand Concourse. It was only two in the afternoon in the middle of that hot July day. I had taken all I was going to take; my skin had already begun to thicken against the slights one grows up with in the inner city.

As kids often do, they home in on the one thing you feel ashamed of and exploit it for the world to see. I had never been ashamed of my Ghanaian heritage until that moment. Isa's insult felt so much like a slap because I actually was African, and Isa knew it. Both of my parents were born and raised in Ghana and imparted in both me and my brother a strong sense of pride in our culture especially because we were born in America. But I felt like I always had to defend it. While Isa had added to my embarrassment that day, I saw something in Isa's face that I would not see again until we were damn near adults: shame.

Isa

"Sage where you going?" I yelled.

"Home! Don't talk to me," she yelled back. Sage gets on my last nerve. I stood by myself watching her walk through the parking lot by herself. She always act like somebody doing something to her on purpose. She always be crying to make somebody feel bad. I do not. Me and Sage been friends since before ever. Then Kim got cool with us and then that's the way it was. Sage real skinny with big lips and a little head; she dark-skinned and cute, but guys like me more cause I'm light and got long hair. She walking away like I'm gonna chase her; I ain't. I'ma stay right here and talk to Cream. Don't nobody got time for her bullshit.

I don't like being laughed at. How was I supposed to know they wasn't laughing at me? I can't read minds. Kim, Billie, and Jewel looking at me like I did something wrong but they ain't gonna say nothing to me. Matter of fact nobody ever tells me when I'm wrong. I get away with a lot of shit. I'm loud and mean and I like getting my way, but Sage makes me feel bad when I act like that. She's my friend but I ain't gonna change who I am for nobody. Cream walked up next to me.

"Isa that shit was funny as hell," he laughed. I looked at him like he was out his fucking mind.

"You crazy? That's my friend. Don't be laughing at her," I told him rolling my eyes. I hate stupid people. He turned red like a cherry Blow Pop.

"Who you think you talking to?"

"I'm talking to you and if you keep on talking shit about my girl I ain't going to be talking to you at all. Call me later," I turned around to Kim Billie, and Jewel, "Come on ya'll, walk me to my building. I have to go upstairs; my mother told me to meet her up there."

My mother didn't need me. I wanted to go upstairs and call Sage and make sure she was alright. Even though she was crying she was kinda acting funny. She yelled at me and stood up for herself; that was new to me.

She didn't answer the phone and she wouldn't come outside anymore. Sage wouldn't answer the phone for anyone but Jewel. After she didn't answer the next day, I was like forget it. I don't kiss nobody ass. Next thing I knew, Sage went to go live with her mother in California; she was only supposed to be gone for the summer. I didn't think I would see her ever again. I was meaner than ever.

CHAPTER 2: *JUNE 1988*

-

Sage

My brother A.J. and I had spent a year in California living with my mother. Living with our mother was hard. I thought it was going to be so much fun; I thought the gifts that she sent A.J. and I in New York during holidays and our birthdays and the summer shopping would be enhanced by living with her. She was so glamorous to me. I don't think I really saw her for who she was; I saw who I wanted to see. When our parents divorced initially, A.J. and I chose to live with our father. I don't think my mother forgave that act of betrayal. She never missed an opportunity to remind us that she knew we loved our father more than we loved her. It wasn't true; unfortunately, we could never convince her otherwise. I believe her position on that took a toll on the relationship between me and her especially.

What I didn't take into account was the fact that A.J. and I would be inserting ourselves into the life she set up with her new husband and his two kids. It probably would have been a better idea if she had spent one year getting acclimated to their new combination before my brother and I came into the picture. A.J. she adored. He was her prince and perfect, which I didn't mind because I felt the same way about him too. Whenever it came to her and me however, we just couldn't get it right. Then she came up with a bright idea. She tried to show me what a relationship between a mother and daughter was supposed to look like by holding my stepsister in the highest regard. *Oh, look at Toni's long hair and her breasts are forming nicely...look at how the boys look at her and she dresses so lady-like.* To me, it sounded like, *you skinny, flat-chested, bald-headed, boy-how is it possible that you are my child?* Her plan to bolster my confidence by highlighting my stepsister failed miserably. I not only resented her; I couldn't stand my stepsister either. After a few months of the arguments and the rivers of tears I shed, I tried to stop caring about what my mother thought and worked on my own self-esteem the best way I knew how: I went back to my father who loved me as I was. My mother actually looked hurt—especially because A.J. was leaving as well. In retrospect I guess she handled things the best way that she knew how. I just didn't have enough in me to wait for her to get it right.

Kim's high-pitched voice cut into my thoughts. "Girl, what do you mean you've never heard of Rob Base?! You lying! You ain't never heard of *It Takes Two?*" panted Kim exhausted. Kim and I were walking to Isa's building. Kim's astonishment at my not having heard of the latest rapper and rap song to hit the East Coast was irritating. It was a constant reminder of

how much I had missed and how far behind I was in New York fashion, music, and slang. There was a bunch of us who grew up together including Jewel, Isa, Kim, Sienna, Donna, and Billie, who visited NY during the summers. But Kim, Isa and I were the closest of us all.

Kim was twelve, a year younger than me and Isa, but more 'experienced' so the rumors went. She was short and had light skin so in her mind that made her beautiful and popular and privileged—Isa was the same way. As with most spoiled children, she was often selfish and wanted her way. She was the youngest of three children by seven years and the only girl. Strangely, her personality was different from Isa's. Kim was always nice to everyone and never did a thing to anyone out of spite. It was her only constant inconsistency.

Kim had spent the better half of the night before teaching me *the Bus Stop, the Kid and Play,* and *the Benetton.* These dances came like breathing to me now. Kim made sure I knew them perfectly. Kim's fresh *Jheri*

Curl glistened about her head as she worked my last nerve. I made a silent wish for her silence as I fingered the braids, I had done myself. I kind of missed my curl too, but it had taken my hair out. Kim and I were going to get Isa because Isa's mother always thought she was up to no good. While that was true most of the time, her mother had no evidence to base that on. Luckily for all of us Isa's mother, who we all called Auntie, thought my father was very strict with me because we were African. I did excel in school and was ever respectful, thusly, I was knighted the *good one*. I was living, breathing, *freedom papers* for all of my friends. But really, birds of a feather flock together. We did everything together.

Isa's pug nose and full mouth met in a pout. Her hair was a sandy brown with sun-bleached blond highlights and in her ever-present ponytail. She had small eyes which became slits whenever she laughed. She and Kim shared the same complexion, but Isa was chunky and taller.

Isa met us halfway to her building. When we got there Isa started the delegation of duties. "Alright ladies," Isa began, "Kim you go in 775 and me and Sage will to 779 and get the rest of the girls if they not outside," Always in charge.

Thankfully, Kim agreed. I needed to talk with Isa alone.

Kim was going to get Donna while we got the other crew members. I had always had some tension with Donna considering she tortured me as a child. There were so many times she punched me so hard it made my mouth bleed. She was just as tall and skinny as I was but her abrasive language and her eagerness to fight even boys struck terror in my heart. She was always so quick to temper and not opposed to making a scene. I wanted to let Isa know if Donna started up with her nonsense, I was out of there. I had no intention on fighting. I never really saw any point in it. I told Isa I was not brawling in the street. Donna was bad by herself but with a battery like Isa in her back, she was a ridiculous kind of mean. Isa was a first-class instigator and proud of it. By the end of the day, the speech I gave Isa was all for nothing.

Everyone except Donna was assembled outside by the time Isa and I came from the building. The smile that spread across my face was immediately erased when I saw my younger brother crying. My brother did not cry. He was a 'boy's boy', so someone had to be dead or something to that effect.

"A.J. what happened?" I asked while trying to hold him still.

"That stupid Donna hit me cause I wouldn't give her my dollar!" my brother shrieked.

"Did she take your dollar?" I asked calmly.

"Hell no! But you know I couldn't hit her back cause she a girl! But ooh!" My brother was punching the palms of his hands and an imaginary target I assumed was Donna.

All eyes were on me. Funny, Donna hadn't done a thing to me or spoken to me in over a year—probably due to the fact that I was living in California. The whole crew knew I was terrified of her. What they did not know was that A.J. was my kryptonite. I would kill for him and that was something no one had ever forgotten. I dried his face and gave him another dollar for his pain and suffering. He rode off on his bike with his friends with the assurance that I would handle the matter. I was his superhero like all big sisters are supposed be.

I marched over to Donna's building and rang her buzzer. She wasn't there—which I already knew but it was more of a gesture to show that I wasn't afraid. Some of the girls were hyping me up ready to see a fight. The meeting we were to have was put on the back burner as I put out the word out that I was *looking* for Donna. After an hour she was still nowhere to be found and the eager crowd went about their business. I sat on one of the benches waiting for Donna to show up. I was silently seething. I didn't know where my mind was. Kim was on my right and Isa was on my left. Both of them were begging me to reconsider what I was contemplating when Donna strolled up with the other half of the crew. Donna's hair was a light brown to an almost orange, bleached by the sun and the inner-city pools. She had strands of hair struggling to stay in the slicked down ponytail on the top of her head. She was easily a size zero. But if there was any doubt, her tight jeans and short sleeve button up *Gap* shirt hugging her pronounced bones would make anyone a believer. She stood over me and sneered.

"Yeah, I heard you was looking for me?"

I stood up and matched her sneer.

"Why you put your hands on my brother?"

"Cause I could," she said completely invading my space.

I clearly wasn't moving fast enough for Isa because just as I raised my hand to slap the smirk off of Donna's face, Isa pushed me into her. Donna shoved me to the ground. I went from zero to rage. I didn't feel as if I had control of my actions. It was like I was outside of my body watching what was happening in slow motion. I jumped up and hit her as hard as I could in her jaw. I actually struck another human being with intent to harm. It was the last thing I remember. I came back to consciousness when I felt simultaneously Donna biting me on my ear and Yo-Yo, Kim's older brother's girlfriend, trying to release my hands from Donna's throat and my knee from her chest.

Yo-Yo was a big girl; standing at a little over six feet and already built like a grown woman, I got myself together. The rush I felt diminished quickly when I came to the instant realization that I could have killed that girl and not have any knowledge of it. I didn't know the amount of violence that must have been built up in me after being constantly been picked on. I always thought of myself as a pacifist. *My* bully lived to see another day; some were not so lucky. In a little less than ten or fifteen years there would be kids who survived attending Columbine High School who wished they would have cut school that fateful day and gone bowling instead. Donna's reign of terror was over. I was never afraid of anyone else again.

The light poles had come on in Concourse Village. That was usually the alarm clock for the neighborhood kids to go upstairs unless we wanted to face our parents coming downstairs in a housecoat and slippers to drag us home. We were pushing the envelope hanging out thirty minutes past that point with the boys, minus Donna. We had just finished an exhausting game of *'go, catch, and do anything'*. For those not quite sure as to what that game is: It's like hide and seek only you're not supposed to really hide all that well so that the boys can catch you and do whatever with you. Mind you, back then, *'whatever'* usually meant a kiss or being felt up. I was always safe from the boys; my ass and breasts were not anywhere near as developed as everyone else's, especially Kim and Isa.

Bilal, one of the chasers tricked me and Jewel into stopping our high-speed run. Everything about Jewel at age thirteen was full figured including her hair which cascaded down her back. She stood further back than I did, boring her coal black eyes into him with disbelief.

"Look, stop running. I don't feel like playing anymore. It's too hot."

Bilal was a milk chocolate brown. His eyelashes were as long as any girl's and his smile was only broken by the silver braces which adorned his teeth. He was tall for his fourteen years and had even begun growing facial hair. He stepped in closer smiling slyly.

"I got a real-live Gremlin in my pocket. I'll show you if you come here." Of course, we didn't believe that he had a real Gremlin in his pocket. But since the movie had come out earlier in the year people all over the country were claiming that they had a real Gremlin. Most could only produce a hamster as proof. So, we dared him to show us his Gremlin. With a swiftness we had never seen before, he unzipped his pants, slid his hand in and pulled out the biggest penis we had ever seen in our short lives. We stood there mouths agape while Bilal posed and grinned.

"You are so disgusting," screamed Jewel, "Come on Sage." She had to pull me away because I was stuck. We caught up with everyone else in the playground that was in front of the main building. Bilal ran up and slapped five with the boys sitting on the monkey bars. We all walked over to the short stone wall which encased the playground. As we talked over each other I began to evaluate my friendship with Kim. She had always been oblivious and that always annoyed me, but that night topped the cake. We were all discussing and lying about our experiences with the opposite sex while snacking on *Bonton* chips, *Now and Laters*, and quarter waters (25 cent juices). Cream was asking everyone if they were virgins or not. He once went out with Kim and dumped her when she refused his sexual intentions. When he put the question to Kim, she was busy daydreaming about something else and completely missed the Q & A of everyone else.

"Hey Kim, you a virgin? Never mind, I know you a virgin," he said with a smirk. But Kim, who had only heard a portion of the question and incorrectly at that, responded to Cream. She turned around and said with attitude and assuredness, "I ain't no virgin, I'm a Pisces!" Everyone laughed except Kim, Cream, and me. Kim was so serious. I think only Cream and I understood the full extent of the 'elevator' saying and we were saddened. We both cared about Kim and felt the embarrassment she should have felt.

Kim

I am not dumb. They laugh at me because I say the first thing that comes into my head. I think it's fun; they never know what I'm going to say and neither do I. I thought I was funny, but Sage and Cream looked like they was mad at me. I walked to my building when I saw my mother standing on the terrace. When she does that, I know that I better get upstairs before she sends one of my brothers to look for me. I sure don't want that. The last time Creston almost pulled my arm out of the socket dragging me home. Chaz threw me over his shoulder the time before that. I don't need no help being embarrassed.

My father died when I was little. I kinda remember him. I got a picture of him in my room. Me and him was at the park. I don't know who took the picture, but Creston and Chaz say they wasn't there because my father picked me up from the adoption agency and no kids was allowed. I cried for like the whole day until my mother got home. She slapped Creston and Chaz for lying to me about our father. The twins are seven years older than me, but they so stupid. They play tricks on me all the time. I wish I was a only child sometimes or that they move out.

I don't really like talking about sex or boys, but it seem like that's all anybody want to talk about. Creston got a different girl for every day of the week. Chaz and Yo-Yo all over each other all the time. I can't help the way my body looks. I see how guys be looking at me different now. I see how my mother try to keep me in the house more. I try to act like it ain't no big deal, but nobody talks to me about anything. My brothers tell me stay away from boys and my mother says I can't have a boyfriend at all. What they say is fine with me because I don't know what to do with them anyway.

Back when me and Cream was going together, he told me that if I wanted to be his girlfriend we had to kiss, and I had to let him feel me up. I was a little okay with the kissing. The touching was okay because I didn't know if I liked it or not. But when he pulled out his thing and tried to make me touch it, I knew that I did not like that. It was all brown and skinny and moving by itself. No way was he gonna touch me and I wasn't gonna touch it. I don't ever care what people say about me. Cream told everybody I was a baby because I didn't want to 'do it.' When his friends started teasing him that he couldn't make me 'do it', he told them that we did 'do it'. He told them he lied about it at first cause he was scared of my brothers. When Creston and Chaz heard about it, they didn't even ask me if it was true, Creston punched Cream in the stomach and Chaz dragged me upstairs by my hair. My mother put me on punishment for April, May, and a little bit of June. I had too much time to think.

CHAPTER 3: *JULY 1988*

-

Sage

Our inner circle furloughed the girls in the neighborhood as the next month began our summer vacation, but our core was still the same: Isa, Kim and me. We picked up Nadia, Jewel and Sienna for the day's adventures.

Nadia was statuesque even as a child. She was taller than all of us. She had a bad habit of hunching over when she walked and talked. She was a little self-conscious about her height. She had a beautiful smile and cute face. Her greatest attribute, however, was her high value for education. Jewel and Sienna both had beautiful brown complexions which never kept company with pimples. Sienna always wore her hair pulled back in a barrette at the nape of her neck. Jewel was a whole other case. Her hair was thick, black, and healthy and cascaded past her shoulders. Whenever her aunt did her hair, it was an all-day event. The washing, conditioning, blow-drying, straightening, and the braiding--by the time she was done, the light poles were on outside and Jewel was *not* allowed outside period. Kim's boyfriend was Mike Colorado-a skinny big mouth kid from the projects up the block. He fancied himself the leader of his friends. Nadia's boyfriend was Jonas-another skinny big mouth, but his head was bigger. Sienna's boyfriend was Jimmy; he was fair skinned with light brown hair and matching eyes. He had no problem letting anyone know that he was sexually active and engaged in the act in the most inappropriate places. His most recent conquest was behind I.S. 151, the local junior high school. My boyfriend was Willie. Jewel was very selective. So basically, at this time she didn't have a boyfriend and I wish I didn't either. I didn't like the sloppy kisses Willie gave me and I was making plans to drop him the very next time I saw him. I was so glad he wasn't there. I don't think that I could have stomached making out with him ever again. I would have called his house, but the phone was disconnected. He lived in Mike's building in the projects across the street from Concourse Village but that day we were heading to Jonas' building: Vietnam.

It had every right to bear the same name of the once war-torn country. At least there were survivors in the country of Vietnam. Vietnam, South Bronx: where everyone was killed just a little everyday in the piss and graffiti, crack and rat, infested building. And we...couldn't wait to get into the first *Tour of Projects*! That's where all the cute boys were. In later years we graduated to dating hustlers, crime syndicate pawns, and kings who were cancers in Harlem, Brooklyn, Queens, Jersey, and B-More.

There was a little bodega or corner store directly across the street from The Vill and one that was two blocks further up near the projects. Nana, Isa's grandmother, had sent us to the store to buy beer, cigarettes, and Pepsi. That was before the age laws of purchase were enforced. The store owners knew us and our parents and knew we had no interest in that stuff. The case would be so different so soon.

On the way to the store two blocks up, the one we were not supposed to go to, Jewel had a premonition. She's always had them and was truly clairvoyant. We ran into Daymon, Isa's boyfriend. He informed us that it was Jonas' birthday.

Years ago, I was in fifth grade with Daymon. I had a terrible crush on him then. He had this blond, curly hair and hazel eyes, light skin and of course that million-dollar smile. But that wasn't why I liked him. He was always nice to me and defended me whenever someone found it necessary to denigrate me because of the dark hue of my skin, which, unfortunately, even in grade-school, was entirely too often. Daymon was cute but I found that it was because of his personality, not because of any physical attribute. Recognizing that was almost too much for my very young mind to conceive so I certainly was not about to share that theory with my friends. I tried to make myself focus on the ridiculous idea that he was trying to get us to go along with that day.

"What's up ya'll?" Daymon said with his million-dollar smile, "I'm saying, it's Jonas' birthday. He's a man today, fourteen. Ya'll gotta come to his house. Ain't nobody home, we got snacks and stuff. I know my girl coming."

He slid up to Isa and started kissing her neck. She was definitely in, which meant we were all in. Ordinarily none of us would be caught dead in the projects. However, we had a quality the girls in the projects didn't have: we didn't live there. I turned and jumped when I felt Jewel jab me in my side.

"Girl what the hell is wrong with you?"

"I don't think we should go. I have a bad feeling," Jewel warned.

"You always have a bad feeling."

The smell of urine and crack by this point went unnoticed in Jonas' hallway. Don't ask how one gets used to it. Jonas opened the door with a key that was on a dirty shoelace around his neck. Jonas' apartment had the echo of an unfurnished one. It was the dull tile floors. No carpet anywhere. The loveseat, couch, end tables, lamps, and center table were all done in early tacky. The boys at *Pier 1Imports* were jumping off the pier one by one each time the sun hit the clash of magnolia and stripe prints. But how soft and comfortable it was!

The whir of air conditioning was all I could concentrate on as I watched the joint slowly coming my way. It was quiet as the joint passed from the left to each waiting fingertip. We each choked after the first deep pull of the joint. This was everyone's first real smoke session. There's a difference between trying weed and having a session. The whole session probably only took five minutes after all it was only a joint the length of a pinky but just as thick. Of course, we were high, so we thought it didn't have any effect. I washed the aftertaste of weed out of my mouth with the best red Kool-Aid in the world. I hadn't even noticed that almost everyone had paired off.

Only twenty minutes elapsed but it felt like four hours. Jewel was antsy. She had already voiced her concern at us being there. Because her mother was not a parent to trifle with, that was her driving force, she announced her departure down the hallway to everyone else in the back bedrooms. As Jewel stood up to leave, it seemed everyone was ready to go. Jimmy, Sienna, Isa, Daymon, Kim, and Mike came lazily walking down the hallway. Then we heard a scream. It was Nadia. She came running out of Jonas' room.

"Oh my God! Oh my God! I felt tongue! I told him *not* to give me tongue and he gave me tongue!" Nadia was quite furious and Jonas, although embarrassed, was the 'man' to his friends. I had thought for a split second that they were having sex. I had heard that it made you scream, but that you liked it. I doubled over laughing at the thought of it because Jonas was also a clean foot shorter than Nadia. Nadia led the way out of the apartment letting the door slam open against the wall. While she fumed out the building we walked leisurely. We were headed down the block when my brother and his friends came whizzing by on their bikes. He had to stop and beg me for a dollar.

"Sis can I get a dollar?" In the same breath he said, "Isa, Nana looking for ya'll. She got her cane," giving Isa his best smile. She smiled back thinking of his future potential. He was happy just to be in her presence. She saw the violence in my eyes and laughed.

"Girl please! Let's get down the hill before Nana comes up," she said just as calm. Which meant Jewel was furious.

"See I told you!" She wagged her finger at Isa.

"Told me what? Shut-up!" Isa shot back. Not wanting to argue, Jewel held her tongue. We made it to The Vill in one piece. Nadia stalked off to her building muttering about mouthwash. Jewel went upstairs to avoid the trouble she was so sure we were in. We walked slowly toward Nana who had been playing spades and cracking jokes, so she wasn't mad at all, just thirsty. Isa was leaning in to give Nana a kiss when Sienna pulled her up and away in the nick of time.

"What is wrong with you?" Isa asked.

"Nothing's wrong with me. We need to talk over here now!" Sienna said continuing to pull Isa until we were all a good distance away from Nana and her friends. Some women age gracefully in their demeanor and others perfect their nastiness toward others. Nana's friends were the latter, especially Mrs. White. If Mrs. White would have had a closer look at Isa, before the afternoon was out, she would have had sufficient evidence to brand Isa the new whore of Babylon. Even though Sienna was still as high as the rest of us, she snapped to when she saw the blemish on Isa's neck; she couldn't let Mrs. White see it. Nana would have beaten us all and then cussed her oldest and dearest friend down to her bones. When we were a safe distance away, Sienna braced Isa for the news.

"Isa you have a hickie that looks like the map of Africa!" Sienna laughed. Isa's very pale skin had a beet-red passion mark on her neck. "What?!" Isa gasped, "My mother is going to kick my ass! Y'all gotta help me get this off!" Sienna volunteered her apartment, so we went up there. Her mother worked as a social worker and she did not have the summer off. That summer the child abuse rate was skyrocketing so she was constantly at work late saving the city's children so that she could support her own but missing out on Sienna growing up.

CHAPTER 4: *AUGUST 1988*

-

Sage

Kim and I went to the Chinese restaurant. We loved to order just chicken wings or just French fries. Ketchup had to smother every section of either item. That day we ordered chicken wings with lots of ketchup and hot sauce. Kim had two wings and I had two. We were eating them as we headed back to The Vill. As we were entering the East side of The Vill, Kim started to wrap up her remaining food and wipe her face and hands. I should have known something was wrong. Nana was sitting on one of the group of benches that had a shade shelter. Nana always made me feel special, even on the days Isa and I thought that we hated each other and would never speak again. In fact, that was one of Nana's gifts: to make everyone around her feel special. That was important to me because all of my grandparents died before I was born.

Kim leaned in to give Nana a kiss. I gave Nana my best smile as I approached her. She in turn raised her cane and brought it down on my hands. The chicken fell to the ground along with my pride. I was so hurt. Nana looked as if she was going to beat me within an inch of my life.

"Young lady, why are you eating in the street? Don't you have a home? And don't you know that you could have gone up to my house and ate? Don't you *ever* let me catch you or hear about you eating in the street again! Pick that mess up."

I could have slapped Kim, sitting there looking so innocent. I picked up the dirty chicken and put it in the trash. I wanted to cry so badly; not because my hands hurt but because my heart did. I did not like the fact that I had disappointed Nana. I hung my head and dropped the dirty chicken in the garbage. Nana walked over and hugged me. All was forgiven and just like that I was okay. The point of this story is that it was during the end of an era when the whole neighborhood raised you and implored morals and values and an occasional *ass whuppin'* where necessary and there wasn't a lawsuit pending because of it. And those extra parents helped us girls and many others skip the federally funded vacations and seasonal homes which served crack up like a buffet.

CHAPTER 5: *END OF THE SUMMER*

-

Isa

Cherry *Now and Laters* are my favorite candy. I will suck on them until I get blisters on my tongue and the roof of my mouth. They make my lips extra red and juicy. We was all going to the store for Italian ices. It was so hot outside; too hot to do anything except find ways to stay cool. Kim and Donna was a little ahead of us. Me, Sage, and Jewel was turning the corner out of The Vill. Sienna was standing on the wall yelling across the street at Mike and Daymon, asking them where Jimmy was. Sage asked me who Sienna was talking to. She couldn't seem them when the C-Town truck rolled passed. I was about to tell her but then I started choking on my *Now and Later*. My eyes was watering and I kept gagging. Sienna ran down yelling for me to breathe and hold my arms up. Jewel was banging the hell out of my back. I thought I was going to die because of the look on Sage's face. I wanted to see what she was looking at but I was bent over in a funny way. I thought if I stood up straight maybe I could breathe. Then I got why Sage was screaming; I caught my breath all of a sudden. The candy flew out of my mouth while I watched Kim being dragged down the street. I fell on the ground screaming Oh my God!

Kim

I was hot but I was hungry too. We was all going to the store. I was counting my money to make sure I had enough for a hero and a soda. Donna was showing me her new name ring. I saw Mike coming down the block. "Mike, come here," I yelled across the street. He didn't even stop. "Nope! I ain't got no money so don't ask," he said. "Your broke ass don't never have no money," I said. Daymon was laughing at him. "So quit begging!" "I hate you!" "I hate you too!" I heard Isa choking and turned around. I wasn't paying attention to where I was going; Mike made me so mad. All I could see was him. I didn't see the Pathfinder coming. I didn't have enough time to jump back all the way; I only took a step back. The back of the truck caught onto my jeans. I was like jerked into the air a little and then I hit the ground real hard. I could feel my back scraping on the street, and I tried to use my other leg like a brake to stop the truck from dragging me away. I heard screaming but I thought it was just me. I saw two buildings, the lines in the street, underneath the truck, a gutter; I felt the heat from the exhaust it was burning my leg. Then the truck stopped. My head banged so hard against the ground I blacked out. When I woke up, everyone was all over me asking a hundred questions.

"Move ya'll. I'm okay. Let me get up." Yo-Yo leaned in and pushed me back down.

"Be still, the ambulance is almost here. Somebody getting Creston, Chaz, and your mother, but don't move." She was so loud, so I went back to sleep. When I woke up the second time that I remember, I was back at home in a cast and in my bed. My room was packed with my friends...Mike wasn't there.

Sage

Kim loved to take everyone through changes. And so did Isa. So why not get a two-for-one. We were all headed to the corner store, not the one directly across the street, when time slowed down. I was standing beside Isa and Jewel next to the curb. Donna and Kim were by the crosswalk, but still in the street. Sienna was bringing up the rear.

Isa was babbling on about something and pointed her finger towards the boys across the street. At the same time, she tried to speak while she was eating a cherry *Now and Later*. (That is a piece of candy for those of you who are not familiar, and it is pronounced "nowlater").

When Isa began to choke on the candy, Sienna and Jewel rushed to her aid. When Kim noticed Isa choking, she too turned to help. Mike and Daymon started to cross the street when they saw Isa in distress but stopped in the middle. A green Pathfinder truck was tearing down the street at the precise time Kim turned. The fender of the Pathfinder was hanging down and out just enough to catch Kim's pant leg and drag her about ten feet. When the truck finally stopped, it was only to shake Kim's now limp body before speeding away.

That forty-seven second break with normalcy was enough to create such an awesome silence that even Isa's constricted throat respected it, dared not interrupt it, so it freed the lodged candy and released the air it withheld from her. The boys that we thought were invincible and all powerful suddenly seemed so far removed from a superhero. Not one of them flew in, or stopped time, or rewound time for that matter. Kim was hurt and we were kids again. We all cried. We screamed. Kim was just as silly as before. That fool tried to stand up and walk it off because she was embarrassed. Yo-Yo showed up and told her to lie down until the ambulance arrived. Some random stranger had chased down the Pathfinder and was able to give the police a description of the driver and the license plate number.

Even in New York City a Good Samaritan can manifest. It's not *that* God forsaken. Kim's ankle was disfigured for life, but she could walk, and dance and she lived, we all did.

CHAPTER 6: THE HIGH SCHOOL YEARS '89-'92

-

Sage

Isa and I were sophomores; Kim, Jewel, and Billie were freshmen. We would begin to transform into the people we would be from this point. Some of us started to reform ourselves from this large group of friends that we began. By the time the college/adult years came around, it would be just me and Isa still struggling to find solid ground. We still loved the projects; however, it was time for a new one. Just two or three blocks to the left were the Melrose Houses. We all were in private/Catholic schools--A lot of good that did; we were still hell on wheels, of course not to our parents' knowledge. Kim was almost over Mike and on to an associate of his, unbeknownst to either of the guys.

Kim and I were coming home from school. We attended different schools but since they were both in the same area we walked together to and fro. As we entered The Vill from Morris Ave., we saw Mike, Bobby, Aheem, and a couple of other boys sitting on the wall. Not one of those boys actually lived in Concourse Village but thugs that they were, they still acted as if they owned the place. These were the Melrose boys. Aheem resembled a younger version of Babyface, the singer. He had a short afro blown out with a hairdryer—one of the latest styles for boys. His eye lids hung so low he looked as if he were sleeping standing up. He was also a very clean dresser. He seemed to take care in the planning phases of getting dressed for the day. Bobby was Puerto Rican and Black mixed. His complexion was a caramel color, and he had a curly flat top hair cut and dimples on either side of his face. He was thicker than the thin framed Aheem. They were both cute guys. They were in some kind of heated debate when I heard them say my name. Bobby was shouting at the top of his lungs, "Ask her! You know *she* ain't gonna lie. I'm telling you Mike over here lying!"

"Ask me what?" I needed to know what I was testifying to now.

"When Kim got dragged by that jeep, what was Mike doing? Didn't he break down like a bitch and start crying? Tell the truth now!"

"Well Mike...what did you tell them? I mean that was kind of a hard thing to see. I mean we was *all* crying..."

"Told you that nucka was crying!" shouted Bobby.

"Nah, man say it ain't so!" exclaimed Butch, someone else from their neighborhood.

"That man soft," said Aheem as he kept a steady eye on Kim.

They were all laughing and giving Mike a hard time about his moment of weakness. Bobby had somehow adopted me as his sister and thought all my loyalties should lie with him. I started walking away and I pulled Kim with me. I didn't even want to see what was about to spark if Kim and Aheem kept staring at each other. I didn't want to have anything to do with it. Which in reality meant, I was going to know everything; Kim wasted no time spilling the beans when they were out of earshot.

"You know me and Aheem is talking right?" Kim said.

"What are you talking about? You're still going out with Mike."

"Please...I'ma quit him tonight when I call him."

"You don't care that him and Aheem know each other?"

"No," Kim said with so much nonchalance, "He don't care, I don't care. And if Mike start buggin' Aheem'll take care of that. Believe it."

I couldn't believe my ears. That girl was out of her damn mind! That was definitely going to lead to some shit. We went our separate ways home. We came back out a few hours later and sat in the back of 775. Kim, Sienna, Isa, Jewel, and I walked to the back of the building. We were enjoying the last days of summer even though it was the first week of school. Mike came over staggering. He was barely holding on to the 80's version of Cristal: a 40oz of Old English. He was already having a conversation with no one and dribbling a basketball that only he could see as he approached us.

"How the hell you gonna break up with me like you all that! Bitch after all the shit I gave you!"

"Mike take your drunk ass home. Your bum ass ain't give me shit!" Kim matched his tone.

"Stupid bitch, that nigga gonna fuck you and leave you and it's gonna be good for you. But then when you finished you could come see daddy."

"Oooh you so stupid! Get the hell out of here!"

"And ya'll conceited bitches didn't tell me shit! But that's okay," he began pointing and speaking directly to each of us, "Because you're a bitch, you're a bitch, you're a bitch, you're a bitch, you're a bitch. Fuck you, fuck you, fuck you, fuck you, and fuck you. Goodnight!"

Mike's antics had of course sent everyone except him and Kim into hysterics. He had already begun to stagger away. What Mike said came to pass. Two weeks later Aheem and Kim broke up and he and Isa were boyfriend and girlfriend. As we joined the world of the Melrose boys, Kim began to distance herself away from us as a group, but she and I still hung out.

Kim, the bounce back queen starting going out with a new guy named Tony. Tony was tall, skinny, and had a bad case of acne. He could dance his ass off though. He had a partner, Omar. So, it came to be that it was me, Kim, Omar, and Tony started dancing at different house parties in the Bronx and Harlem. We were trying to make a little name for ourselves and people were feeling us. We didn't have costumes or anything like that. We just wore whatever was in fashion then completed the outfit with $54.11's better known as high top Reeboks. We were trying to get discovered so that we could do music videos like some of the other high school kids we knew. We would go to the most talked about house party or school dance and dance regularly until the song that we created a routine to was played by the DJ. This would make our routine seem more spontaneous. Then we'd make a circle and do our entire routine and people would let us. After a while people were expecting us to dance all the time. I thought that I would get discovered and my dream of becoming a Luke Campbell dancer would be realized. That was until my cousin made it clear to me what being a Luke Dancer entailed. Knowing that I would need proof, she sat me down to watch one of his unedited videos; I made it through twelve minutes before I felt the need to run to a confession booth. I just wanted to dance—I enrolled in Talented Unlimited Performing Arts High School in Manhattan for a better foundation.

By now, I had been splitting my time between all my childhood friends. Isa and Aheem were a couple and Kim didn't hang around us as a whole anymore. Kim and I didn't walk home from school together anymore either but one particular fall-winter day, I was coming out of the train station on 3rd Ave. and we walked home together. As we entered The Vill we saw Bobby, Aheem, Butch, Red, and Victor were sitting on the benches behind the buildings. Bobby called me over. "Sage, what's up with your girl Aamilka?" I rolled my eyes. He didn't have a chance with Aamilka or Milk which is what we called her. She was two years older than all of us and loved to constantly remind us.

I said to him, "Forget it. Milk is only going to give you a hard on and a headache. And you gonna make her want to slap somebody. Save us all the aggravation." Aheem grinned at Kim. She didn't return the favor.

"What's up Kim?" he said. She turned towards me and said, "I'm going to keep it moving upstairs. Call me later."

"Bye girl, I will." We watched Kim put distance between us; Bobby started in on me again.

"Sage, that's messed up. I thought me and you was peoples. You not gonna talk to your girl for me?" I shook my head no.

"I don't want to get in the middle of that nonsense. And it will be non-sense if you and Milk start dealing with each other. Look at what this ge-nius over here did; now Isa and Kim don't even speak to each other."

Aheem shrugged his shoulders and then volunteered, "Isa and Milk are cool too," then looking at me he said, "You, Isa, and Milk supposed to come over to my house later anyway."

"Sweetie you don't run me. I do not have to be there."

"Yeah right," they said simultaneously, and they all began laughing.

"We'll see." I walked away angry. Bobby annoyed the hell out of me. He thought he was God's gift to the world and the girls who swarmed him gave him more validity—he thought. However, he was right. I would be there that night. I would vouch for him and he would be with Milk.

Kim

I never told anybody that Aheem was my first. I never did it with Mike. He wanted to real bad but I didn't like him enough to do it. Aheem was cute and he had money and he was so nice to me. He made sure nobody bothered me and told everybody that I was his girl. He took me out. He took care of me. I wanted to show him that I wanted to be with him for-ever. I thought I loved him. He picked me up from school, came to my house, and he wasn't scared of my brothers. He called me every night. I don't know what happened. I don't know why he stopped liking me. I don't know what I did. I couldn't tell my mother what happened be-cause she would kill me. Plus, I felt dumb for letting him do it to me and now he was with Isa. Maybe, I shouldn't'tna dealt with him because he was Mike's friend, but I couldn't help it. I really, really, liked him. He didn't care about Mike being his friend so why should I? I cried when he stopped talking to me. I called his house over and over. His mother and cousin lied for him and told me he wasn't there, and I could hear him in the back talking. Then when he did answer the phone he hurried up and got off the phone with me. I heard people laughing in the back. I know they was laughing at me. By the fourth day I was bugging for real. I went to his house and he ain't let me in the house. He talked to me in the hallway like didn't know me at all. He told me he had to do something for his mother so he couldn't come out.

"Kim you not my girl no more so stop calling me and don't come over here no more." I started crying all over again.

"But why Aheem? I didn't do anything," I said.

"I just don't feel like it anymore. You told me you didn't do it with Mike, but he said you did," he said.

"He lying! I ain't do nothing with him! You the only one I did something with ever," I told him.

"Yeah right, you went out with mad guys and you was talking to me and Mike at the same time."

"Just cause I went out with guys don't mean I did it to all of them. And you ain't care about me being with Mike at first. Plus, I quit him and went with you. Just you," I explained.

"Like I said before, I got something to do for my mother so you gotta go. And I got a new girl anyway." After that he opened the door and slammed the door in my face. I went home and cried myself to sleep. A week later, I was walking out the school to go home when I saw him and Isa sitting on one of the cars across the street from our school all hugged up. I stopped, looked at them, and they looked at me. Something turned off inside of me. For like a minute I didn't recognize them. They look like two people that was just sitting there. I didn't feel nothing, so I walked away.

So, I don't know why he keep on trying to talk to me. I can't stand his stupid ass. I'm not talking to him or Isa. I don't know how she can go out with him when she know that me and him was together. She rolled her eyes at me like I did something wrong. I think that's real trifling that she with him. I'm bugging on how Sage act like it's okay too. I shouldn't talk to her two-face ass either, but at least she told me that Aheem and Isa was talking. I didn't tell her that I already knew. Isa still ain't said nothing to me about it.

I really liked Aheem and I thought he liked me. His whole family smiled in my face and didn't tell me that he was talking to Isa. His cousin used to hang out with me all the time and she didn't tell me either. I bet if I told Isa he was smiling up in my face and talking to me she would still blame me. Isa don't think about nobody but herself. She don't care how I feel when I see them kissing on the benches or when Sage can't hang out with me because she hanging out with Isa and Aheem. I wouldn't do that foul shit to her. Why do everybody think it's okay to shit on me? They supposed to be my friends. I never did anything to anybody, but that's cool. I'm gonna start doing me and looking out for just me.

CHAPTER 7: THE HIGH SCHOOL YEARS '89-'92

-

Isa

We were getting older and just dealing with guys and they mothers was one thing. Now we had to deal with these n****s _firsts_ and baby mamas. Me, Milk, Jewel, and Sage spent a couple of hours on the block where the guys did their drug hustling; we called it the block or the ave. We was walking through the projects one day on our way back from the block. We heard about Bobby's ex–girlfriend Juanita and we hated her because Milk hated her. I think she had a place in Bobby's heart that Milk tried to erase but couldn't.

Milk had seen Juanita before in pictures, but this was the first day that we first laid eyes on Juanita together in person. I assumed she was Puerto Rican—I ain't seen no pictures of her. She was as black as the next person. There wasn't nothing pretty about her and her attitude was even worse than mine. She was shaped like an upside-down pear. It wasn't that Juanita was ugly, but she was so average and plain it was hard to see her with Bobby especially because Milk was the total opposite of Juanita. Milk was shapely, pretty, and smart. Apparently, Juanita saw us too, but I knew nothing was going to happen this day.

Milk was standing with her hands on her hips in front of us facing Juanita and said, "You have a problem?"

"No, do you have a problem?" Juanita said.

"Don't ask me any questions little girl. What you better do is keep it moving."

"Soon as you get out of my way."

"You need to go around because we are not moving. So, what do you want to do?" Juanita looked around and noticed she and her two friends were outnumbered.

She sucked her teeth, turned around to her friends and said, "Come on ya'll it's not even worth it." They walked around us and continued on their way. Milk took it as a sign of weakness and laughed loud. Juanita did not turn around.

Time passed by and we forgot about Juanita and her friends for about five months. Milk and Bobby and me and Aheem were on the first year of our relationship. Spring rolled around again. Me and the girls were strolling through the projects again like it was Central Park. Once again, we came head-to-head with Juanita and one of her frail looking friends who we knew was Ruby from the block. Milk hated Juanita just because she existed. This argument was more ridiculous than the first one. You'da thought me and Sage was watching a ping-pong game.

"So, you thought I wasn't going to see you again?" snarled Milk.

"And here I am," chuckled Juanita, "what's up?"

"I know you are not trying to be smart?" said Jewel.

"And if she was, what?" squeaked Ruby.

Jewel couldn't stand it anymore. Ruby made what looked like a move and Jewel knocked her the fuck out. Not down, out; we kinda looked at Jewel for a second. We ain't never seen her put a hand on a single soul. The fight died down in Milk and we all walked away leaving Juanita to revive Ruby. I don't know what made Ruby think she was a match for Jewel. Now I wasn't sure who could beat her. Jewel knew everyone's looks, feelings, emotions, and most of all when we wasn't being honest with ourselves. That was her job. She told us the things that we didn't want to hear. That quality is hard to find in a friend. Someone who will allow you to make your mistakes, have your back, and then when she gets you alone lets you have it—which is what she did when me and Milk started celebrating the victory. Sage laughed along with it.

"So, you think it was right that we was about to fight over Bobby?" Jewel asked.

I stopped in my tracks, "I wasn't fighting over Bobby."

"But you would have jumped in if we all started fighting right?"

"Hell yes. I fight for my girls; that's what we *all* supposed to do!"

"But for what? I don't know that girl and she never did anything to me, you, Sage or to Milk."

"Leave me out of this," Sage said.

"Leave you out of this? You always want to be left out of this, but you in this just like the rest of us."

"She right about that. Sage don't ever want to fight or argue about nothing. You know she's scary," I said trying to keep Jewel off my case. Sage made a weak try of defending herself.

"Just because I don't like to fight doesn't mean I'm scared. I just don't see what it solves unless you're defending yourself," Sage said.

"Girl please, the last fight you had was like three years ago," I said.

"So what?" Jewel brought us back on topic, "Milk doesn't like that girl because she used to go out with Bobby, so what? Who cares? I'm not saying that we need to be her friend, but why do we have to have beef with her? I knocked that girl out for no reason. Bobby ain't my man. I don't even like him."

Milk turned on Jewel and spoke, "You don't have to like him. He is my man and it only matters if I like him."

"You got that right baby," Isa chimed in, "cause I got a man."

"Ya'll just don't get it. Milk you're right: he is your man, and it doesn't matter if I like him or not. So, it won't matter if I don't come around when he's around either."

"That's right it doesn't." I never seen Jewel get so mad. Her and Milk was standing face to face like they was thinking about fighting. I didn't know what was going on, but Jewel wasn't usually like that. She must not really like Bobby.

"All I'm saying Milk is don't expect me to fight or do anything else in the name of friendship when it's really over some bum ass n****!"

"Don't start no shit Jewel," Milk said. I stepped in between them.

"We're family ya'll, family."

Sage

By the time Isa made this statement, our loud discussion placed us in front of Nana's building. I was deep in thought about what Jewel had said. She was right, but I wasn't ready to admit that and I was feeling sorry for myself because she had checked all of us and it seemed I was the only one who got the point. Nana saw us off of the terrace and buzzed down to doorman to send us to the store for Pepsi and cigarettes. None of us had any money so we had to go upstairs and get it from Nana. Jewel, Milk, and I sat in the living room not speaking while Isa went to the back to get the money. We were headed back out of the door when we heard Nana yelling from the back,

"Sage get back in here. You three go on." They never even turned around. I was so angry and hurt and confused. I thought I knew who I was but Jewel's venture into my character shifted me. I walked into the back and couldn't produce a smile even for Nana. Grandpa whizzed past me. I heard him go to the bathroom and then after a flush and sound of running water, the door opened but he didn't return to the room. Nana was lying in her queen-sized bed watching the evening news. The latest Ebony magazine was beside her and an ashtray filled with cigarette butts and roaches, the butts of marijuana joints. Her glasses were perched on her nose precariously and the cigarette dangling from her lipsticked mouth.

"Girl, now what's wrong with you?" Nana asked in what was supposed to be a concerned voice but sounded more like a command.

"Nothing Nana, really, I'm just going to go home now." I was trying my best to be gone by the time Milk, Isa, and Jewel returned.

"Sit down, my granddaughter tells me everything. I know all of you just had a little argument. Listen ya'll need to stay friends. I know she can be a little bitch sometimes..."

I dropped into the antique chair beside her bed. I missed about thirty seconds of what Nana said because I was astonished. Not because she cursed, that was nothing; but to say *that* about who I perceived to be her favorite granddaughter, was entirely too much for me. "...as you two grow to be young women you're going to need each other. I know she's a lot but, stand by her side and hold on to your friendship. I promise all this will pass and you both will be stronger for it, all of you will."

Nana was hugging and squeezing me. I of course was crying.

Nana handed me a tissue and told me to wipe my face. The last thing I needed to show any of them was weakness. Not a moment too soon either. Milk, Isa, and Jewel came bounding into the house full of excitement about some little adventure they had on the way from the store.

Isa asked no questions when Nana and I emerged from Nana's room. Isa immediately grabbed my hand and began to run down the entire escapade with her usual flare. As if the disagreement had never happened. I turned to smile at Nana and found that she was smiling back.

"Give me that Pepsi so I can put it in the fridge." Isa handed it to her, and we all sat down in the living room so Isa could perform her melodrama.

Nana went into the kitchen to prepare dinner. Grandpa was sitting at the dining room table. He had long ago discarded the daily paper and was playing a game of solitaire with a real deck of cards not on the computer. Isa was still reenacting each scene that I *should have been there* for.

In the background we could hear Grandpa aggravating Nana. He was going on about how she was cutting the carrots wrong. Then he said the fire under whatever she was cooking was too high. Now we were all listening to this exchange. We didn't have to see Nana to know that Grandpa was getting on her nerves. She did not like to be bothered when she was in the kitchen cooking. They had been married for more years than our combined ages and he still didn't know her. He kept right on about how the potatoes and broccoli would be too soft if she didn't keep an eye on it. Oh, and wife you are still cutting those carrots much too big. A split second after his last syllable a large butcher knife pierced the air and lodged itself into the wall. There is still a mark in the wall where the butcher knife impaled it over Grandpa's head. He opened his mouth, but we were the ones screaming. Nana never addressed any of us.

"Well, wife, if you didn't want my help that's all you had to say," Grandpa said with false bravado. Grandpa held no fear in his heart for a walking being on the earth- hear him tell it. But we all knew that Nana was the one person he feared even if he refused to outright show it. He picked up his well-read newspaper and began reading from the beginning as if it were still news; all the while peeking over the paper at Nana.

"Husband would you kindly bring me the butcher knife? I need it here for something," Nana said sweetly.

"Of course dear," That was Grandpa's cue that he was forgiven. He pulled the knife out of the wall with the swiftness of a twenty-year old swordsman. As he replaced the butcher knife in the knife holder, Nana placed the knife *she* was using on the counter, reached up and kissed his cheek. He blushed as an adolescent would. He returned to his game of solitaire...quietly.

CHAPTER 8: THE HIGH SCHOOL YEARS '89-'92

-

Sage

The next morning found me tired and dragging. I had left my bookbag over at Jewel's house and had to leave my house early to go get it. On my way down in the elevator, it stopped on the 22 second floor. Bilal stepped on. The boys who get on your nerves when you're younger are the same ones that catch your eye when you're older. The only thing is you never see the change coming. I had just broken up with my boyfriend and things were a little tense between my ex and me because we had the same group of friends Bilal included. In the last few months, I had gotten to know him as more than someone who flashed me in the parking lot.

Bilal was smart, very smart. And he could ball; the boy already had college scouts coming out for him. He went to a private school and pretty much stayed out of trouble. Even with his braces, his smile was nice.

I had been hanging with Bilal for awhile and seeing him now, just this morning, jolted me awake. Bilal was looking so good to me. I could barely concentrate on what he was saying because I was daydreaming. I was having a vision about what our first date would look like, we could go to the same college, and the wedding we would have would be spectacular with an all-cream colored wedding party with lavender accents, and our kids would be beautiful and tall and smart. Bilal on the other hand was basically shooting the shit. He leaned in closer to me. And put his arm around me as we stepped off of the elevator. He smelled really good.

The look on his face told me that he was asking me something and I missed it.

"What did you say?" I asked.

"I said what are you doing after school? You want to come chill with me?" He said waiting for my answer, grinning.

"I don't have anything better to do."

"Wow, it's like that?"

"No, I mean, like I don't have any other plans."

He grinned some more at my reply.

"Stop giving me a hard time boy...where do you want to meet?"

"My house, I'll page you when I get home from basketball practice."

"Okay, cool. I'll probably have to meet up with Milk first."

"That's cool bring her. Jason trying to talk to her too; oh wait, Jason and I gotta stop by my job to get my check and then we'll meet up."

"Okay cool." He leaned in and kissed me like that was what he always did. We went our separate ways, and I spent the rest of the day envisioning what could happen when I got home. I left school immediately after sixth period, skipping chorus. I didn't bullshit like I usually would. I wished I had; I wish I had stayed at school and went to chorus. I wish I transferred to the 5 train instead of the 4 train—I would have been a mile or two out of my way and I would have slowed time down just a little. I was coming down the block and stopped at Ray's corner store and bought a pack of gum. I knew that Milk, Jason, and Bilal would be waiting on me to get home because I came home the latest at 6:30 pm, but today I was on the block at 3:30 like a normal teenager.

The city was building a fence around the new mall over by Concourse Village because there were too many entrances to the mall, and it was inviting an unwanted element onto the property. There was a crowd over by the side doors to the mall. I didn't usually walk that way home, but I wanted to go to the store. I was rushing past the crowd, but Jason caught my eye. There was only a sliver of an opening between two people I didn't recognize, but I saw him; he was kneeling on the floor next to something. In fact, he was bent over and kneeling. At first, I thought he might have been playing cee-low (craps) or maybe he was in a fight. But neither of those scenarios was matching up with the vibe of the crowd. I didn't realize that I was making my way over to the crowd until I was moving people out of my way. I felt like I was pushing against a winter wind. I could see Jason clearly now and his face was hard and there was dried traces of tears and blood on his face. His shirt had blood on it. His jeans had blood on it. Jason and Bilal each had one sister—they were best friends—they were over to one side crying hysterically. Milk was struggling to pull me up. I don't know how I ended up on the ground. I was kneeling next to Bilal. I was reaching out to touch him. I wanted to wake him up because it wasn't funny. He really had a sick sense of humor and okay now the joke was over. People were crying and he had his audience, so I needed him to get up now. I never got to touch him. Milk applied a firm grip around my arms and pulled me up.

The ambulance arrived and the paramedics placed him on the gurney while putting in an IV. Bilal's mother raced to the ambulance screaming that he was her son right before they closed the doors. She had on her nurse's uniform. I don't know if she was on her way to work or on her way home when she got the news. I heard her asking a question about Bilal using a medical term. They wouldn't be able to sugarcoat anything for her; she would know they were lying since she knew more than they did about Bilal's condition.

The police questioned Jason and my ex-boyfriend Ness who were with

Bilal at the time of the incident, but they wouldn't talk to them. The police put handcuffs on Jason and Ness and placed them in the back of the squad car. Milk and other people in the crowd started banging on the squad car hollering for them to let Jason and Ness go. I sat down on the curb carefully this time. Somebody must have called the news because a few news vans were lining up across the street. Male and female reporters with big hair and too much make-up was marching over to where we were. It was getting hard to breathe. Jason and Ness's parents showed up at the same time Bilal's father did. Bilal's dad grabbed both of the girls since they didn't want to be separated and put them in the car. I guess they went to the hospital. One of the other officers who was there trying to keep the peace talked to Jason and Ness's parents. The crowd wouldn't let him speak. He offered to drive them to the precinct where Jason and Ness were. After they left with him, the crowd disappeared after a little while. The news crews didn't stay long after the crowd. It didn't take very long for the blood to turn that burnt brown color. An old science lesson popped into my head about what happens to blood when it comes in contact with oxygen.

Isa, Jewel, Kim, Sienna, me and some of the neighborhood boys waited for Ness and Jason to get home. We were sitting at the back of the building smoking. I don't remember walking there at all. I kept shaking my leg nervously as I smoked. Tears rolled down my face. My heart ached so bad; I had known Bilal my whole life. I couldn't make sense of him not being here. I knew answers to random trivia. I knew why the ocean and sky looked blue. I knew the Pythagorean Theorem. I knew why...I knew the answers to so many things, but I couldn't figure out how I had lost Bilal. We had plans. My daydreams melted like snowflakes landing on my face. They're beautiful as long as you don't touch them; as long as they never touch what's real.

Jason and Ness showed up with two 40ozs about an hour later. Ness still looked shell shocked. Jason poured some beer out for those who weren't alive anymore as was tradition and recounted what happened earlier in the day. As he talked I could see it playing out in front of me. I had to see this dirty trick that time had played on me until the very end.

Bilal had been having problems with one of the security guards in the mall where he worked after school. The guard had gotten into a fight with Bilal and lost. It was a fair one. The guard didn't feel the same. A few days later, the guard brings his friends by the job to even things out. The guard and his friends were members of the Aryan nation. The guard and his friends approached Bilal, Jason, and Ness as they exited the side door of the mall. Because the area does not directly lead to an established business within the mall there were no cameras mounted to the perimeter of the area.

The guard was not the gunman initially. A man to the left of him held the gun to Ness' temple. He pulled the trigger and nothing happened. Sweat poured down the back of his sweatshirt as if he played a full court game of basketball. The man pivoted and pointed the gun at Jason's heart. He pulled the trigger while aiming at Jason, nothing happened. The guard snatched the gun out of his partner's hands. He aimed the gun between Bilal's two eyes. He pulled the trigger. The gun jammed and Bilal laughed in his face. In extreme anger the guard pulled the trigger once more. Bilal's blood splattered all over Jason who was standing right next to him...the sound was so loud and so quick, that Jason thought he had missed. Everyone had ducked and the Aryans ran. Jason didn't realize it was blood that had splattered him until he and the guard started to stand up and Bilal didn't. That's when he replayed what happened in his head and dropped to his knees. Ten minutes before I had gotten there, Bilal had been executed. I ran to the nearest garbage can and threw up. Ness came over and caressed my back as I emptied my soul.

At the funeral, Bilal had an open casket; he looked so dark; so devoid of life and there was a soft indentation in the center of his forehead where the bullet had entered. The morticians had done a wonderful job of covering it up. All I kept thinking of was Milk's question: why couldn't he just wake up? I straightened his tie and Milk caressed his face. I had never seen so many hard-shelled guys break down like they did that day. Jason's voice cracked as he tried to be intelligible in his speech but faltered. Ness's knees gave when he tried to stand. He buried his head in his hands and let out a wail of such deep grief. Guys like him lived a life in which if they were murdered it would go with the territory. But Bilal was a good guy. He went to school and played ball and had his head on straight. What were the odds that he would die such a violent death? What kind of karma was that? What lesson was supposed to have been learned from this? After three days of binge smoking and drinking, we still didn't have an answer. Bilal was still dead, and he wasn't even eighteen. The killer was caught, but it wasn't by the police.

CHAPTER 9: THE HIGH SCHOOL YEARS '89-'92

Sage

In the time it took for the concrete to hold the summer waves of heat hostage again, Grandpa had died and Nana followed not too soon after. Cancer and heartbreak took her. Her funeral was standing room only. People from all walks of life and all ages came to pay their respects to the woman we all knew as Nana. Isa and her family were pillars of strength until it was time for the pall bearers to carry Nana's casket out of the sanctuary and into the hearse for the drive to the gravesite. Isa was saying her final goodbyes when she threw herself onto the casket. It took all of Milk's strength to pull Isa off of the casket. Isa's grief was so intense it pierced our skin like a dull knife. She hadn't cried at all, so we expected it to come at any moment, but we were still unprepared for its affect. To say that we were lost is an understatement. Nana helped to navigate the people we were deep down inside but when she died, we closed that reservoir. We didn't let people in as easily and we didn't forgive as easily. For too long we lost our souls and made no attempts for its search.

Isa

When they brought the hospital bed into the house for Nana, I didn't understand that it was for hospice. Hell, I didn't know what a hospice was. All I knew was that Nana was home from the hospital. I moved in with Nana after Grandpa died and before we found out she had cancer. I wasn't leaving my grandmother alone in that apartment. Plus, my mother was getting on my nerves. I lay in the bed with my grandmother almost every night until she went to sleep. I ain't want no stranger in the house with her. Sometimes I didn't go to school if my mother or one of my aunts couldn't stay with her during the day. Nana was my heart. I couldn't leave her.

I used to sneak and let her smoke her cigarettes. She said they made her feel better. I told her she could only have one a day. I know I was wrong, but I wanted her to be comfortable and happy. I combed her hair every night until it was almost gone. I fed my grandmother her meals cutting everything up into little pieces, then I had to mash everything, then it was just soup. Sometimes I would cry. She'd squeeze my hand, smile, and tell me to 'cut that crying shit out.' She lost so much weight she couldn't fit her bed clothes anymore. Sometimes she had good days. Kim and Sage would come over and we would play card games—spades, pitty pat, bid whist. Sometimes Kim would come over and sing songs for Nana. They went to the same church. I didn't go to church like that and I can't sing. But that wouldn't stop me from singing as loud as I could after Kim finished. Nana laughed so hard she'd start coughing. One time she coughed up blood. I stopped singing after that. She told me it wasn't my fault. I still stopped singing. Me and my mother got into a big argument over Nana dying. She told me that I had to start thinking about it and dealing with it and tell Nana that I loved her and goodbye.

"You need to start making your peace with Nana dying Isa."

"No, I don't because she ain't dying. She gonna be fine. I'm taking care of her. Everybody acting like they can't do nothing for my grandmother, but I can. I'm taking care of her."

"Isa you need to start making your peace with Nana dying."

"No, I don't. I ain't never coming back here again. How you not gonna fight for your own mother? I bet you want me to fight for you, huh? Goodbye."

I told Nana what my mother said, I always told her everything. My mother woulda told on me anyway. Nana told me to remind her to slap me when she had more strength. After that day Nana told me goodbye and that she loved me every night just in case she didn't wake up. She did the same thing for seventeen days, so I stopped being sad about her saying it because she woke up every morning. Four days ago, Nana didn't wake up. I sat in the chair next to the bed. It was 5:37am. I called my mother and told her what happened. I didn't cry at first. After the people came and took Nana, I got dressed and went to school. My mother tried to stop me but that ain't work. I didn't even speak to her. I went to school like nothing happened. When people asked about Nana, I told them she was fine. I took some notes in my classes, ate lunch, talked to a couple of people, and when the bell rang to go home, I went home. I couldn't believe that the world went on like Nana wasn't gone. Nana wasn't here anymore, and everybody treated the day like it wasn't nothing out the ordinary.

The day of the funeral, I got dressed. I made sure I had on a dress, a hat and gloves the way Nana wanted me to. My aunts, uncles, and cousins all tried to talk to me and cheer me up. I ain't talk to them. My mother tried to talk to me, and I just looked at her. My girls showed up at the funeral, but they just hugged me and told me they loved me. They ain't try to make talk. I was mad that the world didn't stop for Nana; I was numb; I was scared to speak because I wasn't sure what would happen if I opened my mouth to say something. I waited for everybody to say goodbye to Nana before I got up to see her for the last time. She looked beautiful and quiet and happy and like she was sleeping. I kissed her on the cheek and whispered in her ear not to forget to remember me. When they closed the casket, it sounded like it echoed through the whole church; I watched them lift Nana in the air and lost my mind. I opened my mouth to take a deep breath but when I let it out, I screamed and screamed. I tried to get them to put Nana back down. I would take care of her. Milk got to me first and then two of my boy cousins held me down while I screamed and cried. Nana had died. So, I died too.

CHAPTER **10**: THE HIGH SCHOOL YEARS'89-'92

-

Sage

D.D.T. stood for _Doing Damage Together_. We wore pink bandanas folded in the back of our jeans. That was our symbol and color. And Lord knows we did a lot of damage together. We had fights; we jumped people, cursed people out, embarrassed people, and wreaked all kinds of havoc in the name of D.D.T. Truth be told, we were worse than the Melrose Boys. They were not the gun toting kind. To say that they never held one, didn't posses one, or wouldn't obtain and use one is not entirely true either, but it wasn't _Boyz in the Hood_. However, the girls and I were so angry after Nana and Bilal's death. We never got a chance to heal from their deaths before three more young men in our neighborhood died tragic deaths. No one really believed that we were as affected by the loss of childhood friends as maybe their parents were we had no outlets other than drugs, alcohol, sex, violence, and rebelling. It was our way of grieving and purging. We couldn't reconcile in our minds that we could live to see twenty-five years of age so we lived life as if we wouldn't; so many unnecessary risks. Our initiation into D.D.T. was a simple example. We all had to do the initiation weekend since we were the founding members. It wasn't as if we were a real gang. No one had to be jumped in or have an orgy in order to be a member. In fact, if someone declined to do it, I don't think it would have made one bit of difference. I was thinking this even as I was about to the stupid initiation.

"I can't believe I'm really about to do this dumb shit."

"Hurry up Sage so we can go meet Aheem and them. You the last one. If we were your other friends you have all over New York you wouldn't have a problem. You need to stick with your girls sometimes. Them other bitches ain't grow up with you, we did. You need to show some loyalty sometimes. Damn!" Isa worked her talent for guilt.

"Isa, save that shit for somebody else. I'm about to do it," I yelled back—mostly because she was a little ways from where I was standing.

Part of the initiation was to find the most expensive car and with dirty sneakers, run across it from trunk to the hood. We were across the street from The Vill in full view of anyone who chose to pay attention to what we were doing. That was supposed to be the risk factor of it. I chose a clean, white, gold rimmed Acura legend with the spoilers. I took a deep breath, said a little silent prayer and took a running start toward the trunk of the car. When I was finished, my size sevens were all over that car. I walked away with a swagger, slapping fives with the girls until the alarm started sounding. We all took off at top speed—the hardcore thugs that we were.

The second half of the initiation lasted the whole weekend. It happened to be Bobby's birthday weekend. We were too young to have bottles of champagne and Hennessey and beer and at least a half pound of weed but we had it. We were going to party and bullshit all weekend and sleeping was not allowed. We stayed in Nana's apartment. Isa's aunt or mom would drop off groceries and make sure the place was still standing and then they would go back to their respective homes. Nana's apartment is the one Isa's mom and aunt had grown up in and it was too painful for either one of them to stay there more than a few minutes at a time. So that summer we were practically on our own in the apartment. The first day of the weekend was okay. It was blazing hot outside, so we went up the block to see if the fire hydrant was on. The fire hydrant was thee way of cooling off growing up in a metropolitan area. Somebody would come along and decide that it was too hot to go to the city pool, which was always overcrowded and there was no way anyone wanted to trek down to the beach. And the beach meant Coney Island or Jones Beach. There were more crack vials there than on the set of *New Jack City*. Therefore, the hydrant was opened up by a wrench and then there was water!

We arrived just as it was full blast. It wasn't that crowded yet, so we were free to enjoy it. Sienna, Milk, Isa, Jewel, Kim, and I were having a great time running in and out of the water. After Nana died, we tried to reach out to each other and squash the beef between us, but this would be the last outing that included Kim. Our t-shirts, short shorts, and sneakers were soaked. We didn't care; we were carefree, and life was good.

At that very moment Sienna accidentally bumped into me and I was knocked into the full blast of the hydrant. Soaking wet I still wasn't ninety pounds; I was so small that time stopped when I realized the full force of the water. I was enveloped in it and pushed clear across the street on my knees with my arms flailing. Opening my mouth to scream, lead to an esophagus full of water. The curb of the sidewalk broke my impromptu water slide. I was out of breath when I finished emptying my lungs of water. In what I thought was long distance, because my ears were clogged, were my friends asking me if I was okay. The second I nodded yes, their laughter burst my clogged ears. We geared up to leave. Walking down the block some guys started calling after Kim; they were a quarter of a block behind us. She turned to say something, but Milk stopped her. She replied to them without turning around. Kim kept her mouth closed as Milk moved Kim in front of her. I turned and saw Kim walking behind me; I thought Milk had it covered.

"She is too young to be talking to any of you," Milk said.

Kim wasn't that young, but those guys looked older than any of us including Milk.

"Let her tell us that," said boy number one.

"Man, fuck them hos," said boy number two.

"Yeah, but you want these hos, dirty muthafucker," yelled Milk over her shoulder. Kim was behind all us at one point and then she started sprinting past us. She never said 'look out' or 'run' or anything. I just happened to look up and saw the Heineken bottle in the air. I told everyone to run. Those clowns were tossing bottles at us and that simpleton Kim didn't even warn us. Luckily none of us were hit.

Later that night was much better. We were all up. We listened to music, played Mario Bros., smoked and drank until our eyes were crimson red; the pupils, not the white area. In the morning, me and who ever did not live in Nana's house went home to shower and change. I had to sneak in a little nap. Luckily for me they were probably just as hung-over as I was, so I was able to get that nap in without a problem.

The second night was so much harder. Two more people came in Nana's house and then four. I was counting heads because I sure couldn't tell you who they were. The next thing that I know Isa comes out of the back yelling at Aheem which was commonplace.

"What the fuck is all these niggas doing in my grandmother's house?"

"Isa calm down, yo," Aheem said in hopes that she would, "those is just my boys..."

"Your boys? Your boys? You know what honey? When these niggas leave, you leave too! Okay muthafucka? Now calm that huh!"

"You always trying to play somebody," Aheem yelled.

Foolish as it was to try to out yell Isa, it was kind of inspiring how he always kept the dream alive.

"Ain't hard to play you, but I tell you what, keep trying to play Billy Bad Ass for these bum ass niggas. These same muthafuckas'll be trying to kill ya dumb ass tomorrow."

I thought for sure Isa had gone too far especially when one of the Das Effects looking guys stepped up. His dreadlocks were as matted as his facial hair. The other guy who came in with him unfortunately looked like his even dirtier twin. The original dirtball spoke to Isa.

"Yo, we see tomorrow how much shit you talk when you come on the ave.," he said with a smirk.

"Nigga you threatening me?" Isa said directly into his mouth since they were nose to nose. Aheem stepped in between them. It got real quiet, real quick. The guy stepped back with his arms raised. He kept his eyes trained on Isa.

"No disrespect love. I would always keep you safe. That's my job until tomorrow." Although there was clear confusion all over Aheem and Isa's face, Isa blinked. And in the millisecond it takes to blink, her face said she registered and comprehended everything that man had just said. I couldn't place who the guy could be talking about. I knew all of Isa's sidemen, but nothing came to my mind. I made a mental note to ask her about it when we were alone.

"Yo my man, be out, bounce, leave," said Aheem.

"Aiight son, gods don't fight with mortals," Das Effects Jr. said.

"What?"

"Learn ya math yo."

"Get ya 5 and 20 percent ass out the muthafucking house." The two dreadlock brothers left Nana's house without any further incident. Isa was the queen of deflecting questions. Aheem may have been street smart but he was no match for Isa's swift thinking or her temper. He would do anything to avoid getting on her bad side. So, he suggested that we all take a smoke break to relieve the tension in the room. Isa was too quick to agree. A smarter man would have known that Isa, who usually liked to argue, was up to something; but he wasn't. About an hour later Aheem said they had to go make a run.

"Bobby! Let's be ghost," he yelled out.

Bobby and Milk were in the back arguing again. Isa, Sienna, Jewel and I all went back there. Whatever the beef was, it had to wait. The boys had to make a run. Isa and Sienna tried to walk in to talk to Milk. Jewel and I stood in the doorway. Milk all of a sudden jumped up and slammed the door in all our faces. She was so loud from the other side we didn't even have to put our ears to the door.

"You are not leaving! No! No! No!" Milk screamed.

We sat on the floor in the hallway listening. To this day, she will not divulge why she wouldn't let him go.

"Milk stop playing. Get the fuck outta the way."

Bobby was quite calm. He needed to be. Milk was a good foot taller and matched him pound for pound.

"Noooooooooooooooooh!"

"Milk stop fucking playing."

"Nooooooooo!"

"Milk, get the fuck..." He tried pushing, pulling, and shoving her human barricade from the door. Like the Rock of Gibraltar, she stood.

"Milk, for real, I'm not playing! Move dammit!"

Bobby balled up his fist and knocked her lights out. All we heard from our side was the initial 'smack' contact and then the immediate bounce, thud of her head hitting the door. And finally, the downward shift of weight. We could hear Bobby drag her from in front of the door. Then he opened the door, stepped over her, and left with Aheem; he never turned to confirm his handiwork. Sienna woke Milk up promptly using a cold, damp wash cloth. No one discussed the incident even at that time; we couldn't. We couldn't digest what just happened. So, we did what we did best: suppressed it. Milk remained in the room, with reluctant embarrassment, she released us from the moment, and we went into the living room.

Isa

I can't believe that Bobby put his hands on Milk like that. We didn't jump in cause this wasn't the first time they got into a fight and she always tell us to mind our business or she start fighting us to leave him alone. This was bad though. I hope she leave him for good. Aheem don't even have one time; he touches me and I will kill him. Kim needs to thank me. She didn't have to deal with none of this bullshit. I'm glad she finally got over me and Aheem being together. I thought I was going to have to bust her ass, but she knew to fall back. This thing between me and Aheem didn't have nothing to do with her. He ain't really all of that anyway but still I been with him for almost a year so he's something. He was there for me when Nana died and I got used to him being around. Next thing I knew I couldn't get rid of him, so I kept him and dipped out with other niggas when he wasn't looking. I let out a deep sigh before saying,
"Girls, I got big problems. I think that dirty nigga tonight knows Kabel. I think Kabel either is getting out soon or he's already out..."
I could see Sage remembered Kabel. He was one of the meanest boyfriends I had. He was doing a short bid, jail term, and I know they was hoping that meant we wasn't together no more. But I still wrote him. I knew none of the girls liked him because he had a bad temper. I keep telling them not to worry—he wasn't crazy enough to hurt me, but now, after what happened to Milk I don't think I could put anything past anybody. Now here come Kabel with his crazy ass. I was gonna have to do something quick before I ended up like Milk or in jail myself.

CHAPTER 11: THE HIGH SCHOOL YEARS '89-'92

-

Sage

The weekend fizzled out into a flat Tuesday. No one knew where the guys were. They would do that now and again, disappear. As a matter of fact, Milk had disappeared as well. She wasn't answering any of our calls or pages. She was gone the morning after Bobby hit her. Her mother said she was okay, so we just gave her some space. Beyond that we didn't know what to say to her anyway. Isa, Sienna, and I were heading to Melrose Ave. to see what was going on. We were talking about nothing in particular when Isa said, 'oh shit' and dipped into a store. She just left Sienna and I talking to ourselves. A three degree turn to the right was the object of Isa's flight: Kabel. Kabel flashed us his thousand-watt smile as he turned to face us and came bounding in our direction. That was the summer of the crazy bald heads and he was well in fashion for someone who had just completed an eighteen-month sentence. He was clean shaven, sporting khaki fatigues, naubuck Timberland boots and a white wife-beater t-shirt, he looked cool as a winter day. He embraced us both with his long arms, which ironically, I was glad for so that I could shake off the paranoia I felt.

"What's up ya'll? A dog like me is happy to see friendly faces. Every face ain't a friend, word," he was spouting jailhouse logic and theory 101.

"Big K, what's up? Looking good, looking good," Sienna was ever the comedienne.

"Yes, I must agree. How long you been out?" I asked.

"Broke the chains three days ago; How long we gonna bullshit here? Where my girl at? I know ya'll still running together so don't front."

It was an honest question and an honest statement. It deserved the same respect. So, we answered in turn.

"She around somewhere," Sienna said.

"Come on. I know she around *somewhere*. But my boo knew I was coming home this month. We been writing each other so..."

"Really?" I asked. It was news to me. He took my answer to mean hesitation.

"Oh, I know she ain't worried about that punk Aheem. Yeah, I know about him. It's nothing. I'm back and on my game. She could consider him dropped. And really ya'll ain't gotta be acting like that either. I always take care of mine."

Isa must have heard his little diatribe because she stepped out of the store. No questions, no consequences they just fell in this kissing embrace. I wished I could get swept up in the little DMXish, us against the world set up, but that was the hood. I knew that before they could fall out of that embrace, the block would be hot. Sienna broke them up when she saw Bobby on the horizon. Isa was a little reluctant until she looked in the general direction of where Sienna was looking. Isa knew Bobby was going to run his mouth to Aheem. We had to put some space and time between what could only be an inevitable disaster. We said our goodbyes with promises to return later. We told him were going downtown to see what we could see, but we would be back. Kabel wasn't having it.

"Baby, I been waiting to see you forever and you going downtown?" pleaded Kabel.

"Kabel, I ain't standing around while you talk to everybody in the damn world. See your peoples and when I get back you ain't got no excuses to leave me to see no body. You feel me?" Isa said, quick on her feet.

"Yeah, yeah, that's what's up. You need some money?" Kabel asked Isa as he was peeling off bills and putting them in her hand. He grabbed her by the head and kissed her hard. He pulled away but didn't let her head go.

"Make sure you come back. Don't make me come look for you," he warned.

"Baby I'ma be right back," Isa said sweetly, moving his hand from the back of her head. She smiled at him and we walked away slowly. Isa was biting her lower lip. I knew she was nervous. I don't know about her and Sienna but Kabel scared the shit out of me.

Harlem was a bust. We saw the same old people and by nine o'clock we were back on Melrose Ave in the good old Bronx. Isa, Sienna, and I were sitting in the basketball court rolling up a blunt. It was easier to smoke in the projects where that type of activity was commonplace than to risk doing it in our own neighborhood. Smoking in The Vill would mean conducting our cipher in the staircase or in the back of one of the buildings; neither of these options were appealing because it involved too many uncontrollable variables including our parents. Beyond that the courts were halfway to our homes and we could air out before we got home.

Two future ballers, NBA or Melrose Ave, just depending on the influences in their lives, were playing one on one. Streetlamps provided enough illumination to make out the basket and cast enough shadow to hide our illegal deed. Unbeknownst to us, that night was about to go in such a different direction. Some others nearby having a fight, thought they too had the cover of the night: Kabel and Elisa, the mother of his child. Now nosey as we were, we had no intention of trying to stop the cipher to see what was up. At the time we didn't know who they were, but we did know they were attracting too much attention to our little oasis because they were arguing loudly. A few moments later Isa recognized Kabel's voice. We realized who he was arguing with swiftly.

"Let's move ya'll," Isa said agitated. As we rose to depart, something that was said between the love birds caught our attention: '*some lightskinnededbitch*'. That slight could have been directed to anyone and been about anyone. However, it was the way Elisa said it that made us think she was talking about Isa. We'd heard Isa referred to as such too many times before. Hell, it could've been about Isa. We listened a little more intently to what was being said.

"I'm saying, *you* wasn't writing me in jail. You ain't put no money in my commissary. You ain't even come see me. Not once. At least she wrote me and was on the block when I came home. Where was your ass? With that nigga Angel. That nigga a sherm-head at that!" screamed Kabel.

"But at least I didn't do no dirt where you could see, but you, you don't give a fuuuuck!" replied Elisa.

"Man fuck this shit. I just wanna see my seed yo," Kabel said flatly.

"You ain't never gonna see her while you fucking with that yellow bitch! Word to my abuela in heaven yo!" hollered Elisa.

I felt Isa get up. She was standing between me and Sienna. We both grabbed for her and missed. Isa stepped out from the shadows to face Kabel and Elisa.

"Number one, I ain't gonna be too many more bitches and number two, how you not gonna defend me?"

Kabel looked startled, confused, and then angry.

"Whatchu talking about?! I know you heard me when I was talking to her..."

"No, you was trying to justify *dealing* with me not *defend* me."

"Hold up, hold up! I ain't gonna let both you bitches speak to me however the fuck you feel! I'm muthafucking K! King of the Ave! You gonna respect me up in this bitch!"

"Bitches?!" Isa and Elisa shouted simultaneously.

"You heard me. Fuck both y'all hos. My paper still right so it'll be another bitch to suck my dick before ya'll hit that corner."

While what Kabel stated was the truth, it didn't sit well with Isa at all.

"Muthafucka you don't ever have to worry about me," because Isa's voice was loud and traveling, a crowd began to form along the gate of the court, "I ain't nobody's bitch... you bum ass nigga! I ain't even one of these dirty project hos. Don't act like you wasn't giving me doe for any fucking thing I wanted! Or how you told me you wasn't fucking with her like that...that all she did was whine and smoke ya doe up and how you wasn't sure if that baby was yours..." Isa didn't just step over the line, she danced on it with tap shoes.

Kabel grabbed Isa by the throat to shut her up, but Isa was prepared to fight. She anticipated his next move and commenced to pounding away at his face with one hand while she tried to free her neck with the other. She kneed him twice swiftly. When he went down Isa kicked him viciously and spat on him. No one jumped in because it began and ended so fast. Nature of the street required that no one intervened. That fight was between that man and his girl. Beyond that, Kabel was a woman beater. The people in the neighborhood had seen Kabel put many a woman in same fetal position he now found himself in including Elisa when she was pregnant.

Make no mistake about it, Kabel was a murderer and would have killed Isa within the hour had he not gone back to jail. While Isa and Kabel were fighting, Elisa ran to "one-time", the cops on the corner, and said that Kabel had hit her and was currently beating on a friend who had jumped in. She had enough recent bruises to substantiate it, but she knew even with that they wouldn't hold him long. But since he was dirtier than Al Pacino in the last scene of *Scarface* when they picked him up, that chump fell under the old Rockefeller drug laws. His release date would deposit him in the new millennium.

CHAPTER 12: THE HIGH SCHOOL YEARS'89-'92

-

Sage

Days didn't get any crazier than the day we tried to change. It began so normally; that should have been the red flag. I met my girlfriend Mary at the 125th street train station on the downtown side so that we could take the 6 train to 68th street. We were going to be on time for school, for once. We met the others from the Talented Unlimited crew. Talented Unlimited was the performing arts sector of Julia Richman High School. As we exited the train station, it was a beautiful day! We strolled to the deli two blocks away from the school and ordered breakfast. We sat on the back steps of the school near the courts and missed first period and a little of homeroom.

With the audacity that only teenagers who have been told how talented they are can have, we swaggered into school. We punched our coded I.d. cards into the computerized mechanism, which along with the date and time read, 'good morning' or 'you're tardy!' We were then allowed to walk through the metal detectors. Finally phase three: random selection of a student to receive a wand and book bag search. When these measures were first implemented, parents and teachers alike rocked the school with protest. We, the students, couldn't have been more pleased. The parents didn't go to school with the Deceptagons, the resident gang, we did. They didn't see blood trailing in the hallways and staircases from the first to the fifth floor and all over the lunchroom. They didn't see the razor blades girls wore in their French rolls and in the insides of their mouths. They didn't see. They never did. Almost instantly the gangs disappeared when the safety measures were implemented. Fights continued to happen as it did in any school, but we were no longer attending the sister school to the famed school Joe Clark wrangled into a semblance of academic success.

I was in love with Hakeem. He was a senior to my junior. He was just beautiful in my eyes. He was very popular he treated everyone with respect. His skin was like a waterfall of deep ebony silk constantly flowing and smoother than a guy's should be. His smile was contagious. His teeth were so white they gleamed. He ran track, he could rhyme, and he was in the mixed choir with me. While I salivated over him, he didn't know that I was alive; well maybe he did. I kind of, sort of, made him think that I hated him. All the girls in the school liked Hakeem. I didn't want to be lumped in with everyone else and he didn't lump me in at all. I was trying to ask Mary if she wanted to hang out after school, but I became distracted by the fight in the hallway. It was broken up as quickly as it had begun, and the hallway cleared. Mary and I continued on to class. We were going to be late, but we had an excuse: there was a fight! All of a sudden there was a little stillness in the air. I felt him; Hakeem was coming near. I could feel my heart beating through my throat. I thought I told Mary to come on. She was in the middle of telling me her plan for cutting school and skipping Lebo's class, (Mrs. Lieberman, the T.U. choir teacher). I fell back and ran in the opposite direction. By the time Mary caught up with me on the first floor, she was fuming. I was still sweating profusely standing next to another friend Darneice. She was a senior and, in the choir, as well. Mary was so angry she could get her words out initially.

"*Darniece*, let me tell you what this chic did," Mary said without looking at me.

"Mary, I told you come on..." I tried to explain.

Darniece tried to listen through fits of laughter. Mary turned her body away from me and continued to speak to Darniece.

"Anyway *Darniece*, I was in the middle of my story when *that* one dips out. Which would have only made me a little mad, but I almost bumped into Hakeem and Ramik. Again, not a big deal, except they caught me talking to myself. The more I tried to explain, the more they looked at me like I needed to be in Bellevue," fussed Mary.

"Sorry..." I mumbled trying to hold in my own laughter. Darneice didn't share in the empathy and finally exploded her guffaw in Mary's face. I had to make it up to Mary, so I said I'd cut school with her. We headed to the movie theater on 59th street where Anderson, Darniece's brother worked. As we strolled along, we bumped into Ashford and Simpson, the Motown singer-songwriter married couple. They were so gracious and sincerely nice. They gave us autographs and then asked the dreaded question: why weren't we in school? Mary quick on her feet, told them we had lunch double periods on Wednesdays because as T.U. kids, our day was extended until 5:30 on Wednesdays. It sounded so good, *I* believed it. She went on to say how we were on our way back, but that *I* just had to have a pretzel first. I was thinking this girl has a future as a PR person. Was she a spin doctor or what? Ashford and Simpson waved us goodbye as they wished us luck in singing and in school. Having a school in the same neighborhood as wealthy real estate moguls, television and music studios, we would occasionally run into celebrities. More often than not, they were not as nice as Ashford and Simpson. When we got back to the school, Lebo cancelled class—amazing. For the first time we left school at 2:30 like everyone else.

Isa

Me and Jewel was in front of 840, a building on the Grand Concourse across from Sage's building, when Sage and her friend Mary showed up. I started seeing this new guy after I dropped Kabel and Aheem. He didn't live nowhere near us and I liked it that way. I was tired of all the fighting and arguing with people. I wanted to chill. I know I'm a instigator and the girls got my back no matter what so when I stopped they stopped. Besides I think they stopped hanging around me so much cause we was always in some shit. Kim been stopped dealing with me. So, I was trying to change some of my ways. I wanted the girls to meet him and maybe some of his friends. I wasn't expecting Mary, but I told her she could come too. She was cool.

"Mary look, you don't have to go. In fact, you should go home. We always wind up getting into some kind of beef," Sage said, playing me.

"Mary don't listen to Sage. We don't do that DDT thing anymore. We just trying to chill. No more jumping people and that other dumb shit. So, you do not have to worry." When I finished Sienna walked up.

"Let's roll out ya'll," she said.

We hailed a gypsy cab. Four of us squeezed in the back and Jewel sat in the front with the cab driver. We used to catch a cab and then jump out without paying—and we had money. We got so good at scamming the cab drivers over the last few months, that when we were about a couple of blocks away from our destination, instead of jumping out of the cab, Jewel would begin an argument with the driver. That day she went on and on about that wasn't the place we asked to go. The man got confused and flustered. Jewel broke on him; yelling take us back to where he got us or let us out immediately. He let us out I'm sure just to end her loud tirade. We exited the cab like we were so angry and distraught at being let out in the middle of nowhere.

As he pulled off, we laughed walking down the half block toward Bronx River Projects. The cabbie saw us patting ourselves on the back in his rearview mirror. He made a sharp u-turn and hollered out of his window, "I'm going to kill you!"

It looked as if he reached under his seat for something. We didn't wait to find out. We each ran in different directions. Sage actually ran into someone's yard. The people there just looked at her like they saw that shit everyday. We all met up in the projects laughing through our fear. Murder was nowhere to be found; my new man's name was Murder.

Sage

There was a group of girls in front of his building. Since we were not DDT anymore, it should've been easy to ask questions nicely and we did. Yes, they had seen Murder and in fact he was in his house. The girls showed us the hallway to the apartment. We walked away with the feeling that not every female is trifling. Murder opened the door himself. He was tall with dark brown skin. He was a muscular slim with a thin layer of hair on his upper lip. The apartment was furnished with over-the-top items. The wrap around leather couch took up the majority of the living room. The walls were a bleached white. The framed paintings displayed splotches of red, silver, black, white, and green in abstract. The aquarium was six feet in width and took up three fourths of the wall. The sound system was directly beside the aquarium which I had no doubt contributed to the two fish floating at the top of the tank. The oval shaped glass table had filled ashtrays, Hustler and *Word Up!* Magazines, and rested on top of a zebra rug. The black curtains gave the unnatural blue light more substance. It was a drug dealer's den. He stepped back to allow us in and closed the door behind us.

"Glad you made it. My boys on the way back to here from the studio." He put their newly pressed cd on and showed us a poster of them; all four of the guys had bald heads and screwed up faces. They had named themselves *Onyx*. While we were waiting, Murder takes out his gun to show off for an already gun-happy Isa. It was a new silver plated nine-millimeter. He demonstrated to us how to break it down, load the clip, the safety, and the rules of recoil.

"All of you need to try it out for yourselves. A woman should know how to protect herself, but more importantly her man." Murder looked young but his words belied his age might be considerably more than what we were used to. Minutes later, Murder's brother, Killer, dropped by. He dumped about an ounce of weed on the table and told us to roll up so we could get the cipher going. Mary did not smoke. So, she sat away from us in an armchair. She didn't know about getting a contact and we weren't going to tell her. Murder and Isa took two blunts and disappeared into his room.

As soon as we finished our second blunt there was a pounding on the door. We just knew it was one of those angry boys from the poster. I crossed over and sat on the couch next to Mary so that I could have a better look as they entered. When Killer opened the door, a girl was in front screaming,

"Tell those skank hos to come out here now!"

I walked to the door not because I was brazen, but amazed. When I looked out of the frame of the door, there was a sea of girls in the tiny hallway. All I could think to myself was "fuck!"

How was this possible? We had started on the right path and beef comes anyway. But I understood; this was Karma. Jumping people, spitting on people, all around degrading people would revisit us in that dingy project hallway. And we probably deserved it. However, lives were going to be taken if that was the way we had to go. I moved back into the room and had a pow-wow with the girls about Mary as we handed her our jewelry and rubbed Vaseline on our faces. I plead Mary's case.

"Mary is not a part of DDT and we shouldn't make her fight." They agreed. I knew that Mary would have fought but she wasn't much of a fighter. I had become as volatile as my friends and Mary was my anchor in sanity. Killer was trying unsuccessfully to reroute the hoard at the door. It was almost as if he was more worried about what would happen to them than to us. Of course, we didn't know Murder for the three months that Isa had known him. And his brother knew Murder best. Murder bounded out of the room when he heard all of the commotion. He nearly tripped over the rug trying to determine which group he would deal with first; he chose us.

"Whatch'all doing? Ain't gonna be no fighting up in here. Ya'll going home and ain't nobody gonna touch ya'll."

We each searched one another's face for a retort. There was none. Murder wedged himself past his brother to address the mob. So, we followed Murder out the front door with Killer bringing up the rear. A grown woman, at least twenty-one or twenty-two, mirrored Isa's features and body type plus a gap in her top row of teeth; it was unclear if this woman was Murder's ex-girlfriend or current girlfriend, but we were clearly teenagers. She took a fighting stance in front of Murder.

"Conesha, move and get these hoodrats from in front of my door and out my hallway." He was alarmingly calm, and the crowd was instantly hushed as we pushed through. One of the girls recognized me.

"I know you! You Kim's friend! Yeah, you live over by Concourse Village!" The crowd erupted again. I reached for the girl and mushed her head back. Killer grabbed me with one arm and carried me out of the building. The crowd followed us out to the sidewalk. Conesha, did not like to be ignored. She was again in Murder's face.

"I been with you for years! When you was a nothing! I helped you get that rep and that name nigga! I ain't going nowhere. When this young bitch up and leave, I'll still be here. You don't know how to let me go so let's not do this. Not over this little girl. Is she even legal?"

"Conesha leave. You making me angry." Murder said softly.

"This bitch don't even look sixteen!"

Conesha mushed Isa in the face unexpectedly. Jewel punched Conesha on her temple. One of Conesha's friends swung at Jewel and missed. She was quickly knocked down by Sienna. The brawl was in full swing when Murder started shooting his gun in the air. Rat-a-tat-tat and the whole crowd scattered. Murder placed the tip of his nine to Conesha's temple. I had never seen anyone so scared. I had never seen such a cold menacing in anyone's eyes as I saw in Murder.

I guess over the years Conesha and Murder had had their spats and maybe it even became physical sometimes. However, it looked to me as if it had never gotten to that level. Tears flowed from Conesha's eyes shamelessly as he slowly forced her to her knees.

Jewel was dealing with her own demons and very upset at having been put in this type of situation again. Jewel wasn't usually violent, and she respects all life. This was just a dark era for her. She doesn't even recall 85% of what went on during her high school years; she blocked it all out. People across the street could hear Jewel yelling and goading Murder.

"Shoot her dumb ass! Simple bum-ass-project ho! Shoot her mutha fucking ass!"

Isa placed herself between Conesha and Murder. I thought I was in a nightmare. I couldn't reach Isa to pull her back because Killer still had a tight grip around me.

"Isa what the fuck are you doing? Move!" I yelled.

"No, I don't want my man to go back to jail on the strength of this bitch!" Then Isa turned to Murder. She placed one hand on his face and guided his icy stare away from Conesha and toward her own face. Using her other hand, she helped Conesha up and pushed her toward her friends. Isa began to speak to Murder. There was not a drop of fear or anxiety in her voice.

"Baby listen to me so I don't have to say this shit twice. If you go to jail over this bullshit, I will not be coming to see you. I will not be writing you. There will be no money in your com from me. You will not be my man. And please believe I will get rid of this baby faster than you can bust that gun. I love you and you need to focus on that. I'm telling you, you kill her, you will never see me again and you better damn well know that I ain't bringing no kid to no jail honey. So, make your mind up now."

Murder lowered the gun and hugged Isa. He didn't know Isa was pregnant and neither did we. He was elated and moved to think he had an heir to his assassin organization. Killer let me go when he saw that I had calmed down and caught Conesha before she fell to the ground again. She looked so defeated. It was more than the pregnancy which let her know it was a lost battle. It was the respect Isa demanded of Murder and his willingness to give it to her. The affection and love he showed her in the simple hug. She knew it well and knew that he was sincere.

That young girl saved her life. Murder would have killed her without hesitation. Through a distant connection between Conesha and us we learned a few things about Murder and Conesha's relationship. She was just like Isa a few years ago and when it came time to save someone's life, she not only stood aside, she encouraged him to shoot. In retrospect, I can see her flashing back on the blood splattering that never came out of her Polo shirt. She threw it down the incinerator as she would many items of clothing from both she and Murder over the years. She watched in agonizing silence as we got in the cab home and he lovingly kissed Isa before he closed the door. Killer came behind him and spoke into his ear. They jumped immediately into Murder's BMW two cars down and veered out. That cab ride was filled with tense silence. My friends kept changing on me. When did we become this angry, this comfortable with drugs and guns and jail and murder and violence? I kept changing. I didn't like how I felt after we would erupt with so much anger, but while I was immersed in it...it was intoxicating. I was losing myself and I couldn't seem to find the road back to me.

Riding the subway to school a few weeks later, I read in the Daily News that Conesha had turned state's evidence against Murder when the police caught her trying to throw away a small duffle bag, gun and a blood-soaked shirt down the incinerator. The police had been watching her and Murder for some time now. Some of what I read, I already knew because of Isa but I was also able to pull out some of the lies. Such as Conesha still loved Murder even after the gun incident so she stood by his side and showed solidarity even though by then, Murder had put a ring on Isa's finger. Isa wasn't mentioned in any of the articles I read and good thing too because Isa's family had no knowledge of her involvement with Murder or her pregnancy. Even when the detectives told Conesha that it was her brother that Murder killed and showed her the evidence, pictures of his dismembered body parts, she continued her silent vigil. She believed that Murder would be grateful and show some gratitude. But when the detectives told her the duffle bag, she attempted to throw down the incinerator was her brother's heart she took a deal with the prosecution. Murder was indicted on thirty-two counts of murder and conspiracy to commit murder.

Isa

I wanted to kill Conesha but the detectives moved her out of the city. No problem, I would catch up with that bitch at the trial. Me and Sage skipped school and went to Murder's arraignment. The judge had denied Murder bail. We were sitting in the row of seats directly behind Murder.

I tapped him. He wouldn't turn around. So, I tapped his lawyer to get Murder's attention. Murder ignored his lawyer too. I started to hit him in the back, yelled his name, and he refused to look at me. Murder leaned over to speak into his lawyer's ear. I calmed down hoping for a word too. The judge instructed that Murder be removed. I got hysterical. Sage tried to calm me down as the court officers escorted Murder out of the courtroom. The judge called for order in his court. I sank into my seat and cried my eyes out. Murder's lawyer, a short bald white man, walked through the swinging doors which separated us and spoke. His deep voice didn't match his body at all.

"I'm Nathan Freeman, Mr. Beach's attorney." Sage looked at him with confused when he said Murder's real name.

"Mr. Beach...um Salim? I will not use his street moniker." I nodded with understanding but looked out of the window with tears rolling down my face. I know he would speak to Sage like he was speaking to me. "Salim has instructed me to give your friend the money he was going to use for bail and tell her that he loved her and that he was sorry." I still looked away.

"Isa don't you want to send a message back?" Sage asked. I shifted in my seat more.

"No worries," he said, "I've been fired." He walked out the courtroom. Me and Sage walked out a few minutes later. We took the train home and I cried on her shoulder. I went back to Nana's house. What else could I do? I fell asleep in front of the TV. The phone rang. I picked up the remote control to turn off *In The Heat of the Night*. Then I picked it up. It was Killer.

"Isa, what's up? I gotta make this quick. I'm leaving town in the morning. You wanna go?"

"You not in no trouble. Why you leaving? Where you going?" I rubbed the sleep out my eyes.

"Long Island. My family got a house there."

"Look I ain't going."

"Me and my family can take care of you and the baby. It ain't nothing."

"Let me think about it. I don't know if I'm keeping this baby or not. Call me in the morning before you leave. Maybe I can work something out with my mother or something. I don't know what I'm doing about anything anymore." I had to hang up on him because I was sick again.

Sage

Later that week called Isa called me crying. Killer was about to go on the run. He asked her to go with him to the 'family home' in Long Island. He said he would take care of her and her child. He also told her Murder died in a prison fight earlier that week; he never even made it to trial. Killer died himself when pieces of a plane leaving JFK airport crashed onto his family's home a month later.

True to her word Isa terminated that pregnancy. I had underestimated relationship between Murder and Isa. I thought Murder was just another guy. Isa really loved him. I even thought Isa was running the okey doke, tricking him, about the pregnancy or at the very least about Murder being the father. We didn't see Isa for about a month. She went to spend some time with Milk in Jersey.

CHAPTER 13: THE HIGH SCHOOL YEARS '89-'92

-

Sage

It was senior year. When Isa came back, it was time for school, and we continued to follow her through the tumultuous relationships she had with guys. Almost always if she started dating a new guy, he would have friends that at least two of us would wind up dating as well. It was strange, but more often than not, when one of us stopped dating the guy it caused a domino effect and the other relationships would fall apart as well. But the drama realm would forever have Isa as its reigning sovereign.

Day was giving way to night and shift changes. Have to be in the street to see the street. It moves, breathes, and breeds. You can hear the wind whispering: 'I'm on my grind cuzin'. Its aroma is a mixture of steamed crabs,

Chinese food, the chicken spot, hair grease, blood, steel, sweat, cooked crack, booze, beef patties, Cuchifrito, and weed. This is New York City. The noise: car horns, loud ass-drunk ass old men in front of the bar. Eastern Star sisters dressed in all white emit a quick hush as they float by. Doors slamming, kids crying, moms yelling, fathers denying all in a syncopated rhythm. Their lead singer is the coco/cherry man-he sells the cold ice treats. His hustle is the most honest. This is New York City. Everyone's rushing because everyone's late because everyone's suspicious about everyone who touches their money. Welcome to New York City.

We were on our daily trek to Harlem; this time to see Isa's newest conquest Wayne. I already knew he was stupid. We went to the same high school, but we never spoke to each other. I thought he was a fake drug dealer. He flashed too much and did entirely too much talking. He was so polite whenever he called Isa's house and she was just as nasty to him. Isa's mother loved him though she had never laid eyes on him. She decided since he had mastered the English language, unlike the thugs Isa usually went out with, she would always take a message from him. The rest she didn't give a second thought. She usually hung up on them if they lacked simple phone etiquette. Isa was prepping us about him.

"Ya'll he so dumb! He does whatever I say," said Isa.

"What's new?" I said. She acted like all the guys she dealt with weren't dumb in some way.

"No, I mean Wayne is an asshole! I never even kissed him! He's all fat, black, and ugly..."

"Funny, you dealing with Biggie Smalls now?" joked Jewel.

As we come upon the block, who do we see but Bucky Beaver. That wasn't his given name or even his nickname. I nicknamed him that behind his back. I never knew his real name and it wasn't important. His teeth protruded so badly he couldn't close his mouth without impaling his bottom lip. At least that's what I envisioned since I had never seen his mouth closed. He went to my high school too. Isa knew damn well that none of us would be dating *him*.

He gave me dap, a handshake, as if we actually spoke in school. Then Wayne came laboring out of the building. He was just as how Isa described him: fat, black, and ugly. Looking back now, he was basically a good person. He fell really hard for Isa. That man wound up crying over her and everything. I kind of felt bad about being a party to Isa's mistreatment of him. However, people only do to you what you allow and he damn near gave her permission. He loved the attention he received from the people on his block; People who felt that no one would want to be with him, for any reason.

Isa

He was in awe of my light skin and blond hair. I was a fly girl and I let it be known to any and everyone that I got down for him and I was his girl. Because I so proudly proclaimed my allegiance to him, people treated him differently; girls approached him like he Denzel Washington. I had that affect on people. I could make anyone believe that what I had was solid gold when it wasn't nothing but wood. I was his status symbol as far as him and his hood were concerned. Now behind closed doors, Wayne hopped to it. He was constantly begging me to at least give him a kiss. After three weeks of seeing each other, I had racked up a little over $2000 worth of jewelry, clothes, sneakers, hairdos, dinner, and weed. All Wayne had to show for it at the end of the third week was a broken heart. About four months later he met someone else. She could have been my twin. The most unbelievable part of the whole thing was his deep denial. He really thought that I was just so torn up about her Murder's death that I couldn't be in a serious relationship. To take it a step beyond ridiculous, Wayne named his first child Isa. Dumb, dumb, dumb, dumb, dumb...

CHAPTER 14: THE HIGH SCHOOL YEARS '89-'92

-

Sage

I was trying to find a way to put some space between my home friends, school friends, and my common sense with little success. I could see the escapades we sought were nearing an end that would not be beneficial to my peace of mind, but still I rode that crazy train and paid the fare; Kim got on board too with no escape route. Isa knew this guy from one of her many high schools named Pudgy. Pudgy was supposed to be this rising producer and he knew all the money men like Country, Supreme, and Alpo. We knew them too, but apparently not like he did. Pudgy's cousin Butter had a fully equipped studio. Butter was against any new acts but when he saw Kim, he changed his tune. They told us that they wanted to make us stars. It would be me, Isa, Jewel, Billie, who was now living in New York permanently, rapping and Kim on vocals. When we first started out, we would rap about nonsense. We would get a nice flow and then dive into gibberish. We weren't rappers...we were funny and had charisma. We were young and cute and why not?

Pudgy set up an informal meeting between The Fly Girlz, that was our name, and some cats that were interested in new acts. He didn't tell us; he just made it seem as if they were some of his boys just hanging out. Then we did what we always did: rap about nonsense. One of the guys thought we sounded ridiculous. He was immediately cursed out by Isa. The second one thought we had chemistry and little flow, but we needed to focus. The last one said we were terrible because we wanted to be. He told us to take the suggestions we heard that day and apply ourselves. But in that business, we would only get one shot and three just walked out of the door.

We were furious when we found out who the guys really were. Pudgy explained he wanted us to be ourselves and not feel pressured into performing. Rolled eyes were his only responses. We were aptly learned. So, the next few times when we were supposed to be hanging out with Pudgy, we stayed ready. In fact, we started to gear all situations toward rapping so that we could demonstrate our skills. We were getting better and a lot of Pudgy's boys were feeling us. One of Pudgy's friends gave us the best advice we ever had: rhyme about what we knew. If we could bring it closer to home, we may come up with a hit or two, and maybe even get on someone's mix tape. We already knew that if we rhymed about what we knew, we wouldn't be any different than *Too Short* and we wanted desperately to be different.

Pudgy and Butter introduced us to one of his other acts, a Spanish rapping duo, Lisette and Tanya. Pudgy and Butter were paid by their boyfriends, a couple of mid level drug dealers Noodles and Earl.

They weren't runners on the street, and they didn't have a block. They were transport experts. They would get young girls still in high school to transport from New York to the Hamptons, Jersey, Philly or Delaware. Delaware needed coke too. Lisette was Noodles and Earl's Spanish connection. She spoke the language so that there was no beef between the guys and the Puerto Rican and Dominican connects. She was also Earl's girlfriend. She rarely transported. Her duties also included recruiting and researching the recruits thoroughly. She did a better job of checking than the CIA.

Lisette's girls were always honest, loyal, young, down on their luck, and most importantly retail hoes—they worked for clothes and shoes. The girls never got a whole lot of money. They would get something like fifty or a hundred dollars and some type of jewelry or a leather jacket, or Reeboks. Lisette got the big bucks. While she was just like the girls she recruited, she had more street sense and damn near a black heart. She loved Earl but didn't trust him as far as she could throw him. She wasn't new to the game. Her mother was the one who put her on. Her mother, "Esposa", to everyone, schooled Lisette well. She was doing Fed time in the Midwest somewhere. She had just gone away a year ago.

Lisette said she and Esposa were very close while Lisette was younger but going into her teenage years Lisette started feeling herself as most girls do when some young boy smiles and slides in her. She started feeling like she was a woman and she and her mother stood on the same ground. In Lisette's case, she said it out loud. Esposa beat her ass like a grown woman in the street and then left her there. She couldn't come in the house to retrieve not even clean underwear. Lisette stayed with another cousin and then Earl until Esposa went to prison. She then moved back into the apartment she lived in for seventeen years once her mother was gone for good.

At that time, she was eighteen and could care for herself and the rent. That was Spanish Harlem anyway, 151st and Broadway. The block protected her as if she were the lone resident child. Earl was half Dominican and half Black. Otherwise, they would have run him off of the block. They did shame him for never having learned the language.

Lisette tried to tell us how good the drug life was and that we would make crazy dollars and wouldn't need a real job. It sounded really good and tempting. It never occurred to us that we had agreed to be drug mules or the amount of jail time that would come from such stupidity. Even Jewel, our moral compass, was intoxicated by the money and danger. All we had to do was go to school and then cut; something we already did. We were supposed to meet Lisette at the Port Authority at 1:00 pm so that we could catch the 1:30 to Delaware. She already had the coke. We were told to meet her in the downstairs bathroom with our book bags. If any of us were stopped, we were to say was that we were going to a cousin's or a grandmother's for the weekend and we already had clothes there. It made sense. Isa, Kim, and Jewel were still in private so school they were in uniforms; Billie and I were in plain clothes.

Lisette was already at Port Authority. She sent a SkyPager message telling us where to meet and for us to separate from each other. It was a scary and exciting time. We were so busy talking we forgot to separate. We were everything Lisette told us not to be: loud and raunchy. It was a good thing we were being ourselves. There happened to be a water main break at 42nd Street. There almost always was. We didn't know it, but Lisette had two other girls with her. She had already given them their packages. We recognized one of the girls as Tanya, Noodles' girlfriend of two years. She had no business being there. She was at least four or five months pregnant. We didn't know the other girl, but she looked really nervous and scared. We nicknamed her Scary.

What happened next happened so fast. Because of the water main break some type of alarm was sounded for the workers there. There was a loud, rushed and indecipherable announcement on the P. A. system. There were train officials within the station giving more clear directions. But Scary didn't listen to any of that. Her nerves were already on edge. Cops were running toward her general direction, but not *to* her. She became undone when she saw the police dog. It was all just a coincidence. The officers were headed upstairs to the in-station precinct after a safety drill they did to show the Mayor and the people of New York that Port Authority was safe.

Scary started behaving erratically. She was screaming in Spanish don't let the dog get her, she was afraid of dogs. She said she would never do it again. Lisette was telling her to shut up, but she kept on talking. One of the cops was holding Scary trying to calm her down when the dog smelled the coke in her bag and jumped on her. She became inconsolable. Lisette stopped talking to Scary altogether. Lisette turned and took Tanya by the elbow and made her stand up. When Scary saw that Lisette meant to leave her there, she started screaming and pointing at Lisette and Tanya. She was yelling out their names. Lisette pushed Tanya away and turned around toward Scary. Lisette reached into her Gucci bag and shot Scary at close range in her head. She quickly dropped the gun. She managed to only be shot twice by the cops. One bullet went through her shoulder and the other was lodged in her thigh.

Tanya was screaming and fell to the floor. She wasn't shot, just scared. From where we were standing, we could see everything. We were all thinking the same thing: a few more minutes that could have been us. And we all of a sudden couldn't think of one reason why we needed the money or what the allure was. We turned around and got back on the subway home. Earl didn't go looking for Lisette. Nor did any of us think that he would. He and Noodles denied knowing the girls when Tanya called from the precinct. No one from her family would come and bail her out. We sure didn't have any money. The detectives told her that Lisette blamed everything on her. Tanya was in shock, but she straightened her face and remained silent during her entire interrogation.

After seven hours of her sitting in silence and refusing even water, she was sent back to her cell with a swollen face and a bruised lip for her silence. Since she didn't show any suicidal tendencies, they didn't see a need to check on her regularly. Later that night she hung herself in jail. Noodles didn't claim the body of Tanya or the child and he didn't go the funeral.

He never made contact with Tanya or her family again. The detectives had lied on Lisette. She never said a word either. But Tanya believed it because she knew how grimy Lisette was and she watched her shoot Scary. She didn't even know that Lisette was capable of killing anyone. Tanya left the earth thinking that everyone in the world had betrayed her.

Lisette called Earl from the hospital only to plead Tanya's case. She knew he wasn't coming for her and she didn't care. She knew that the phone was probably tapped but she thought that way she could get Earl and lessen Tanya's time. Tanya was only sixteen. Earl pretended that she had the wrong number. Lisette apologized for having dialed the wrong number and hung up. That call was for Tanya. When the news that Tanya had killed herself reached Lisette, her rage for Earl grew. She was able to call Isa somehow and told her all this.

Lisette's smiling picture ran in all the papers, news broadcast- Spanish and English alike, and of course the hood news—word of mouth. Each medium had the story completely twisted, as usual, but we damn sure weren't about to fix it. Lisette was branded like some kind of female drug lord. She had enough money to hire a greedy, narcissistic, media-whore of a lawyer. There was not one bad picture of Lisette anywhere. Even in her mug shot she posed like it was the cover of Vogue. Scary died and they gave Lisette life for the homicide and more time on top of that for possession, trafficking, conspiracy, and lack of remorse. A few months into her sentence Noodles and Earl were found hung off of a pier by the Jersey shore. Lisette became a legend.

Kim took the opportunity to spend more time with her boyfriend Sean and put some distance between us; she didn't seem that fazed by what happened. However, truth be told, those first few nights found us all fighting an asthmatic type of breathing and praying to God that it wouldn't be our last night in our bed in our house. Lisette might have killed us all if the need arose. We knew that. We saw her enjoy killing Scary. She enjoyed it—a true sociopath.

CHAPTER 15: THE HIGH SCHOOL YEARS '89-'92

-

Kim

Once upon a time...

I was supposed to be a star. In most people's opinion, including my choir director, when I was going to church, I could sing. I was not an Aretha, but definitely a Mary J. singer. I was one of those people who was constantly told that she was cute and that she could dance and sing. No one ever emphasized the importance of an education at least not the same way they emphasized my beauty. And then when my body began to fill out, forget about it. For me, it was more important to have a bunch of name brand handbags, shoes, jackets, and toys. Even my underwear was name brand. If people knew me, they would know there was nothing to be jealous of. I was sweet and kind. I was very popular with the guys from all over, but I had no use for them after they couldn't buy me anything else. I definitely was a Harlem Cat's girl. The one I loved though was Sean. He lived in Harlem and he rose to be one of the biggest names around. I had other guys on the side just like he had other girls on the side, but we belonged to each other first.

Sage

Sean let go of her first. He had to. Kim was trying desperately to get a record deal. She knew that school wasn't her thing and she needed to be discovered and quickly. To that end, she was on dates with producers, writers, artist, whoever he may be that claimed to be in the industry or who could hook her up. Not saying that she slept with them all but, the point is if it was one, it was one too many. She ran into the wrong one. We don't know what he promised her, or if she had knowledge of what was getting ready to happen, but if she had one regret, it was meeting Butter. Hell, many people regretted meeting Butter including us, but we didn't lay down with him; Kim did. Butter was short for a guy. He was about 5'7-5'8. His brown skin was smooth and baby fine. His dimples, full eyebrows, long lashes, naturally curly hair, and light brown eyes overshadowed his yellowing, crooked bottom teeth, for most; not for me though. There was nothing like a man with nice, clean, white teeth. Hell, there's nothing like a man who brushes his teeth. A little toothpaste a day would have made all the difference in the world. With all of the money he laid claim to, I often wondered if he knew what a dentist was. Damn, I digress. He more than lived on 109th and Seventh Avenue; he was the grime from the gutter of that corner.

Kim

Sage always joked that his alias was Butter because of his teeth, but he said it was because of his skin and his game: smooth like butter. Sage said he was a piece of shit and tried to tell me the same thing, but I was obsessed with him making me famous. I started to ignore Sean. I guess Butter's game was like that after all. He started feeding into my ego and telling me that he would make me a star. He put money in my pockets and treated me like a queen.

Sage

Meanwhile on the other side of Harlem, 125th and Morningside, Sean was truly trying to make a way for her. Sean knew this guy who went to school with Puffy. They all got together and did lunch. Puffy at the time was with K.Ci of Jodeci. They told Sean's friend to tell Sean to bring Kim around so that they could hear her sing. K.Ci said that Devante' was looking for some girls to make a group and if she was all that Sean was saying, then he would see how she did in the studio and put her on. Kim had a better shot than we did. She had real singing talent. Everyone's seen the behind the music with the stars. Devante' had a group that involved Missy Elliot and in fact he had a house full of different artists. Kim could have been there. And her foot was in the door. Kim thought she was grown and yes, at sixteen she should have some kind of common sense.

Kim

I was at Butter's house when I checked my pager and saw that Sean had been blowing me up. I called Sean back from Butter's home phone and jumped up and down when I heard the news about a possible audition. That was a Thursday in August. I was set to meet with Puffy and Devante' by Saturday. I kissed Butter and prepared myself to leave. I needed some money to go shopping so I emptied his pockets and motivated toward the door. Butter wasn't pleased or happy with this situation. I felt sorry for him, so he was able to guilt me into having sex with him. I didn't know he had a video camera going and filmed the entire episode. There wasn't anything raunchy on the tape and I didn't even perform oral sex, but you could see my face clear as day. When we was finished, Butter was still pouting.

"You going see that nigga? Now? After we just...?" Butter questioned.

"Yes I am."

"You don't need him. I got whatever you need," he said. He was pressuring me again to leave Sean, but I wasn't that crazy. Sean would never let me go.

"I'll call you later," I said. I gave him another kiss. I left Butter lying in his bed alone with four dollars in his wallet and walked out the front door. I called Sage from the nearest pay phone and told her that Butter finally talked me into having sex with him.

"Girl I did it to Butter just now."

"Why would you do that?" Sage was stunned.

"Please he spending money, he stupid over me, and he *is* going to get me a deal."

"No, what he is going to get you is killed if Sean finds out."

"Sean ain't going to find out."

"What if Butter tells him?"

"Okay you and Butter both crazy. He said the same thing. He keeps trying to get me to leave Sean. I told him he better play his position because he don't know my man."

"He doesn't know Sean? Everybody knows Sean."

"He just knows I got a man, he don't know his name. I'm not that stupid."

"I can't tell."

"Look nevermind that. I got an audition with Devante Swing!"

Sage

I tabled my concern for her love life as our conversation switched to irrational stardom swiftly. Meanwhile Butter was having his own irrational moment. If he couldn't have Kim, then he would destroy her. He made copies of the tape and made a small fortune by Saturday. There's never been a Harlem cat on his grind like he was at that time. Butter was trying to bury Kim alive. Kim had no idea what was going on because after shopping in lower Manhattan for the perfect outfit, she went home to the Bronx and then on to Sean's house to make nice. Saturday morning Devante' called off the meeting. He basically said Kim was too hot and freaky. He didn't do porn stars as artist. That's something coming from someone whose next group single was entitled '*Freakin' U*'. That was the word on the street.

Sean was steaming. He called his homeboy Jokk that set up the meeting initially. Jokk said that he didn't know what was going on but that he would find out. I arrived at about two to help Sean comfort Kim. Jokk was ringing Sean's house bell within the hour with a copy of the tape. Sean didn't know what was on the tape and had spent the afternoon consoling Kim who felt she had lost all hope. Jokk didn't even know what was on the tape. It was a struggle to get the tape. He had to promise to harm the guy's family in order to get the tape. The guy who gave it to Jokk just said that he should sit in between Sean and Kim when it was played because it might be too much for them; we all sat and watched together.

Kim

When the camera focused on the room, I jumped up and me and Sage screamed together, "Oh my God!"

Jokk saw what it was first and tried to run to the VCR and stop it before Sean could process into his mind, but it was too late. He saw enough. Jokk pulled the tape slowly out of the VCR. When Sean turned to face me, my tears were fresh, and I was scared shitless. It was hard to talk but I tried.

"Sean, listen...I..." Sean slapped me so hard I flew into the end table and broke the lamp which used to sit there. Shards of the glass cut my arms and neck. Jokk ran to block Sean from doing anymore harm.

"Sage, get her into the bathroom and lock the door!" She didn't need all of his instruction because she was already moving to help me to the panic room. As Sage moved me down the hallway, I could see Jokk's grip on Sean was loosening because he still had the video tape as too. Sean snatched it out of Jokk's hand, pulled the tape ribbon out, threw it on the floor stomping it, and broke down and cried. I closed the door and Sage tried to dress my wounds as best as she could with peroxide and toilet tissue. I did lock the door. A few minutes later Sean's door-rattling banging made us jump.

Sean asked, "Who is he Kim and where does he live?" Sage shook her head for no, don't tell him. I told him quickly the correct information, "His name is Butter and he live on 109th and seventh." He didn't say anything else. Sage slowly opened the door, and no one was on the other side. The front door was wide open. Jokk came through the open door panting. He had his hands on his knees to balance himself and catch a breath. He stood with his hands on the back of his head like he is being arrested and faced me. Sean was gone.

CHAPTER 16: THE HIGH SCHOOL YEARS '89-'92

Sage

A functioning crackhead pretended to be in a dope fiend's nod in order to avoid questioning. He would be the unreliable witness that destroyed the case before it got off the ground.

About a little after four in the afternoon Sean went to the smoke spot on 110th and Lenox. He walked down the block and found Butter sitting on his stoop. Butter was so stupid. He never knew what Sean looked like. He was so wrapped up in Kim, he never asked her what her boyfriend's name was. She always referred to Sean as her "man". There were five guys sitting around Butter. They recognized Sean and Sean assumed Butter did too. But as Sean was giving pounds to everyone around, Butter didn't flinch. Sean's game plan of confrontation immediately changed. Even from sitting in Jokk's car a few cars up across the street, we could tell that Butter didn't have a clue who Sean was. We had beaten both Sean and Butter to the block, but not in enough time to do anything but watch from the back seat through tinted windows.

Sean

Butter felt this was his block and he was confident that no one would try him. Butter watched a girl from the block give me a sexy hello while I nodded back. Butter gave me his attention when I walked up.

"What's up man? Butter," Butter introduced himself.

"Ain't shit. Sean," I introduced myself and saw that there was no reaction. The crack head on the block was stupefied. Even he knew what danger Butter was in. The guys who surrounded Butter when I arrived tried to leave, but I half ordered them to stay. So, they sat back down on the stoop. I pulled out the twenty sack of green and began to roll up.

"So, what's the word y'all?" I questioned.

"We just shooting the shit," Butter replied.

The tension could be cut with a knife. The only ones talking was me and Butter. By this time Butter could feel it, but he couldn't understand it. He was surrounded by his ride or die boys and they wouldn't let anything happen to him. He made them rich, that is, hood rich. He treated them fairly because he knew a tyrant could be overthrown any day of the week over a quarter, twenty-five cents. I know he was trying to figure me out, plus I rolled up dolo, alone. He chuckled at his paranoia. I woulda shot, but I'm a different man. I thought beyond five minutes—I thought five days into anything. I dried the homegrown rolled up in the Garcia y Vega cigar paper with my lighter. When it was dry, lit, and sending the familiar fragrance wafting to the fire escapes above them, I passed it to Butter first since he was sitting to my left.

"Always nice when niggas come bearing gifts," Butter said between exhales.

"For sure, I ain't been around these parts in a minute. Used to come around here when I was a knucklehead with my brothers," I reminisced.

"Yeah, that's cool," said Butter. The blunt was now one man away from me.

"Yeah, my brothers used to run Harlem. Those niggas knew how to do it. Niggas respected them and they gangsta. They never did no dirt in they house or on they street. Niggas lost they lives if they even tried to pull that wack shit on this block," I said.

"This block?" Butter was puzzled. I could see him flipping through his mental rolodex. The only brother team he knew were the Beach brothers; four altogether. They did more than deal drugs, they were murderers, assassins. They held no fear for the boys in blue or men in black. One of my brothers died in jail. The only reason why the rest died was a freak accident. They bought a house in Long Island. An airplane had some kind of engine trouble and crashed off the Long Island Sound. Part of their house was crushed along with four other homes. They died instantly. They had built that house to move our mother into. They were in the house painting when they died. Probably a blessing for Butter; otherwise, how could he have possibly prospered?

I noted that Butter was trying to process the information and figure out if all of the brothers died in the crash. They did, except me, the last of the brothers, was at home in the projects with my mother. Before Butter could think anymore, the blunt was back to him and there went his short-term memory. He exhaled it with the smoke.

I made sure to buy some sour diesel weed, very potent. Not one member of the cipher noticed that I wasn't inhaling. This time around I just passed on the blunt. I was thinking back to that day my mother took a baseball bat and tried to kill her father, uncles, and my brothers.

We were in Louisburg, North Carolina visiting her father. He owned acres of land. I didn't want to come back to New York. My grandfather had horses and chickens and rows of cornfields. His backyard looked like a park to me. I couldn't understand why my mother would want to live in the city when she grew up with all of that. Every summer I would beg to stay down there, and she would say no. There would be no explanation and we would head home.

The last time I was down there, my grandfather and his brothers took me and my brothers further out on his land closer to the forest. They were teaching me how to shoot and helping my brothers to improve their skills. My mother made granddad promise not to teach me how to shoot a long time ago. That was the condition of us coming to visit every summer. Of course, my brothers only stayed eight days at the most as they became more powerful, but they stayed that day. My mother was supposed to be out visiting relatives overnight. But this time, as soon as she left, we headed out too. I was a swift learner. I only needed instructions one time. Granddad said I was a natural—better than my brothers. I didn't even buck when I fired the gun. My aim was sick. I never missed, and my speed was incredible. The entire clan of men stood mesmerized by me. And I got caught up in the hype from my brothers, Granddad and his brothers. So much that we didn't hear my mother and her two aunts coming up on us until my mother was yelling.

"You will not corrupt this baby! He's the last one! I have four sons! Four sons! And you, my own father, my uncles, you turned three of them against me! They worship your life of violence! I lost their father because of this shit and then you take my sons. Their father was a devout Muslim and then you pulled him into your world! That element you deal with came after him because of you! Look what you've done. They killed mama because of what you do! You see Sean? Don't you see what this family is? Don't you see that they are evil? I thought maybe they were telling the truth. That they changed their ways. But no, Daddy ya'll didn't! You lied to my face! You boys don't think I know what you do in Harlem? You ain't doing shit my father and uncles didn't do my whole life! If it wasn't for your father getting me out of here, I might have been killed. I didn't want to live their lifestyle which made them remember all over again that I was a girl. That was a sin all on its own, huh Daddy?"

I stood motionless. My mother was a devout Muslim herself. She was a demure woman. She never raised her voice or cursed. She carried herself like a lady at all times. My mind was blown by the lioness I saw before me. Before I could open my mouth to apologize for hurting her and to let her know that I would never go against her, the youngest of my older brothers who was twenty, spoke.

"Okay, so you know, what's the big deal? We've always kept you safe..." He never finished those words. Granddad didn't react fast enough. My mother took the baseball bat and cracked my brother's ribs. Before she could be subdued by the aunts, she had broken an arm of each son, except me, a leg of each uncle, and knocked Granddad senseless. I was horrified. I never knew my mother could embody such violence, rage, and speed. Every man who had surrounded me now lay on the ground. These sharp shooters were no match for my miniscule mother. My mother's aunts, who were easily two hundred fifty pounds a piece, were literally lying on top of my screaming and panting mother. I stood mortified. I dropped my gun. Repeating in my ears was my great aunt's voice saying 'Sandy you could have killed them all. I thought you got rid of that thing in you at the hospital.'

Soft nervous laughter being overpowered by a loud guffaw going around the cipher brought me out of my reverie. The blunt was now down to a roach.

"What's the joke?" I asked.

"Nah," Butter answered, "ain't nothing. Just this stupid bitch I used to fuck with." I remembered why I was there and so did the guys surrounding him. By this time Butter's mind was gone. He was good and high and running his mouth.

"What about her?" I calmly asked.

"I'm saying, she was cute and had a fat ass, but she was trying to play me, so I had to check her ass quick. I told her I could hook her up singing and shit so I could hit that. So, she finally gave it up the other day and acted like it was nothing. After all that shit I bought her stupid ass. That bitch was going to pay. She tried to act like her man was all that. If he was, then why was that bitch with me? Huh?"

Butter was loud and laughing now. The crack head watched intently from the sidewalk. No one noticed him crossing the street for a better look. I stared straight ahead. This time when Butter's boys started to inch away, I allowed them a few feet.

"What you do man, you slap her around a little, get her jumped?" I inquired.

"Nah, I got that stupid bitch on video tape, fucking her brains out. Her ass all in the screen. My best work if I do say so myself," Butter bragged.

"She let you tape her and then dissed you?"

"Her dumb ass didn't even know it was there. I'ma send her a copy and see if maybe she want to go into acting now," Butter howled at his own joke. The guys eased off another few feet.

"I'm saying man, what about this cat she fucking with? What if he sees the tape? Could be trouble, you know how these bitches be," I prodded.

"Who gives a fuck about that nigga? I wish he would do something. I wish he would *think* about doing something. This Calico right here," he patted his left side, "will take care of any beef he wanna bring."

"Now that's what I'm talking about."

"Huh?"

I pulled out my Smith and Wesson and released two bullets into Butter's head via his temple and eye socket; the way my family taught me. It was the family mark left on all victims. Butter's boys were kicking rocks long before I stood to place the second bullet through Butter's right eye. The crack head slumped on the floor near the car he was already leaning on and pretended to nod off.

Butter's brain matter mingled with the blood on the steps of the brownstone. His body slammed against the railing and slid two steps before coming to a stop. I bet he thought that when he left this world it would be in a blaze of glory or behind some young thing. His last vision was of the last of the Beach brothers. For the first time, he didn't see the big picture.

I stood up and walked away quietly shaking my head. I had stood in the blood spray. I made a mental note to be careful next time. Leaving on only my wife beater undershirt, I pulled my hoodie off and set it on fire in a nearby trash can. I walked down the street and pulled a bottle of water out of my oversized jean pockets and rinsed my hands of any residue or blood. I took my bandana out of my back pocket wiped the bottle off and entered a bodega. I turned the bottle in for a five-cent refund but bought a piece of Bazooka gum instead. I purposely dropped my bandana in front of a pit bull tied up in front of the store. The dog tore the bandana to shreds; the remnants of blood incensed the dog.

I hailed a cab to LaGuardia airport and flew to North Carolina. I would lick my wounds and avoid jail while in the loving comfort of my family. I killed over a woman. Granddad was going to kill me.

Kim

I went into a little bit of a depression after everything that went down. I didn't leave my mother's house for any reason. I didn't go to Sage or Isa's graduation. I didn't go to the junior-senior prom. I went to school and came straight home. When I was in the house, I stayed in my room, watched TV, and ate French fries and chicken wings. I couldn't tell my mother or anybody what happened. I was hoping nobody around The Vill knew what happened in Harlem. Chaz found out somehow. He kept dropping hints, but he never said anything straight up. I know it would be any day now before I did or said something to get on his nerves and then he would tell my mother. I wanted to die. I was tired of crying about it. I felt so violated but I thought it was part my fault too. I never shoulda messed with Butter. I ain't sad he's dead but I ain't happy either. I can't see why that man had to die but I did feel like killing him myself. I'm all mixed up inside. This was the conversation I had with myself everyday in my room alone, with the curtains closed and the lights off. Nobody was home today so I was in the living room with the lights off eating an ice cream sandwich when the doorbell rang. I looked around for someone to answer the door but since I was alone, I had to get it myself. It was probably Isa or Sage.

When I answered it, I stood there staring at him. He looked at me wearing baggy sweats and a tee shirt tied at the back. My loose ponytail came to life as I swiveled my head to say no. He looked exactly like my father. I thought I was seeing ghost. He grabbed my hand before I could close the door.

"Hold on there baby girl, I ain't your daddy. I'm your Uncle Cane. Don't you remember me and your daddy was twins?"

"I...don't...I really can't handle this right now." It was hard to talk.

I turned away from the door and walked into the living room. I plopped down on the couch and stared wide-eyed as he glided into the living room as well and carefully placed his blazer on the arm of the overstuffed chair before sitting. Uncle Cane was a tall and big man. In his face, all you saw was regular. Nothing about him seemed threatening except maybe his height, but Chaz and Creston were the same height. He kept an unlit cigarette dangling from his lip. He dressed really classy. He was a dapper don. He was never without his trademark Fedora. He always smelled nice and had some nice-looking woman on his arm. In truth, he looked like a pimp; an expensive pimp, but a pimp non-the-less.

Uncle Cane never sold a woman in his life. He loved them too much, hear him tell it. He called himself an artist, a life-coach. To him, every woman was beautiful and if she didn't feel that way, he did all that he could to make sure that she did. Some would call him a kept man. He never asked a woman for a dime or even suggested it. They all loved him and showered him with gifts. Uncle Cane made his money running clubs with back room activities. When it came to his business, he was serious. He had been known to make people who cross him disappear. Men copying Uncle Cane usually had bodyguards; Uncle Cane always walked alone and did his dirt alone. Another reason he's never seen the inside of a jail. He was well spoken, had a wealth of knowledge, and believe it or not had several degrees.

My mother hated him. In her eyes, he was the total opposite of her dearly departed husband. He was always around the family when my father was alive. But right after the wake, she banned him from the house. She didn't want us kids influenced by him; which is part of the reason he didn't know what was going on with me, at first. The other reason was he looked so much like my father my mother couldn't stand to see him. I couldn't tell because my mother took down all the pictures of my father. My memories of his face faded a long time ago. Uncle Cane loved my father so much, and he was gone so long I thought maybe he died too.

"I'll get to the point Kim: you need to get your shit together. You're barely passing high school, so you need to get your GED. You're not following the wonderful example of what a woman should be that your mother is setting. I know that because of all the nonsense you caused up in Harlem. So, you'll be coming with me. I'll help you fix the mess you've made of it so far."

"What makes you think I'm just going with you? I don't know you like that." I had enough trouble with men including family.

"You are coming with me. You can pack some things or not. It's up to you. I'm not a man to be trifled with and I don't care if you are family. I'm going to do the right thing by you for my brother's sake."

Somebody was always trying to save me. The last time I saw Uncle Cane I was nine years old. I don't remember anything about him. I know that's how he remembered me, a nine-year old girl. But he lived in Harlem and word spread fast about the tape, Sean, and Butter. I didn't call him; he came to find me at my mother's house. Maybe this time I was gonna be saved by someone who could teach me to save myself. My mother walked in the house calling my name.

"Kim, come help me with these groceries." I jumped up to help my mother and try to let her know that there was company, but she beat me to the living room. I watched my mother standing there akimbo and my uncle lounged in the chair. My mother's face twisted into a sneer.

"What the hell are you doing in my house? Nevermind, just get out."

"Evening Peaches, long time no see." My uncle grinned from ear to ear revealing several gold teeth. One tooth had a diamond encrusted in it.

"Don't call me that. Get out."

"My apologies...Eve. I'll leave as soon as Kim is ready."

"What do you mean? She is not going anywhere with you!"

"Eve, I don't have any idea what it's been like to raise these kids on your own. But I do know that you're already a grandmother. I just want to help you out with Kim. This neighborhood is fine, and I know you're a great mother, but you know she'd be different if my brother was alive."

"You come into my house to disrespect me?" I was praying my mother didn't slap him.

"I would never disrespect you. This girl is on the brink of dropping out of school. Who else is going to get her where she needs to be?"

"Cane, my husband thought you could do no wrong. He loved you like that not me. I don't like the lifestyle that you lead. You a hustler. You don't know what honest living is about. You ain't never have to struggle and you just live off of other women. What are you going to teach Kim? How to be a whore?"

I looked at my mother frozen. It had just occurred to me how much I really didn't want my mother to know about the drama in Harlem. I didn't want my mother to think less of me. I loved my mother and wanted her to be proud of me, but school was just not interesting to me; especially not now. I didn't want to explain to my mother what went down in Harlem. I told her that me and Sean broke up and that's why I'd been in a funk.

"Ma, I think I'd like to go with Uncle Cane," I almost whispered.

"What?" My mother twisted to face me.

"I think I just need a break from everything. Maybe somewhere new I could do something better with my life. I won't know anybody so I could study for the GED. Maybe I could even get a job."

"What you say Eve? I can guarantee she won't know anybody because we'll be in upstate New York until she passes her GED and then we'll come back here and talk again about what she wants to do."

My mother swept us both up in her eyes. She wasn't a foolish woman. She knew that something was wrong with me, but she didn't know what. Me and Sean had broken up plenty of times before; he would always call or come by or try to get her to plead his case to me. This time was different. Me and her used to be so close. She tried to support me with me singing, but she had to work to support the whole family. The money she made had to go to food and shelter not demos and studio time. I know that's when we parted ways. She tried to explain to me that it wasn't that she didn't believe in my talent, but her words fell on deaf ears. I didn't want to her it. My mother bit her lip to keep from crying.

"You giving up on school Kim? You would rather be with this low-life than with me? Of course, you want to go with him. You miss your father. I always knew that I was always a far second to your father in your eyes;

so much in fact that you prefer to be with his low-rent understudy than with me."

She turned her back and spat her words over her shoulder. She put her hands over her face and wiped away her tears. I ain't see my mother cry in years and I felt worse now.

"You don't even know this man Kim. He's not your father. He's nothing like him Kim. Your father was a good man."

I turned away from my mother and stared off somewhere.

"I'm tired of fighting with you and your brothers about the decisions you make with your lives. I don't have it in me anymore. Seems like you made up your mind no matter what I say."

My mother walked into the kitchen and put the groceries away. I walked into my bedroom to pack a suitcase. Uncle Cane caught me by my arm.

"Hope I'm making the right decision. Young girls are always a problem, even family, but I have a feeling that you're going to be different. I saw how quickly you took in the situation and made a decision. I like quick thinkers. Don't make a liar out of me." He was definitely not my father. I started packing. My door was open, and I could hear my mother sit down to the dinning table. She was talking, but I wasn't sure if she was talking to Uncle Cane or just talking out loud.

"I should throw away this curio and buy a piano or maybe rent one. We used to have one when Chaz was alive. It was the last thing we argued about before he died; told him that it would be silly to have a piano in the dining room. We needed space for the kids. Since Kim is leaving though and both the boys gone, I could rearrange Kim's room and put the piano in there. I was the one who taught Kim how to play the piano from the time she could sit up on the bench. Chaz got us one so me and Kim didn't have to go to my mother's house in Long Island or my father's brown-stone in Harlem to play. It was second-hand but Chaz was proud of it. It was some of the best moments of my life with Kim; we would do mother-daughter things."

I remembered that a little bit. Uncle Cane started talking. I didn't know if he was talking to my mother, but it sounded like it.

"I remember that; Kim was a natural. We thought that Kim would become a classical pianist. She was so gifted. She couldn't read music, but she could play by ear."

"I remember the first time I heard her sing. It was a few minutes before choir rehearsal at church. She was acting like one of the soloists. The mic wasn't even on. I was floored by how raspy and raw it was. That girl sang from the seams of her soul and it was terrible. I made a mental note to give her vocal lessons when I got home from work the next day, but by the time I came home Chaz's melodious tenor was ringing through the house. He was already teaching Kim. I loved to hear him sing. That's how he eventually won me over in high school, but he didn't care about me until he heard me play the piano and sing. The rest was history."

It was quiet for like five minutes. I thought she might be coming down the hall. So, I started packing things I didn't need like Cabbage Patch Kid clothes. I started taking the clothes back out when they started talking again.

"I used to blame the music for the rift between me and the kids. The twins have no talent for music, singing, or dancing. They just blasted that awful rap music until my ears bled. Creston is just like you. I can't stand to look at him. Might be going to hell for disliking him so much. You know he plays basketball overseas? He never comes home. He never writes. He never calls. When he was drafted into the European league after high school, the family ceased to exist to him. My letters came back *return to sender*, all forty-three of them. I had to let him go."

I didn't know that Creston didn't call or write. Chaz is ignorant enough to me and I didn't miss him, but I didn't know he was treating Ma like that.

"I thought you, Chaz, and Kim was going to be like the Winans."

"Yeah, well music brought Kim and her father closer than ever but left me out in the cold. This family was more like regular people than I cared to be. I don't blame anyone for the way my life turned out. Probably shoulda took more interest in what the twins liked and supported them too. Maybe if Creston would open just one letter, he would know how sorry I was and maybe forgive me for not being there for him."

Where the hell was I when all this was going on? I musta really been in my own world. Never thought of my brothers like people; they was just pains in my ass. I closed my suitcase and walked into the hallway. I could see my mother and Uncle Cane reflected in the curio glass. They weren't looking at each other at all. I walked back out carrying one suitcase and two winter coats. Uncle Cane took my things from me and walked toward the door. My mother cocked her head to the left.

"I never seen him lift a manicured hand to help a soul. Maybe he means you some good Kim." Uncle Cane cracked a smile.

"I'll be in touch Eve. I'll try to be better." Cane let his words drift. My mother continued staring at the curio as she spoke to him.

"Cane...I know you loved him. Love her the same way."

"I will Eve. Kim I'll wait for you at the elevator."

I nodded my head and he turned to leave. I stood behind my mother's chair and placed my hands on my shoulders.

"It won't be that long, and I'll call you every Sunday. I think that he probably needs me too Ma. I'll do better upstate and I'll make you proud of me."

"Baby, I'm already proud of you and I'm sorry if you don't already know that. Please don't give up your dream because of me. I'll see what I can do about helping you."

I bent over the chair and hugged my mother. I placed my face on her face.

"I love you Ma. I won't give up and I'll be back."

My mother held back a sniffle and breathed in deeply.

"Darling you do what you need to do. I'll always be here if you decide to come back."

I squeezed my mother tighter.

"Ma I..." My thought got stuck in my throat as my mother moved my arms from around her. I took a step back to avoid being hit with her chair. My mother stood up, went to the door, held it open, and looked down the hall at Uncle Cane getting on the elevator. I felt a pang in my heart. She started talking real softly.

"I used to think me and your uncle might have a different relationship if he didn't look exactly like your father. But that ain't true. He makes me feel like your father wanted the life that he lived. If your father could trade it all would he? Was life with me enough for him?" I didn't know what to say to her. I couldn't figure out my own shit. She wiped her eyes with the back of her hands and dried them on her slacks.

"Get moving. I need to start dinner."

I walked slowly toward my mother and tried to hug her. She blocked the hug.

"Don't misunderstand, if I hug you, I won't ever let go."

I nodded my head and walked out of the door and rushed to close it. I pressed my back on the door for support. All I needed was five minutes and then I would be able to support myself. I heard the phone ringing from inside. I could move if I could hear her talking. She didn't answer. It was Chaz's son, my nephew, leaving a message on the answering machine.

"Grandma, daddy says you're too busy, but I wanna come stay with you tomorrow please? I..."

My mother must have picked up the kitchen phone.

"Hey Grandma's baby! I'll come pick you up myself!" I stood up and walked down the hallway.

Sage

Kim had moved out of New York with her uncle. Everything that happened with Butter and Sean left her half crazy. Isa and I would wind up going to the same college in North Carolina. Jewel and Billie went to college in different states. A few weeks after Lisette was sentenced and Butter was killed, we wrote our one and only rap. It was put on a couple of mix tapes before college and life sent us on our separate ways. We dedicated the song to all the Kims, Lisettes, Tanyas, and Scarys out there who let money and men ruin their lives.

Mommy Dearest

Baby I'm a star
Your mom's the best
Not half
But all the checks
Smile pretty

Look nice
You'll see
It's not hard
To trick these
Dummies, dummies, dummies
G's, cheese
The cheddar
You better
Come offa that green
Mutha fucka
Platinum, gold
Whatever it is
Bearer bonds
Leather bags logoed out
Full length furs
Empty the vault out
Now I'll empty my nine till the clip is out...shout
I don't question how I came to this place
Just why we're sitting face to face
I'm looking at you
You looking at me
And in your eyes
I think I see
My rise to the top
Was not in your plans
But to stay in the palm of your hands
You dealt
I felt
It melt
My heart for you
But you know we're through
I was your girl
Your ace boom
Never do you wrong

Had your back
In long or short cons
They never saw me coming
Sick with sweat
Puny little girl
How could I be a threat?
But you know
I know
No bodies yet
Had a taste for that doe
Had a taste for that blow
Had a taste for seeing that blood flow
You was my idol
The highest title
Numero uno
Walked in your footsteps
In three-inch heels yo
So good in my G
Started to believe
I was greater than
Even you conceived
From pjs and ojs
To villas and whips
Excursions with Persians
Milan on a whim
Princes of nations and hoods
Synonymous
Evil thoughts
Profit my motis
Gifted in speech
Inflection in my tone
You just ought to
Vacate the throne
I watched you

Heard you
Felt you
Smelled you
You showed me
Told me
Molded me
Sold me
On the idea
There was money to be got
A nonexclusive club
Nonelusive club
Til four in the morning
Tear the club up!
I watched you murder
And maim
So thusly did the same
All in the glorified name
Of the dollar
My pimp
The dollar
The mighty, the mighty, the mighty
The dollar
You found salvation
I'm glad
No, really I am
Want you to feel all the guilt you can
Your tears mean nothing
All in vain
This poison and my blood
Are one and the same
Like Frankenstein's monster
I'll follow you to your grave
I want you snatched out your sleep
Screaming my name

I have no conscious or heart or desire to live
Don't even know how to repent for my sins
And in my final thought
I have no regrets
But every night
Before you get your rest
Always know this
I loved you mommy dearest

CHAPTER **17:** *If people want to believe something badly enough,*
they can make it into reality.

<u>*Isa*</u>

With so much happening in our lives at home, none of us really got into
what was happening in school. I mean like running for class president or
the senior trip. I was kicked out of so many schools that I didn't think I
was going to graduate. I had a C average, and I was cool with that. Sage
did okay but she always did okay. She gets good grades without studying. Kim, I don't really know about. I know she was failing a couple of
classes but now she moved with her uncle. So, I guess maybe she could
start over. My mother made me go to my prom. Especially after she found
out Sage went to hers. I coulda kicked her ass showing my mother all the
pictures. But I knew I put my mother through a lot of shit since Nana
died so I went. I wore the dress she picked out. I went with the boy I knew
she woulda picked out herself. And I wound up having a great time. The
guy was one of my people's brother and he was decent to me the whole
night. He didn't try anything sexual—he just helped me have a good time.
When the prom was over, we went and got something to eat. After that
the limo took us to my house. He kissed me on the cheek and told me
goodnight. He was decent.

When graduation came none of our parents was having it. We had to go, period. Mine was the same day as Sage's. She came to mine first because it was in the morning and I went to hers in the evening. After the graduation both our families took us to City Island to celebrate. City Island had the best sea food in the world. We told our parents that we would be going to Shaw University in North Carolina. Sage's father was so happy. My mother was happy I was accepted somewhere. Sage made me apply. I think she was worried I wouldn't go and wind up doing something stupid. I think she might've been right so in the fall that's where we would be. I still didn't know what I wanted to do with my life. But *School Daze* and *A Different World* had me thinking that maybe it would be a different world.

Sage

The last day of Harlem week was the setting. Harlem was even more ridiculous during Harlem Week. It's like a long ass block party during a week in August. It covers several avenues from Lenox to St. Nick. Cars are bumper to bumper. Even the celebrities are out. There are celebrations, parades, dance contests, basketball tournaments, car, and fashion shows. Street vendors are selling foods from their native countries for reasonable prices and flags representing the people of various nations who inhabit New York are waved. There was an altruistic purpose for having Harlem Week; more than likely pertaining to the Harlem Renaissance and that whole movement. The youth of the day reduced it to a block party where they show off every damn thing they value. It was off to college for us in a couple of days. The whole crew dressed to kill, but soon became bored. Jewel, and Sienna went home. Isa, Billie and I stayed.

We were on 125th in front of Mart 125 taking pictures. Then we walked down the block to cross the street so that we could parade up that block. We had to be seen in our outfits. I had on a white skin-tight dress and white high heels with the white rimmed sunglasses. Billie was wearing a yellow number with her back and stomach out with yellow heels and matching sunglasses. Isa wore a pink tube dress with pink heels and pink sunglasses. We were gold and iced out, that is, by ghetto standards. All eyes were on us. We thought we were hot shit. Billie and Isa were taking turns running the scam that I had invented because they were trying to be faithful to their boyfriends...again.

A group of guys tried to get our attention at the corner. They were really trying to get Billie's attention. When we crossed the street, there was a row scaffolding there. Some renovations were being done.

"Yo, I'm saying we chase you all across the street and ya'll can't speak. What is she deaf or something?" said the biggest man we had ever seen in our lives. He was asking about Billie, but I answered him. I looked at him, straight in his eyes, and said, "Yes she is."

I tapped Billie to turn around while Isa looked like she was ashamed of him. His friends were just astonished. Billie pretended to be confused. He still wasn't convinced.

"Get the fuck outta here!"

"No, she's really deaf," I reiterated.

His eyes darted between us trying to gage if I were serious or if one of us would break revealing the truth. That was the second week of that scam so by then we were so good at it, that he would need to have ESP to determine the truth. He continued his interrogation.

"How she gonna be deaf and be out here then?"

"Are you trying to say that deaf people have to stay in the house? They have to be retarded or something? You know, I know she gets tired of explaining, but I really get tired of it." I said in mock anger.

"She really deaf? Then why it looks like she understand everything that we saying?" This was a reoccurring question, and I wasn't swayed.

"She's looking right at us, reading our lips. She wasn't always deaf. She had some kind of operation when she was six because of ear infections and then something went wrong and here we are."

"So, can she speak?" I could tell by the softening of his voice that he was starting to believe me. Hell, I almost believed it myself.

"A little bit, but she's self conscious because her voice isn't as clear as ours because of the operation too."

I added that bit on the spot. He believed it. Now, it was time to go in for the kill. He looked sorry. Isa played her part.

"I thought you wanted to talk to her or did you change your mind now that you know she's deaf?" Isa said.

"No, I still want to...how do I say sorry?" He was priceless.

I made up some gesture. I taught him a fictional way to say 'sorry', 'pretty', and his name. Everyone was so amazed. All Billie had to do was repeat everything he did starting with herself. Then, his friend wanted to throw salt in the game.

"That's fly and all but how ya'll talk on the phone?"

Last week, that would have stumped me, but I was on my game cuzin'.

"When you call her she'll see your voice, or really it's your words on this screen in her phone. Then she types in her response and you hear a computerized voice. I wish I had something like that, but that machine costs a grip!" I shut his friend down swiftly. I had no idea if what I was saying was even remotely true about the phone, but it sounded good. So, he and Billie exchanged numbers, and everybody went their own way.

We were on our second tour of walking up the block when we were stopped by some guys on bikes, Kawasaki bikes. It was the latest rage with young Black males. Of course, the bikes had to be loud, fast, and colorful. The only thing sexier was a female on the back of the back as he did tricks with the bikes. We ran the same routine on them. One of the guys thought it would be a great experience for Billie to ride his bike. Well Billie thought it would be a great idea if we all held hands, in the middle of Harlem Week, in the midst of all those people, on 125th street and say a word of prayer. A couple of the guys refused but three of the guys, Billie, Isa, and I held hands. So, there we were saying the Lord's Prayer and asking the Most High to keep them safe. Isa and Billie got on the backs of the bikes, but I declined a ride. While they were gone, I talked to the other guys. When Billie and Isa came back, their faces were flushed, and their hairdos were windblown. This was the time before there was an enforcement of helmet laws. They were smiling and giggling.

A strange look came across Billie's face; she began making eyes at me. My back was to the street, so I didn't know what she was talking about. Billie made some kind of gesture to the guy to wait a second and then dragged me away.

"He's getting ready to pass us by!" she said in an excited whisper while making hand signals so she wouldn't tip off the other guy.

"What the hell are you talking about?"

"The guy in the silver Altima."

I was sick of this Altima guy and her. For weeks now, Billie had been looking for him. She spotted him when we were at the Pologrounds watching a basketball game and decided she was in love. Because there was so much traffic during Harlem Week, it was easy for me to walk over to his car without it passing me by.

"I need you to pull over," I said. He must have thought I was a cop or crazy or maybe he read the agitation on my face and in my voice. He pulled over and got out of his car. He sat on the hood of the newly waxed car. He smiled at me pleasantly. I was thinking don't waste that smile on me because I'm so not attracted to you. I wasted no time.

"Look, I know you don't know this, but I'm tired of looking for you and I'm not even the one who wants you. See my girlfriend over there, she spotted you a few weeks ago and we keep missing you. So, what's up?"

I knew he was going to look at Billie's pretty face, head full of hair, almond eyes, curvy body and fall to pieces. And he did. He actually licked his lips.

"Uh, tell her to come on and I'll take ya'll home or wherever you want to go." The two cars behind this guy belonged to his friends. While I was explaining to William, or Billy as he liked to be called, one of his friends slid up behind me. I whirled around.

"You can ride with me shorty. Don't worry we don't bite," What a shame I thought, and he was wonderful to look at. Yes indeed.

"Unless I asked you to right?" Flirting was like breathing to me.

"Yeah," he said remaining in my personal space. I motioned for Billie and Isa to come on. They didn't even say bye to the guys on the Kawasaki bikes. Isa walked up trying to focus her eyes on her new conquest.

"Which one is mine?" she said seductively. I stepped around my new friend to see what she was talking about. My new friend Kareem pointed to a Puerto Rican cat in the latest Legend, dark blue-cream interior. That was enough for Isa. I jumped in the red BMW with Kareem. When I looked out of the passenger window, I could see the look of astonishment of the biker guys and the first crew we ran the scam on. Billie was yelling at the top of her lungs for Isa to give her her pocketbook. I just turned my head and gave my attention to Kareem.

We all headed to Jackson Hole for dinner and then to the Shark Bar before we ever made it home. I wished we had never met them. I dealt with Kareem until I was about one month into college. It didn't end well. A girl who lived down the hall from me in the dorm was from New York too, but she was from Brooklyn. She was looking at all the pictures I had up and saw picture of me and Kareem hugging. She asked about him by name. We started comparing notes and discovered that he was *our* boyfriend. I called him up and told him someone wanted to speak to him. He thought it might be Isa. We went to the same school, so it made sense. But the second he heard ole girl's voice he knew what was up and hung up. I called right back and left him a message. He wasn't answering the phone. I simply told him it was over.

Billie and Billy did not end well. It would seem that he thought his mother would not think that Billie would be good enough for him. The mother never actually said this and never alluded to it. In Billie's eyes that made him weak. But Billy felt he knew his mother better. His mother turned out to be some big-name actress who was the mom in a long-running television show.

CHAPTER **18:** *If people want to believe something badly enough, they can make it into reality.*

<u>Isa</u>

Our freshman year was like a continuation of our senior year. Those country boys fell like dominoes for me and Sage. We couldn't do no wrong. All we needed was a couple of months and we were going out with the best of the best from our campus, St. Augustine, North Carolina State, Central, and a couple of smart guys from Duke University. Every guy had a purpose. The best part was, we learned not to have sex with everybody. All we had to do was tell them we were virgins, and they would back off. Nobody wanted to be our 'firsts'. If that didn't work, we would tell them we were seventeen and we were. Our freshman class was the youngest, largest, and smartest freshman class Shaw had ever seen.

I tried out for the cheerleading team and got on. I was the captain of the cheerleading team at my third school when I was a sophomore in high school. I remembered I liked it. I didn't make captain here, but I had time. Sage joined the modeling troupe, acting troupe, and the university choir. I had my eye on joining a sorority. I couldn't be involved with too much otherwise people would know if I made line. I had enough time to pull up my grades and start working on my community service work. By the time Homecoming came around the following November, I was a proud member of Alpha Kappa Alpha Incorporated.

Being in a sorority changed my life. I started having opinions about things I didn't think of before like voting and politics and reputations—having a good one. I stopped smoking so I could actually study. I stopped cursing out loud like my mother begged me to. I tried to work on not speaking Ebonics all the time. There were times I couldn't help it. Sometimes somebody had to be put in their place and they weren't understanding me unless I was cursing and using slang and with my New York accent, that shut everybody down.

Sage didn't pledge but she was crazy popular because she was involved in everything. If it was a play, a concert, a fashion show, a party, or political rally, you better believe she was there to support. She supported me when I pledged even though she couldn't understand why I wanted to do it. She even bought me some paraphernalia and my first pearl. I couldn't believe we been friends since we were little and now, we were in college. After all we been through, she never left me behind.

Sage

I fell in like. That's how it started. He loved the hell out of me and gave me the world. I didn't appreciate him until it was too late.

Sophomore year had me thinking that I was super beautiful and sexy. I always had a safety net. People always seemed to want to help me and I played on that. I was a manipulative bitch when it came to men. And frankly I couldn't care less. I believed that there would always be another man to replace the current one. I did not believe in investing any real time, patience, or love into them because I never wanted to be disappointed. I was never surprised when they cheated but the men would always be surprised when I walked. No hysteria. No crying. No going after the other woman. Just me leaving as I promised would happen if I was cheated on. It was pure logic and there was no need for the drama. On some level one must respect my gangster. I make no bones about taking care of myself above all others. But I found out in the most unforeseen circumstance what it meant to put someone else's feelings above my own.

His name was Frank Allen, but everyone called him Joon. He was tall, handsome, lean, with amazing brown eyes, warm spirit, and really laid back. He was a senior from Howard University who was doing his internship at the local radio station in Raleigh. Apparently, the internships were saturated in D.C. and found a way to be paid for his internship in Raleigh. Plus, his family had a little money. He loved me blindly and that was his downfall. If my eyes scanned it and my voice whispered it, whatever it was became mine. In my mind it was a perfect relationship. I did the devoted girlfriend thing with him and why not? It allowed me to have all that the world encompassed. And because of his self-induced glaucoma, I could see whomever I wanted without fear of losing him.

One time in particular I was talking to God and thanking Him for my coma thanks to my resolve to become the Queen of Shots the night before. When I came out of the coma, I just knew that I would die. I had lost the shot game. Isa had won. We were at this little hole in the wall country bar that took pretty faces as proof of i.d. We had just finished finals and were celebrating. Isa had seventeen shots of tequila and bounced off of the bar stool as if she had just been given a V-8! Her tolerance was incredible! Around my sixth or seventh shot I sat in stunned silence as Isa knocked them back with grace and flare. I, on the other hand was carried to a cab and Isa held me up while she gave our destination to the cabbie. So, when the phone started cursing and yelling into my ear, I wanted to kill it! I answered it only to have the berating continue. Isa had picked up the other line at the same time. From the way the conversation was going the caller didn't know that I was on the phone as well. He thought he was speaking to Isa.

"What the fuck?! I thought you bitches was supposed to be my girls! How you going to let Sage play me like that?! And when I saw ya'll last night at Ray's you had me talking about getting her a ring. You bitches was playing me to my face. You knew she was out with some other nigga'! What's up with that yo? What's up with that?!"

"First of all, stop yelling. Second of all don't just start cursing and carrying on the minute you hear hello. I don't know what the hell you're talking about..."

"You know what this is about Isa." Joon said with a little more softness, pain actually.

"Joon, you acting stupid and calling me everything except a child of God because you can't find Sage. She's at her aunt's house, the one who lives in Greensboro. You know she is damn near Amish and doesn't allow any gadgets in her house including pagers. Sage is hung over and probably asleep like I was until you called," Isa lied. She knew exactly where I was and never thought twice about covering for friends over minor things like this. However, that morning was more about survival than anything. Isa just wanted to go back to sleep. This was a normal nonsense call from Joon and I could smooth it over later since a great lie had been told.

"Naw, naw, ma, it's a little more than that. My boy Dean saw her getting into some cat that he know car," Joon explained.

"So what? Maybe he was giving her a ride. I don't know."

"Naw, he said it looked like they were going out," Joon accused.

"Did you say Dean?" Isa was setting up for the indignant lie.

"Yeah," Joon replied.

"Joon, you told me that Dean was feeling Sage. Maybe he was just trying to throw salt in your game. And I bet you lost it right in front of him too. And think about it Joon, did he tell you in private? Did he call you at home? Or did he tell you when other people could hear?" Isa was reaching.

"He told me this morning when we was all playing basketball. When my team started winning, he started talking shit. We all did and then he hit me with the Sage thing. It took mad heads to hold me back. And everybody kept saying 'why would he lie, why would he lie?' I started believing that shit."

"Be smart Joon, think." Isa added for effect. Joon began to calm down and soak in the lie. He needed to believe the lie.

"Damn, I'm sorry really. I have to make this up to her. She gonna think I don't trust her and shit."

"Yeah, you do that. Now I'm going back to sleep," said Isa.

"Okay and when I come around later, I'll bring something over for you and Sage."

"Alright, goodbye." He hung up first and then I did. Isa hung up the phone last and rolled over only to roll back when the phone rang again. Tears formed in my eyes because I wanted to sleep so badly. Isa and I answered at the same time, but she spoke.

"Hello?"

"It's Billie. Is Sage on the phone too?"

"Yeah, I'm on here. What do you want?"

"Don't be nasty Sage. Isa you need an award! That was Oscar material. I didn't know what you were going to say. All I could tell Joon when he called me was let's call you Isa. Sage you don't deserve us."

"I know. Since I'm up, I have a date with the toilet bowl. Bye."

I hung up for the second time that afternoon. This time when I rolled over, I threw up in the garbage can next to the bed. I only emptied it right then and there because the smell was going to make me sick again. After cleaning up, then I went back to sleep, but not before turning off the ringer. I fell asleep wondering if we actually got into a cab last night or was it the car of some guy I was talking to? I would sort it out later.

Isa

Shit like that continued to happen over the course of their eighteen-month relationship and he continued to become more enamored with Sage. She could do no wrong it seemed. He gave her money, paid for her car insurance, and gave her jewelry. He even paid her portion of the rent when we moved off campus. His generosity surpassed all, and he did it with a sincere heart and that's what makes my part in what happened so fucked up; because had he been told the truth from the beginning he probably wouldn't have changed so dramatically.

At the end of our junior year, Billie and Jewel came to visit us at school. They went to Virginia State. I knew they knew something was up when Sage didn't say anything about Billie smoking a cigarette. She couldn't stand them. I gave them a knowing look and then we all looked at Sage. Jewel sat next to Sage and spoke softly.

"I had a dream about fish last night. We all know that means someone is pregnant, but I thought it was this girl at my job. What the hell are you thinking about doing?" Jewel was wasting her talents at Virginia State. She needed her own psychic show.

"Jewel, why are you always accusing me of some foul shit?" Sage pouted.

"Because you or Isa are always doing some foul shit and getting us involved," retorted Jewel.

"I haven't told the father yet," said Sage.

"Why the fuck not?" I asked.

"Because this baby belongs to this local cat I was dealing with, Bukaii. But he thinks he's thug life and he's acting stupid."

"Girl, take your ass back to New York and get that shit taken care of before Joon take care of you and him," Billie said what everyone was thinking.

"I have to tell you the truth about something," Sage hesitated. Tears streamed down her face. I hadn't seen her cry in years. She was really shaking and scared. Snot was running freely and then she slumped to the floor. We waited for her to drop the bomb on us.

"I did tell Joon...but I told him that it was his baby. Bukaii was acting stupid and I was scared. But I thought Joon was going to give me money to get an abortion, but he was like no and he was all happy and shit. He was like I could keep going to school until I had to stop and then he would go to the professors and get my work. He said we could move in together. He said if I wanted, he would bring my aunt down here until I got used to having the baby around and then when I was ready, we would get married. He already ran out and bought a ring and told everybody. Tonight he's going over to auntie's house with his grandmother, grandfather, uncle, mother, and his two older brothers. You know his family was already giving me a hard time because I'm not even a little bit Puerto Rican like Joon. Abortion wasn't even an option. He must have called everybody he knew because they been calling me ever since; getting my address and shit so they could send me stuff. Ladies, I just don't know..." Billie was good and angry. So was Jewel. I couldn't even look at them.

"What the fuck is wrong with you Sage?" Jewel asked as calmly as possible. "Why do you do this to us? Why can't you think about anybody else beside yourself? Joon is not some bum off the street. That man loves you. He damn near worships you. Running the okey doke is one thing, but how the hell are we supposed to pull this off? I mean we are not going to let you hang out there by yourself, although that is part of your problem, but damn!"

Billie chose to lighten the mood.

"Okay the shit is over with. She is having the baby and we have to agree that it's Joon's otherwise we gonna fuck up say it's Boo Boo's baby..." she rolled her eyes, "we don't know what we would have done in the same situation so let's not judge her. What we need to work on now is the baby shower and the strippers! I got five on it!" We laughed and hugged but I could see Sage was still sick. We should have been better friends and made her tell the truth.

CHAPTER **19:** *If people want to believe something badly enough, they can make it into reality.*

Sage

"Ladies, I'm nervous and scared. We're only a week away from the baby shower and I'm due next month. I think before...it's already too late to stop this from hurting him but at least he doesn't have to be embarrassed in front of his friends and family and my friends and family." The month before I was due, I moved back to New York to be closer to my father. I also wanted my child to be a native New Yorker. Jewel, Isa, and Billie flew in for the baby shower. Kim's mother brought a gift from her and Kim. Kim seemed to have fallen off the face of the earth. Her mother never said exactly where she was whenever someone asked. She always said Kim was fine or she'd tell her that we asked about her. We each had gone through something where we needed some time away, so we tried to give Kim the same respect.

"What are you talking about Sage?" asked Isa.

"I think I'm going to tell Joon the truth. I feel so guilty and sick. I can't sleep at night or in the day. I can barely look him in the face and when he starts talking about getting married, I really want to throw up. He put a ring on my finger." Isa the Scam Master reached back to her former self and interrupted me.

"Girl shut the fuck up and let this shit happen. That's the hormones talking. When that baby doesn't have to want for anything, you'll remember how you almost fucked it up."

"But Bukaii called and he's talking about claiming this baby and he says he wants to be with me and be a father to his child and _his_ family has been calling me too talking about they want to be a part of their grandchild's life."

"You gotta be shitting me!" screamed Billie.

"Look at me," said Jewel.

"What?" I feigned innocence.

"This is me, Jewel. You can't bullshit a bullshitter. That shit is exciting to you. You gonna have Joon sitting under the jail. Bukaii ain't no match for him and it doesn't matter if you tell him now or later, he is going to black the fuck out. Don't ever tell him if you want everyone to live."

"Ain't nobody scared of Joon," I said sarcastically.

"Bitch, you better understand something, you tell and keep a lie like this it will change a muthafucka and the way he deals with everyone. So, keep your mouth shut! Okay get out now. The rest of us need to talk about your gifts and you don't need to be here," commanded Isa.

"All riiiight! Gifts! Toodles!"

I barely closed the door when they all spoke up at once; I could still hear them. "Something's wrong with that lunatic!" I laughed and left them discussing the contributions for my baby shower gifts.

The day of the shower was wonderful. When we were younger, we didn't have any money for our other friends' baby showers. But now they were prepared for my baby shower. My girls were there early to decorate and to help me and Joon's family set up the food. People started to arrive around two and brought beautiful gifts. Even Milk showed up for the shower. The shower was in one of the banquet halls in the community center of the apartment complex. I took my sweet damn time arriving. I felt great when I was getting dressed. Then a wave of guilt washed over me when I looked in the mirror; me in my beautiful mahogany dress with the plunging neckline. Ever the diva, I completed the outfit in three-inch black high heeled boots. I couldn't believe I could fit in them, never mind walk in them. I wondered if I would have the nerve to actually walk into the party. The pressure was getting to me, but I forced myself to open the door.

The decorative plate was made for me and we played shower games. We ate and danced and opened gifts. It was a wonderful time and then Joon took the knife and slit my throat...figuratively that is...and as my accomplices, my girls went down too. All we could do was wear plastic smiles and die inside as he spoke.

"Sage, I love you. This is the best gift you could ever give me. I never loved anybody before. I thought no one could make me feel this happy. You're giving me a chance to be in my child's life like my grandfather is in mine. I want to teach my child like he taught me. I want to love you like he loves my grandmother...forever. I would never leave you or our child alone. I will always put you first," he pauses to wipe his nose and eyes, "let me have that ring back."

He takes the ring from my finger and takes out a blue and white box and pops the question as he placed a ring, 2 ½ carat, emerald cut, in a platinum setting on my finger.

"I remember what your girls told me about your ring. You got good friends who know you. They always look out for you. So, with their blessings I hope, and that of your family, Sage, will you marry me?"

I thought I was going to miscarry. I turned on my heel and left the shower. My aunt, dad, Isa, Billie, Jewel, Joon's two older brothers, and his mother all followed him as he chased me upstairs to my aunt's house. The girls wrapped up the party and sent the gifts with Billie's aunt to the next building. I made it into the house and ran to the nearest window for air. I looked through the window and watched the girls file out looking like Goth extras. They sat in the back of the building and smoked a quick blunt before they went to the front and sat on the benches. I walked around to the front and looked off of the terrace. I wished I could've been down there with them. They sat there completely stunned and looked up at me. I knew they were wondering what was going on up here. They didn't have to wonder long. Joon stepped on to the terrace and hugged me really tight. I pushed him away gently. I just didn't know how it was going to go down, but I wasn't about to make it worse by marrying him. I already was sick everyday. I was a 'get money' chic and now my conscience was running the okey-doke on me. I turned around and walked inside and talked to him.

In a matter of seconds, a slow-motion scene exploded on to the terrace: Joon managed to hurl every part of his body off of the terrace with exception of his left leg which was miraculously snagged by both of his brothers. They had placed their feet against the paneling as an anchor to catch him. Joon's body violently slammed against the other side of the terrace. The entire community watched in horror. His mother's screams could be heard for what had to be miles. Joon begged for his brothers to release him, but they held on as his mother fell to her knees and prayed. I was stunned. I couldn't move.

Joon's brothers pulled him back over the railing and helped to hold him down. Someone had dialed 9-1-1 because the cops and an ambulance were already there. When the EMTs emerged from the building they had Joon strapped to the gurney. I was following but his grandparents stopped and gave me such a harsh look it halted me mid-step. Thank goodness the girls were there to hold me up just as I was about to fall. We went back to my aunt's house; it was empty while my aunt had taken my father to his house thinking I may have gone there instead, so we were alone.

"Sage I'm so sorry," Jewel said to open discussion. I could hardly breathe. "For what? I know right from wrong. I should have told him from jump street. He could have died tonight."

"Talk to us Sage what happened?" Jewel asked. I stared straight ahead as I spoke.

"He grabbed me the minute we came in the apartment from the terrace. He was asking me what he did wrong and why did I leave...I just broke down. I had to tell him three times before he understood everything. When I told him the third time everybody else had walked in and heard everything. Then he started choking me. I wasn't even fighting him back at first. His brothers were pulling and tugging but couldn't get him off of me. I thought I felt my bones cracking. I deserved to die, but not this baby so I started holding my stomach and groaning. That's what made him stop. He looked at me and was like he was sorry and that even though I hurt him he would never hurt the baby. He said that it would take some time, but he would get over it and it would be alright because no one knew but us. We could still get married and he would adopt the baby and later on we could have another one. Then he asked me again....but I said no. I told him that Bukaii wanted the baby and his family wanted to be a part of the baby's life and that I loved Bukaii. Joon looked at me like I wasn't even there. He turned his head and walked real slow at first. Then he broke into a run and his brothers chased him on to the terrace. His mother was calling me all kinds of names in Spanish and she spat on me. She ran outside and was praying over him. His grandfather wiped my face with his handkerchief. I didn't realize I was screaming until his grandfather was telling me to hush. Next thing I know, the paramedics busted in with the police. At first, they thought I needed them and then they saw

Joon. The EMTs said the hospital might hold him until he's stable and then let him go but what have I done?"

I moved back down south after I had the baby. Bukaii was true to his word and supported me, for awhile. After I finished college Bukaii started acting funky again. After all he was still young, and he was just playing house, but this was my real life. He did what all young guys do: he thought about himself. Almost four years later, I found myself face to face with the person who could make or break my career...someone so unexpected.

2

⌘

Book Two: Slipping

CHAPTER **19 Still Reinventing:**

Sage

I was consciously trying to do the right thing. God worked in my life and I knew it. My plans always failed and His always came to fruition. It *was* easier to do things His way and be happy. I was a nicer person today than I was even five years ago. I knew what it meant to suffer. I knew what it meant to forgive even when I wasn't forgiven. I knew what it meant to love even when I wasn't loved. I knew how to appreciate what I had even when it was ripped away from me. I was grateful and positive, and my friends were better people too. We each had come through a separate hell of our own making with scars and bandages and held firm to the fundamentals which bonded us as children. We loved each other and accepted each other as is. A twenty-year relationship, which watched us emerge as mothers, wives, successful, and reflective women.

My heart broke into one thousand pieces the day I laid eyes on my son August. He was perfect in every way and I realized at that moment that I didn't love anyone as much as I loved him. I was all he had in the world and he looked at me as if all he expected me to do was love him. My pregnancy was uneventful. Bukaii was the best; he proposed to me on Valentine's Day and gave me a moderate diamond ring. His family was moderately wealthy, and he worked at his mother's moderate property management company. Then out of nowhere Bukaii was the worst. He stopped going to work on a regular basis, but he kept receiving a paycheck. He was lazy and spoiled. But I *chose* him over Joon. I chose a life with Bukaii and he chose a life of leisure. He played dice and Madden; played basketball and sick; played his mother and other women; played me and I played myself by staying until August was well after a year old.

I supposed I wanted to prove to everyone I hurt that I had made the right decision. This was the man that I was going to marry, and we were going to have a good life together as a family. I needed to believe that I could make it work with Bukaii and he would work to make us a family. I sometimes worked as a substitute teacher at the local high school, but I was coming home from my first job as a copy editor when life decided it was time for me to reap what I had sewn. I entered the living room of the two-bedroom apartment I shared with Bukaii, to find my fourteen-month-old son watching TV alone. I found Bukaii's cell phone and car keys lying around—evidence that he was in the apartment somewhere. I picked August up and nearly dropped him. His diaper was full of urine and dried excrement. I felt my blood begin to boil. I took him to his room and removed the decrepit soiled diaper. Deciding he needed to immerse in the tub, I ran his bath and cleaned him the way my aunt taught me.

After securing August in his play pen with his sippy-cup and some apple slices, I went looking for the super idiot. I picked up the phone and called my next-door neighbor on the right of us (he sometimes played cards or video games over there with another deadbeat dad) and Bukaii's parents—no one had seen Bukaii. I tried to always keep our business private, but he left our child unattended and that needed to be broadcasted. I needed his family to know that I no longer trusted him.

I went on the balcony for some air after I fed August and put him to sleep. When I looked to my left, I found Bukaii. The balcony adjoined to ours had two chaise patio chairs pulled closed together. He was asleep on one of the patio chairs in nothing but boxers, white tube socks, and the herringbone chain that I bought him for his birthday two weeks prior. His long lanky legs were dragging on the floor. He was lying on his stomach, but his face was drooling in my direction. He was so comatose that when one of his eyes opened and focused on me, he smiled and continued sleeping. My neighbor was sleeping on the chair next to Bukaii cuddling with a body pillow; that was all she had as a means of covering. She had a really nice curly weave—she always bragged about going up to New York to have it done and then flying back down to North Carolina again. She said the whole experience was *tre`*expensive, *tre`*was her trademark, but I know for a fact that the farthest she went was Durham to her cousin's in-home beauty salon. She liked to show off the dragon tattoo which began at the base of her ankle and wound itself around her entire caramel-colored leg terminating in her Garden of Eden—again as she would boast. I thought how snake-like the thing looked now. I used to think that she was so mysterious, beautiful, and glamorous. I won't take anything away from her, she was an aspiring model, and she did get a lot of exposure. I suppose she loved her husband and that's why she kept coming back to live in these apartments; one step up from the projects.

There was evidence of weed and half a strip of ecstasy pills on the table beside them. I personally had never tried ecstasy and had no desire to, but there was also a little mirror on the table with white residue that I could only conclude was cocaine. I was so blown away. I was standing there like a first-class fool with my mouth open. In retrospect, I could have had myriad thoughts; oddly enough my first thought was of her 340-pound muscle-bound professional body building husband...and then he walked in. He looked across the patio at me from his doorway and saw the mix of emotions on my face and put a reign on his rage. He motioned for me to meet him in the hallway. I locked the patio door just in case Bukaii woke up and tried to hop back over. He could stay out there all night for all I cared. I met the husband in the hallway. He looked at me I guess waiting for me to cry or yell or have some kind of breakdown. I think it made him nervous at first because I looked at him as if we were about to discuss NC State's chances of making it to the final four during March Madness.

"Are you okay?" he asked.

"I'm easy like Sunday morning." I replied and I was.

"I'm going to have to kill your man you do know that?" he said.

I nodded. "I understand. I think I'm numb to this bullshit. Don't worry, whenever the cops show up the only thing, I'm going to tell them is how he left my child alone in the apartment for God knows how long. In fact, if you give me a few minutes, I'm going to grab August and leave this place altogether. He left his keys and cell phone inside so literally he's assed out."

He chuckled and lit a cigarette as I went through my door.

I grabbed my 'just in case' bag which now included seven days worth of outfits for August, grabbed my son, left all of the lights on, locked the door, and walked out to my car. I was just reversing when I heard the first screams of horror.

I had no intention of going to Bukaii's family's home. They would only protect him and blame me for his outside interests. It was a Thursday night. I went to a Holiday Inn for the night. I didn't have any idea what I was going to do so I called my dad and told him what happened that night and many nights before that one. Like the king that he is, he told me without out a shred of judgment in his voice to come home. I went to the bank in the morning after checkout and withdrew what little money I had in the savings account since it was my money. I'm glad I didn't marry his simple ass.

CHAPTER 20 Still Reinventing

Isa

I had to get my shit together. That was easier said than done. After Murder died, I went to college and earned my degree in Criminal Justice. I almost did not make it because I was insane. I kept doing the same thing over and over again expecting things to turn out different. It was my senior year, and I was so confused about my life. I did not know what I wanted to be, but I knew that I was tired. I was tired of not caring about anything or anyone. I just wanted to escape. I felt like I could not breathe. I was suffocating on myself and I did not know how to save myself. That is when I met Rodriguez.

Rodriguez was from a small town in Oregon. He only attended my college for one semester. He was a philosophy major. The only Black people he had ever seen were on TV. He said when he was younger, he did not think that we really existed. That is why he was attending Shaw. His father refused to pay for it so Rodriguez found a scholarship that would pay for the semester; he saved up money to travel and for incidentals. Did I mention Rodriguez was Black? Well, he was mixed, and his father was raising him out in Oregon. His father kept him in an all-white community and Hispanics who were so pale they could pass for white. Rodriguez was the strangest person I ever met. He listened to jazz like I listened to rap and R&B. He read books I never heard of like Dante's Inferno—I knew a guy named Dante...He could recite lines from the Bible, the Torah, and the Koran. I was trying to keep my head off the desk during my residential law class. And the way he dressed was so crazy! He literally put on a clean shirt, pants, a pair of socks and shoes and walked out of the door. He did not try to match anything, and he did not care about name brand items at all. His hair was this wild blond looking afro thing and he was tall enough to play basketball professionally but could not be so bothered to know the name of one team.

Everybody at school liked Rodriguez. He changed the vibe when he walked in a room. People felt calmer, more confident, like everything would be alright. Out of all the people at my school I could not figure out why he hung around me or why I hung around him. I did not stop cursing or smoking or being loud and he did not do any of those things. Sage called him my funny valentine. He was a big flirt, but he never tried anything with me. The most he would do is give me hugs or hold my hand. Once or twice, he kissed my cheek or forehead, but it always felt like he was my brother.

I talked to him about everything and he talked to me about everything—I thought. The week before the semester ended me and him were sitting in Estey Hall, the university's theater. We were helping Sage out with the lights and sound for her one act play and she was late as usual. I was sitting on the stage in the spotlight. He was in the second row trying to decide if he liked the gel lights he had in the background when it hit me that he would not be here the next week.

"Rodriguez, why do you hang around me? We are so different," I said. I could not see his face because of the spotlight, and I think that is what gave me the courage to ask him.

"We're not different Isa. We are exactly alike. We say whatever we want, we do whatever we want, and we are not afraid to be who we are good, bad, or otherwise. Most importantly, we were both lost when I met you. I think that we might be about to find our way soon. What do you think?" He asked.

I did not know what to think. I guess he took my silence to mean I was thinking because he kept on talking.

"My mother is—

"Is?" I interrupted; I thought she was dead since he never talked about her.

"Yeah, *is* in a mental institution. My *father* is really my grandfather. My mother is his daughter. She was raped by this Black guy and she snapped. It was too much shame for her especially because my grandfather kept telling her that it was her fault for wearing a short skirt. When she found out she was pregnant that pushed her over the edge and she tried to kill herself. My family doesn't believe in abortion so that's how I got so lucky. My grandfather would've given me away, but my mother kept asking for me. The doctors said that it was helpful if she could focus on things that were in this reality. Maybe she could one day find her way back to sanity. That fell apart the older I got. I started to look like my father, and she got hysterical and withdrawn. By that time my grandfather already loved me, and he had to tell me truth about my conception because I thought I did something to make my mother hate me. I finally got why my grandfather hates Black people so much. I'm not saying it's right, but at least I know what happened to make him feel that way."

It was too much for me to handle so I asked something to pull away from it. "Did they ever catch your fath—I mean the guy who did that to your mother?"

"Yeah, he was already in jail for some other rapes. I wonder if I could turn out like that or crazy like my mother."

"I don't know much Rodriguez, but I do know that is bullshit. We design ourselves. Rape is a choice. Your mother had a mental breakdown because of that man's bad choice. Now if that is what you want to do with your life, let me know so I can remove myself from you right now. No one is born a rapist. You are already a better person than him and your grandfather. I am not going to lie, we Black people definitely have some shit with us, but everybody does and that is why you have to take people for who they are as individuals not based on who their parents are or their race and sometimes not even on their past. You have to concentrate on how that person treats you."

That is when I figured out what I wanted, who I was, what was wrong with me, and how I was going to fix it. I told Rodriguez about my life with Murder and my history with men. I told him I did not know that I was looking to fill something up inside of me until I met him. I never tried to kiss Rodriguez or have sex with him or manipulate him. He told me that I was beautiful inside and out. He told me that I was perfect the way that I was and always follow my own mind. There was not a man anywhere who could say I was with him during my time with Rodriguez. He was my first real love. The kind you feel unconditionally. The kind that you know you have to let him go or you will ruin him because you are not all the way sane yet. He came on stage and sat behind me on the floor. He wrapped his arms around me, and I cried and cried and cried. He kept whispering in my ear, "It's alright. *I* love you. It's alright. I love *you*."

The door creaked and I saw Sage slowly backing out of the auditorium. That night Rodriguez and I stayed on the phone all night. In the morning he caught his flight back to Oregon. He did not call or write me anymore and really, I was not expecting him to. I got focused on school. I started getting A's from professors who did not give A's. By the time graduation came in May, my term GPA was a 4.0. That was enough to boost up my cumulative GPA to a 3.7 and I graduated cum laude. Rodriguez did not come to the graduation—I *was* expecting him to be there. I wanted him to see what I accomplished. I wanted him to be proud of me. I wanted him to see that I was proud of myself.

A week later, I was taking the train to New York. I was accepted into the police academy at College Point in Queens. Sage stayed in North Carolina with Bukaii. I told her she was stupid for staying with that asshole. She needed to come back to New York with me and I would help her with the baby, but he talked her into marriage, and she said yes. I told her point blank that I was not sure if I would be at that wedding. Bukaii makes me sick; it was just something about him that was not right, and I never passed up an opportunity to let him know it. Sage was mad at me, but she would be alright. I called her when the train reached D.C. We both were still getting used to our new cell phones or rather having one. We made plans to see each other Fourth of July weekend if the academy let me out; otherwise, she said she would be at the academy graduation.

The train would be stopping for about forty-five minutes so after I hung up with Sage, I went into the station for something to eat. I loved Sbarros. I was fiending for a calzone. I could not wait until I got to New York. I could smell the oregano and sauce before I could see the restaurant. I was daydreaming and bumped into a lady. She was actually a young girl—maybe eighteen or nineteen years old. She had huge hips, huge behind, and big breasts. Her waist was squeezed tight with a white belt that barely fastened. Everything on her was tight: jeans, shirt, shoes, and face. She looked like if she unbuckled her belt, she would be one round size all around like the Kool-Aid man. She had large silver bangles on her arms and matching earrings. Her eye make-up was heavy black with shades of silver. She wore black lipstick lined with a silver pencil. Her hair was cut short with little curls and it was dyed sky blue. I meant to say sorry, but I was buggin! She looked crazy especially with the eye piercing and the nose ring. She did not like me staring or the fact that I did not apologize.

"Damn, you coulda least say sorry! I know you see all this," She said that running her hands all over her body. I kept looking at her like she had lost her mind. She leaned into my face and snapped her fingers in my face. That did the trick.

"You are right. I am sorry for bumping into you," I said.

"You need to be sorry," she said.

"Little girl, you better find somebody else to play with. I am not the one! I said I was sorry but do not get it twisted. We can do this however you want to do this," She and I were eye to eye. She was bigger than me but when I looked in her eyes, I saw fear in there. I took a step back. She was only a little girl. She probably was younger than what I thought—maybe sixteen. Did I want to ruin my whole career over this? I turned and walked on to Sbarros. She kept on cussing me out and threatening me. I got in line and waited my turn. A deep voice interrupted my thoughts of a pepperoni and cheese calzone.

"There was a time when you would've punched her in the face even *if* you were wrong. I'm really proud of you," the voice said. When I turned around, I was staring into a broad chest. I had to take a step back to see who it was. He was smiling that same smile from over a year ago.

"Rodriguez."

"Isa," He grabbed me and hugged me so hard I could not breathe. "I've missed you so much."

"Yeah right! You missed me so much that you never called me." He put his head down.

"I couldn't see you, so I didn't call. My father got really sick and I had to spend all my energy on him."

"I am sorry about that."

"I believe you. Where are you going? Are you here in D.C.?" He asked hopefully.

"No, I'm on my way to New York. I'm going into the police academy."

"I see."

"What? You have a problem with that?" I was ready to defend my career because I had to keep doing it. I loved him and all, but he could get it too.

"Relax Isa, I just can't believe somebody is going to put a gun in your hand legally," he joked. I punched him in the arm. I had to massage my hand a little because his arm was solid as a rock. I was going to ask him about his new body when the announcement was made that I had ten minutes to get back to my train. He smiled that sad smile at me and pulled out a business card.

"Call me or email me...soon Isa. I leave for South America in two weeks."

"What? Why?" I looked at the card. "You work for the United Nations? Already? You had to have just graduated."

"I do and my father had an old friend who hooked me up. I can speak four languages, so they snatched me up. Come on let me walk you to your train." I could only follow him with my eyes popping because I just noticed that he cut his hair too and so many women were looking at him like he was some kind of model. I started to feel, I guess, jealous. I hooked my arm in his and let him talk so I could keep looking at him. I never noticed that he was cute before, just strange, but I loved him just like he was. I had to find a way to guarantee that I saw him again. I was dipping into my master manipulator files.

"Listen, Sage is supposed to be getting married sometime soon and I need a date."

"Didn't I just tell you that I'm going to be in South America in two weeks?"

"You do not even know when it is. Hell, I don't know when it is. If you do not want to go, just say so."

"You can just say you miss me; don't pick a fight and or try to manipulate me. I know you Isa," I giggled to myself—he did know me.

"I miss you and I will call you," I said. I looked over and saw the blue hair girl coming toward us.

"Excuse me, I don't mean to interrupt you, but I was wondering if I could say a few words to Mr. Rod? I'm also sorry about our encounter earlier." I did not know how that hood rat all of a sudden could speak English, but I was not about to let her steal my last few minutes with Rodriguez; he decided differently.

"It's okay Tasha. How are you?"

"Great! I'm catching this train. I got early admission into Delaware State.

They have a good social archeologist program. I think your letter of recommendation might have gotten me in. Thank you."

"It's nothing and I'm so proud of you. You know I only missed *your* graduation because *I* had to graduate right?" She clearly liked my man, and he had no idea.

"Thank you, Mr. Rod. Well, I'm getting on now and I'll send you a letter to the program's address."

"Cool Tasha. Do good things in Delaware." She gushed a little and stepped onto the train. I looked at him to explain.

"You want to explain?"

"Sure, as soon as you call me." He leaned over and kissed me like nobody's business. He squeezed me, helped me on the train, and then stood on the platform until I left. When I could not see him anymore, I realized I had no idea why he was at the train station. Maybe it was not for me to know.

CHAPTER 21 Still Reinventing

Kim

I sat restlessly in the passenger seat of the Pathfinder. My uncle traded vehicles with a 'girlfriend' for the trip upstate. He gave the 'girlfriend' the fully loaded Caddy. Girlfriend was none too pleased that he was going with me. She didn't believe that I was his niece until he showed her a bunch of pictures that I didn't even know that he had including school and holiday pictures. The woman immediately tried to be my friend. I started to tell her how dumb I thought she was but decided to just disregard her. I couldn't gather up the strength to educate her. Sitting in the car watching trees and mountains go by, (I didn't know New York had mountains), I wondered if other people did that to me. I thought about how many mistakes I'd made acting crazy like that lady. I wondered why I felt so old all of a sudden. I was tired and felt like I didn't have any real joy in my life.

I leaned the car seat back and took in a deep breath. Uncle Cane barely said a word to me in two hours other than to ask me if I was hungry or had to use the restroom. I said no to both. Now I wondered what he was thinking. What made this man with no kids of his own want to be with me, a crazy, mixed-up teenager? Why would anyone want to be with me after all the things that I did? I knew what happened to Butter. I still wasn't sure that I was sorry that he was dead because it felt like he killed me first. But still, who I was to be glad that someone lost his life? It was my fault this man was dead, and that Sean was on the run. I knew I didn't pull the trigger, but still...

Uncle Cane sat there looking straight ahead. He had no idea what he was doing.

"If my brother were alive, I would have been around more. I was halfway glad when Eve told me to stay away. I couldn't take the grief anyway. All of you look exactly like your father. I left your mother to fend for herself. Yes, she was a strong woman, but I was wrong for walking away so easily. Now I have a nephew overseas that no one sees, but he's fine. I have eyes wherever my family may be. The other nephew is in the city and became a father much too early, but he has a city job now and the streets aren't so sweet to him anymore. But you, Kim, I never saw you coming."

I was kinda afraid to interrupt him. So, I just kept quiet hoping he would go on. People never speak to me like they expect me to understand anything deep and I didn't want it to end.

"You're so street smart, I never thought you would be caught slipping. That was my fault entirely. The streets are my domain. It's my business to know everything that's going down before it's going down. That young boy moved faster than I did; talking about your little boyfriend Sean. I sat in my dark blue Jag and watched the whole thing go down. I saw you drive up; thought maybe you would get him to jump in the car. I waited for young buck to keep it moving. I thought at first, he would approach Butter and maybe shoot the fifths, but then Sean sat down. Butter's crew tried to warn him by stepping back, but Butter's head was too big. He let young buck slide right in. I could see from where I was sitting, three cars away, that young buck had a piece. Then again, I'm an O.G. I respected young buck's gangsta. He came in alone and left alone-just the way I would have. Young buck never took his eyes off the prize. He looked that man in the eyes and pulled the trigger twice."

I tried to swallow but it was so hard. I wish I had some gum to pop but then Uncle Cane would probably remember that I was sitting there. I sat frozen and let the words fill up the car.

"The style he used looked really familiar to me. I made a call an hour later to confirm my suspicions. I knew young buck's grandfather from way back in the day; told him to thank his grandson for me, but he should never kill over a woman not even my niece. I got the boy's record straight so that if he ever wanted to come back to New York he could. He and I are even.

Now, I have to do something about you."

I thought it might be safe to take a breath now. I wanted to crawl inside a hole. I was so embarrassed, but at least I wasn't dead. I *was* broken. I stared out of the window like I had never seen anything except concrete. I remembered visiting upstate when I was younger. But I was sixteen—be seventeen in a few weeks—I needed to concentrate on his plan of action. I know me, sooner or later I was going to be out of this mood and give him hell. I don't think I can even help myself. He reached above him to his sun visor and selected a c.d. to pop in the player. *I Who Have Nothing* by Luther Vandross and Cheryl Lynn came through the speakers first.

Uncle Cane's rich tenor matching Luther's octaves brought me out of my daydream. He sounded so much like my father. I missed him so much it hurt. I didn't even know that I had picked up the female lead until Uncle Cane wiped the tears from my face. We rode for the last hour and a half singing duets. It was a good wash for both of us.

The house was on an incline. It was cream with black shutters. There were leaves everywhere. Autumn had come early to Plattsburg. The street was very quiet. It was nearly ten at night. I looked at the house skeptically. The porch light was on and there was smoke coming out of the chimney. Uncle Cane noticed me hesitating and chuckled.

"I pay a guy to be the caretaker of the house. I called him earlier and told him that we were coming up. He's the one who put on the lights for us."

"What about the fire? How did he know what time we was going to be here? The house could have burned down," I answered.

Chuckling again Cane replied, "Darlin, he lives next door. I told him what time we might be getting here. He probably lit it and went home; through the back door when he saw us pull up."

"Actually, I came around to see if you needed some help getting in." A frail-looking white man stepped out of the shadows. I nearly jumped out of my skin while Cane turned to hug the man.

"Sorry to frighten you miss," the stranger said.

"Kim, this is Mr. Bagby. Bagby this is my niece Kim."

I gave him a half-assed wave. Bagby grabbed my bag and took it inside. When he was a safe distance away, I turned to my uncle.

"What's wrong with him? Is he dangerous? Should I be worried?"

"Everything. Yes. No. You never have to be worried with me as your uncle. Bagby is a certified genius. He went to M.I.T. and he's going to be your teacher."

"You mean tutor."

"No teacher. He knows everything and how to make sure that you know everything. We'll be home-schooling you so you can have your regular diploma. It's not a discussion. And you should do yourself a favor. If you have a thought about disrespecting that man or trying to play him, I suggest you change that plan. But I know *my* family, so I know you won't understand until after you try him tomorrow. You'll remember real quick that I warned you." I scrunched up my face.

"Why would you leave me with someone who would be a danger to me?"

I was starting to regret coming with Cane. He put an arm around my shoulder and steered me toward the house.

"I already told you that he is not going to hurt you."

"But you said he was dangerous!"

"And he is. But if you do the right thing, you'll never have to find out and I won't have to lose a very good friend." Uncle Cane winked at me as we continued into the house. Closing the door behind us, he hung up both of our coats on the coat rack. I took the house in. I immediately loved the country home feeling I got from the house. It smelled like cinnamon and warm apples. The furniture was soft, plush browns, golds, and reds. Bagby came to the bottom of the staircase.

"I put the bags in the rooms. Cane you have your room of course and I put Kim the guest room down the hall. You have your own bathroom within your room Kim. Class begins promptly at 8:30 am. Please be ready to go."

"Where we going? I thought we was going to do this right here." I looked at him questioningly.

"Did you just learn English? Never mind good night to the both of you." Bagby turned and went through the kitchen toward the backdoor. I was facing my uncle now with my hands on my hips. I was waiting for answers.

"You better get some sleep. I'll have breakfast ready at 7:50 am. You won't blame me for being late. There's an alarm clock in your bedroom. Make sure you set it to a time that allows you to do everything you need to before breakfast. Call your mother and tell her you made it here safely. Good night." Uncle Cane kissed my forehead and quickly turned around. He grabbed my purse and took out my cell phone and broke it. He handed me back my bag and went upstairs.

"There's a phone in your room." I stood at the bottom of the stairs in stunned silence. Was it going to be like this the whole time? I ask questions and they act like I didn't say anything?

CHAPTER **22 Still Reinventing**

Sage

The first thing I did when I got to New York was find a childcare program for my child. I didn't have to look far; my cousin Ama had an in-home daycare two stops away on the 4 Train. My dad said he could pick August up on days that I had to work late. Ms. Evelyn, Kim's mom, watched him sometimes on the weekends or holidays that fell on a Monday. The second thing I did was join a gym to get rid of the baby fat and the layers of red velvet cake that I added to my waistline because of Bukaii's nonsense and my self-pity. Isa had already gone into the police academy. And Kim was still M.I.A. I got a letter from her once saying she was in upstate New York and she was getting better. I was glad to hear somebody was recovering from their breakdown. I felt like mine would never end. My boss in NC had referred me to *Shine Magazine*'s owner and he hired me as a copy editor too. Sometimes it is who you know. However, he let it be known quickly that I needed to find a way to make myself invaluable. I had no idea what to do.

Isa

The Police Academy was like bootcamp, but I did not know it at first. I was walking and talking with some girl from Atlanta. Her accent was killing me while she was loving mine. We just got off of the bus that picked up thirty of us and took us to some place that looked like an army base but somewhere in the but-crack of Queens. This short, ugly, woman who looked like a man came up to me. She had on a grey t-shirt with PO-LICE written across the front in black letters, matching sweatpants, and sneakers. Her hair was pulled back in a short ponytail. I heard her before I saw her. She was yelling at everybody but here she was starting with me, so I stopped.

"Where the hell do you think you are? The club? You think you gonna wear all that jewelry and tight jeans?" I walked away laughing and talking. "Who this bitch think she talking to?" I strolled my happy ass to the open field where the other recruits were. Super-ugly walked to the top of the platform in front of us and started talking to the crowd.

"There are numbers on the ground on which you should stand. Sergeant Snow will help you out."

A large white woman with dark hair cut short walked in between us to make sure we were on the numbers. When I looked around I saw rows and rows of people. Sergeant Snow shoved me back toward the front. I was not about to fight that big woman. I was hoping that Super-ugly would not tell Sergeant Snow about what I said. Snow kept pushing and shoving people until everyone started to get themselves right without her help. Super-ugly spoke to us again after everyone was standing on a number and not moving.

"I am not your friend, homegirl, sister, aunt, mother, or your bitch. I'm not your psychiatrist or spiritual advisor. Your well-being concerns me only in that you are well trained to serve and protect the people of this great city and that wherever you go bearing the badge and robe of blue that you are an exceptional reflection of me: Lieutenant Mary B. Sallye. You may only call me Lt. Sallye. It is my goal to pull only the best and the brightest out of what I've been given. Some of you will be on your merry way before dinner tonight at oh-eighteen-hundred hours. If you have it in your head to be a champion of your group, defy the rules of this outfit, cause mayhem in anyway Sergeant Snow will have a one on one with you. It would be in your best interest at all times not to defy me. I'm not what you want. Some of you may last until the end of the week. The cream of the crop will complete this six-month training plotting what you will do to me because you refused to be broken. However, comma at that point, you will be officers of this great city."

Lt. Sallye stepped back from the podium microphone and Sgt. Snow stepped up and gave us some basics of survival. She told us rise and fall times. She told us mealtimes. She told us where we would sleep and eat. She told us about the restricted areas. She told us how to answer questions when we were asked. She told us about fraternizing with each other and commanding officers. She told us to forget about our life before we came. She told us we can leave whenever we wanted before the six months were up, but we could never come back. She said we were dismissed only when she and Lt. Sallye left our presence. When they were about twenty feet away, we got a little courage and started looking around to see if we could move or not. Sgt. Snow blew a whistle and yelled that we dismissed. I was definitely going to have check myself and my mouth before somebody got hurt. I was trying to do something with my life.

Kim

I noticed neither one of them locked the front doors. They may be comfortable up here, but this was the setting of all the murders I saw in movies. I locked all the doors and windows that had locks. Then I turned off the porch light before going upstairs. There was a room at the end of the hall with a light on. The door was open so I assumed it must be my room. I walked toward it and saw one of my suitcases on the bed. I opened it up and pulled out of pair of flannel pajamas my father used to wear. I closed the bedroom door and called my mother while I was changing. The answering machine came on. I left a message wondering where she mother was or if she was sitting there listening to the message. I brushed my teeth and then wrapped my hair up in a doobie wrap before putting a scarf on. I closed my suitcase and placed it on the floor. I decided I could unpack after my lessons tomorrow. I set the alarm clock and then walked over to the light switch which was by the door and turned off the light. I slipped my tired body underneath the down comforter and laid my head on the pillow for the next hour in deep thought. I never thought that I would ever have trouble sleeping in a place so quiet. I was used to the lullaby of the street: horns, yelling, music, and life. Nothing was going on here. My last thought was that I would more than likely die of boredom. So, I was surprised to find that I was awakened by the alarm at 6:30 am and it was a year later. Obviously, I had fallen asleep.

CHAPTER 23 Still Reinventing

Sage

The second month that I was there I was pitching a story idea to the editor, Anya Merker, who was a major witch; and I'm being nice in that description. She was super skinny with big curly black hair. Her head was big, but it was nothing compared to her mouth. Her pale white skin always made me think she might have been a vampire in her former life. Everyday, without fail, she wore bright red lipstick, blush, dark eye make-up, and a gold necklace with The Star of David pendant. She was tapping her red acrylic nails on her desk as she was ripping my idea to shreds. She looked like Cher gone wrong—which is saying a lot.

"Sage, your idea lacks depth. I don't think that you can make it work. Female rap artists are almost obsolete; try again. I know that you had this job just handed to you, so you don't know that it takes hard work to be a writer. You don't just come up with some flim flam and presto chango there's a story. You have to do research. And who's going to write the story? You think the other writers have nothing to do? You think rap artists and interviews fall off of a tree? Please honey stick with your job. You're doing a marginally good job with it. Do what you know."

I was in the motion of giving this Brighton Beach reject a piece of my mind when a man in a tacky grey suit appeared at Anya's doorway. The suit was choking him at the neckline, under his arms, the waist, thighs, and terminated at his ankles. Anya and I stared at him. He cleared his throat.

"Sekyiwah Mensa?" He pronounced it the way it was spelled—which was wrong. Very few people outside of my family call me that and definitely not this clearly recovering alcoholic. Sage is my pen name and the nickname derived from my Ghanaian name. Already irritated with Anya, I turned my fury on him.

"It's pronounced seh-chew-wah."

"Whatever, you've been served." He placed a subpoena in my hand and left as swiftly as he had arrived. Confusion was leaving little room for anger until I read the subpoena. Bukaii was suing me for custody of August. My anger came back with a vengeance. Anya cocked her head and threw me a sly grin.

"One of your homies trying to get street credit getting arrested for blasting somebody. Or was it one of the street pharmacists falling victim to the hood? And let me guess, you're not a snitch huh?" I leaned in close to her. I smiled as if I were telling her something hilarious. That way anyone watching would be hard pressed to believe that I was telling her to go to hell.

"Listen, living in Harlem doesn't make you an expert on all things urban. I would stop with those remarks before you get slapped…you know by one of your peeps." I left her fingering her pendant and ended my day at four. I had skipped lunch and came in early, so it wasn't an issue. I went directly to a cab. Normally I would take the subway from the SoHo office to 34th street. I would power walk to 36th street where my gym was located as a pre warm-up to my work out. But today I needed to work off some steam immediately.

I went to the locker room and changed into my work out clothes. I did thirty minutes on the treadmill and thirty minutes of arm reps with five-pound weights. I still couldn't sort anything out. But by that time a kick boxing class was starting so I joined in. Aerosmith's "Dream On" was blasting as I was getting my rhythm. I almost had some idea of what I was going to do about Bukaii but not about my failing career. We cooled down and then I went to the shower. I was almost done dressing when the woman next to me started talking. She had her head down drying her hair so I couldn't see her face. My back was to her as I pulled on my socks and fastened my jeans.

"Somebody musta pissed you off the way you was kicking that bag today." I started talking without thinking and brushing the tangles out of my weave.

"Please believe! First my ignorant editor of the no-risk taking *Shine Magazine* says that female rap artists are obsolete, so she basically kills my story and then my ignorant baby daddy served me with a subpoena today trying to fight for custody of my son. Now I got to go to court next Monday for a hearing. I can't afford to miss work especially with that crazy broad trying to fire me every chance she gets."

"Wow. I would hire you as my bodyguard, but it sounds like you already have a job. But I think I can help you out with that 'crazy broad'. Are you a good writer or are you gonna make me look stupid?"

I chuckled and started pulling on my boots with my back to her.

"I'm an amazing writer and I'm not going to make myself look stupid. Do you know somebody I can interview? I ain't too proud to ask for help."

From over my shoulder the woman grabbed my cell phone, dialed a number, made a call, and hung up. It happened so fast that by the time I turned around she was done.

"Call that number by seven tonight to tell the driver where to pick you up tomorrow morning. Be ready to roll at eight. He'll bring you and your photographer to my house. No matter what you've heard about me, I am very professional, and I believe in being on time."

I was almost speechless. "Thank you."

She put on her motorcycle jacket, Jackie O glasses, and walked out of the locker room. I sat stunned as I watched the bodyguard, I just noticed follow Lil' Kim around the corner.

I hate to admit it, but Anya was right about my idea not having any depth. That day I learned that it would be the last time I give Anya any room to criticize my work and be one hundred percent right. I would be more thorough. By the following morning, I had a photographer who was in love with Lil' Kim so that would guarantee beautiful pictures of her. I had an angle for my story and questions that would allow Lil' Kim to tell her story the way she saw it and give the readers something they had never read before. The owner loved it...I sent a copy of the story with the pictures to him and Anya at the same time for insurance. I was taking a risk. He could have fired me if he felt I was going over Anya's head. He believed in protocol, but he also knew that I had been taking her shit without complaining to him like everyone else in the office did. The story ran that month with Kim on the cover and my name in the byline.

Kim was pleased with the job I did and that led to an interview with The Lox and The Firm for our *Battle Royale* issue a month later. Three months after that I was in Long Beach with The Dog Pound for the *Great Smoke-Out* issue. I could barely enjoy any of my success because I was always in North Carolina defending my job as a mother to some judge or following the orders of the first judge to bring August down to North Carolina for every other major holiday to Bukaii on my own dime. This was my punishment for thinking of my child's safety by moving him to New York. I needed a better lawyer.

CHAPTER 24 Still Reinventing

Isa

I was four months in the program with no problems. We trained like we were in the military. I stayed clear of Lt. Sallye and Sgt. Snow. I did what I was told, and I did not try to join any clique. I helped out the people in my class when they were falling behind and I made everybody study because we all needed to pass the written test during the fifth month. My favorite training was gun skills. I learned everything that I could about every gun we had on the compound. I could take any gun apart and put it back together again. The best part though was distance shooting. I found out later that it was called being a sniper. I could see the target no matter how far I was and nail it. I used to hate math when I was in school but for some reason, if I got the coordinates of a target I knew exactly where the target was without looking.

The fourth week of training until the fifth month, I made an enemy. Laura Juarez. Apparently, S.W.A.T. was recruiting, and she thought I wanted in. Juarez was 5'4 with curly black hair and bleached ends. I couldn't tell you what color her eyes were because she was squinted all time. She drew her eyebrows on even though we wasn't supposed to wear make-up. She looked surprised as hell when you looked at her. I did good not to talk about her or to her. She stayed in a bad mood and I'm not the one she wanted to mess with. I think she had a little bit of a Napoleon complex. I don't know if women can get it, but she had it. She got it in her mind some kind of way that I was her competition. I just wanted to be a police officer. I was not thinking about specializing in anything. I told that crazy woman that, but she didn't believe me. She approached me in the mess hall.

"Steney what's up? Let's talk outside," she commanded. I looked at her like she was crazy. I was not going outside with her. I wanted to finish eating my tater tots and pizza. After that I was going to the shooting range.

"No thanks Juarez...still eating." She grabbed my tray and threw it in the nearest garbage. I closed my eyes and prayed that when I opened them, she would be gone. Otherwise smashing my milk into her face was the next step. Sgt. Snow walked by, picked up my milk, and told me to follow her. I pushed away from the table and Juarez bumped me as I passed her. I stumbled a few steps and turned to face Lt. Sallye. I know that I was red. I wanted to choke Juarez, but Lt. Sallye had Juarez face down with her foot on her neck. I do not know where the Lt. came from. I did not hear her approach or Juarez go down. Lt. Sallye looked me in the eye. I wanted to say a lot, but nothing would come to my mouth.

"Steney don't keep Sgt. Snow waiting. Double-time now!"

"Yes, Lt. Sallye." I turned and jogged to catch up with Sgt. Snow. I followed her to her office. She opened the door and entered with me following behind. There was an older black woman sitting behind her desk. She had on a military uniform. I could not tell if it was Army, Navy, Airforce, or Marines. I was too scared of not knowing what was going on. I just followed Sgt. Snow's lead. She was standing so I stayed standing.

"Commander Brown, Isabelle Steney," said Sgt. Snow.

"You are dismissed Sgt. Snow." Snow turned and left the office closing the door behind her. Commander Brown stood and extended her hand, and I shook it.

"I'll be brief. We need all of our forces prepared for any level of attack. Lt. Sallye isn't a woman of many words and neither is Sgt. Snow. They both, however, have the highest praises for you. You've made top scores in every area of the program. You're a leader and you know how to work with a group and alone. We want you—Special Operations."

"With all due respect, I don't want to be in the military, Commander Brown," I said. I hoped my voice did not crack.

"It's not the military. We'll be in contact. You're dismissed." I walked out of the door while she put her head down to write something. I was extra confused. I walked to the range to get some target practice. I was on my second clip when I saw Commander Brown being driven to the helipad on the west side of the base. I felt a presence behind me. I knew it was Lt. Sallye. She did it again and I did not hear her until it was too late.

"You did not teach us how to do that," I said without turning around.

"Be specific."

"Arrive without being noticed."

"The only one who can teach you is Commander Brown," she said.

"But--," I said, but I was talking to the back of her head. She was already ten feet away walking in the other direction. I couldn't concentrate on shooting anymore. I wanted to be a cop. I didn't want people to start trying to make me more than what I was. I was going to be a police officer and work my shift and try not to kill anybody if I didn't have to. There wasn't anything special about me. I wanted to be regular and that's it. I don't want to be bothered with no man or kids or drama. Special Forces sounded like a quick way for me to die. No thank you. I walked back to the dorm. I walked through and saw Juarez cleaning her gun on her bed. Across from her was Lumet, the crazy white girl from Montana. She was tall the way Juarez was short. She had short brown hair, long arms and legs, long face, blue eyes, and her skin was splotchy all over. When they stood next to each other they reminded of those guys in that book *Of Mice and Men* we had to read in high school. The only difference was Lumet was mean as hell. I already knew she was going to be a dirty cop. I just had to make sure I didn't wind up in the same precinct as her. She wasn't wrapped too tight. She looked at me and made a shooting motion with her fingers and pulled the trigger three times. I walked past them shaking my head.

"Juarez, you think I got her between the eyes?" she asked.

"No doubt."

I didn't know what the penalty was for fighting. I didn't pay attention to that rule because I wasn't trying to fight nobody. But I could see sooner or later I was going to have to shut one or both of them up or I wouldn't get any peace. I could just do something and say I didn't know any better, but I did; I knew ignorance of the law was no defense. I had to think and do some research. A girl I was cool with, Melinda Grove, walked into the dorm heading straight for my bed. She's the one from Atlanta I met when I first got here. I think she wanted to be a cop just to meet guys. That's all she ever talked about. She treated the academy how some girls treated college like its only purpose was to find a husband. If they got a little educated on the way then hey, that's cool. But she probably *would* get a husband here. No matter what she put on, sweats or a uniform, she looked like a body model playing dress up. Her body wasn't meant to blend in like the academy tries to make the women do. I was struggling a little with it, but it was impossible for her.

"Stenayyyy," she yelled."

"What's good Grove?"

"Girl, everything! This academy must be like the Harvard of police academies or something."

"That would be West Point."

"What? Oh, whatever. They got this fine man on the base with some of the commanders and shit. He gonna be heading up a new Scared Straight program on this campus for like kids. I'm thinking about making him my baby daddy or getting a baby daddy and then send my kid here so I can get next to him." I want to judge her, but I can't. It wasn't that long ago that plan would've been just fine with me. I did need to tell her the flaw in her plan.

"If you have a baby to send here it would be years before you would see this man again. By that time, he might be old or fat or married or you might be married or fat or old. Just talk to him and see what's up. He's not a recruit or commander, right? So, step to him."

"You right. You know those stupid rules about fraternizing is the only thing that's keeping me from trying the rest of these fine men out, but you know me, I'ma get my freak on one way or another."

This chic was giving me a headache, but she *was* distracting me from killing Juarez and Lumet.

"Come on, let's go," she said.

"Go where? I just came back from the range. I'm taking a nap. You should too. They barely give us breaks here."

"Girl you have to see this man for yourself. He ain't nothing like the men down south! He don't look nothing like the dudes in New York. I ain't saying it right. Come see," she said.

I wasn't getting a nap so I got up. We walked past Juarez and Lumet and Grove and looked back at them. I kept going. Juarez and Lumet weren't going to say anything to her or do anything to her. Grove was a black belt. She grew up with five older brothers who kept beating her up. Her mother put her in the class, and she started beating up everyone. She wound up in a group home because she was so uncontrollable. She did the National Guard and then came here. Just because she looked like a Georgia Peach didn't mean she wasn't a Tasmanian Devil. She caught up to me. We walked about thirty yards with Grove talking non-stop in my ear. We reached the basketball court where a game was going on.

I learned a few things in college. One of them was basketball. I didn't play for Shaw, but I played on the court behind the boy's dorm. I'm pretty good too. It was only two or three girls the guys would let play ball with them. I won't lie. I was trying to get close to one the guy who teaching me. He was the point guard for the school's team. I didn't know I would start liking it or be good at it. If I wasn't so busy running the street in New York, I might've played a lot sooner. I started practicing without him and eventually being without him. Now I couldn't resist a pickup game. Grove grabbed my shirtsleeve.

"We don't have time for a game Steney. We on a man hunt."

I couldn't hear her; I took off the long sleeve shirt she was holding on to and ran to the court in my tank top and sweats. They needed another player for three on three.

"Just give me ten minutes Grove. Somebody else should show up by then." I yelled over my shoulder.

"But you gonna be all sweaty."

I ignored her and kept going. They wouldn't let me in the game. A tall, lanky black guy stood over me blocking my way on to the court.

"You guys are short a man so why can't I play?" I asked.

"Yeah, we short a *man*. You're not a man," lanky man said.

"Neither are you and they letting you play," I said. He made a move for me. One of the guys held him back.

"Let me find out, you okay with trying to hit me but you got a problem with me playing ball?"

Grove was behind me and the guy really backed all the way off. Grove could beat everybody on the base, men too. She didn't like basketball and didn't play. But she didn't like anybody saying that women couldn't do anything because they were women.

"Let her play," she said. She could be a bully sometimes. I loved that about her.

"She ain't playing on my team," lanky man said.

"I got you Steney. You can play on my team," the guy who held him back said.

"She gonna be calling foul every five seconds," lanky man said.

I checked the ball so we could play. He ran his mouth worse than Grove. I shot a three over his head. Let the shit talking begin. I had to guard him, and he was giving me hell. Ten minutes into the game he did this pivot with his hips and his elbow busted my lip and knocked me down. Before I knew what was happening, I had snatched him by the shirt and twisted it underneath his neck. The other players broke us up and I was allowed two free-throw shots. That put my team up by four. Lanky man was hating me more and more. But with Grove standing there cheering for our team, Lanky man behaved as much he could. Plus, Grove was bouncing so hard she was distracting every player on the court except me. I had to give her a head signal to calm down so *my* team could concentrate.

The ten-minute game turned into a full game with a good portion of the academy watching the show. Even Grove forgot what we came out of the dorm to do. Our teams went past playing Horse, we were going for twenty-five points. My team was one shot from making twenty-five; they were four points from it. The guy on my team was going for the winning shot and he missed but he was fouled. He went to the foul line and missed one of the two. We were one point away from winning. Lanky man got the ball and faked me out. He banked a three and now we were tied. We played a passing game, and I got the ball. I went for the easy lay up and Lanky man elbowed me in the stomach. The shot went in, we won, and I crashed to the concrete.

"I'm going to whup your ass now," I said struggling to get up.

"That's no way for a lady to talk," said a familiar voice.

I stood up right and looked up into Rodriguez's face.

CHAPTER 25 Still Reinventing

Kim

My bags were packed and there was an airline ticket on my dresser. I examined it like it was the first time I had ever seen one. The sun was out early that July day. I forced myself out of the bed just as I had every day since I'd arrived, went to the bathroom to brush my teeth, throw on my sweats, and get ready to run a mile or two around the neighborhood before breakfast. Being in Plattsburg had done wonders for my attitude on life, my body, and my education. I didn't all of a sudden love school but at least I had a new purpose for it.

I laced up my sneakers and threw a cap over my head. My uncle would go crazy if I went out of the house with just a scarf on my head. I learned that hard lesson the second day I arrived. The lecture he gave about how Black women needed to be presentable at all times was one I did not want to have him ever repeat; especially not at the decibel he chose to use.

I opened my door and quietly tiptoed past my uncle's bedroom because he was a light sleeper. But that morning I didn't need to bother. I could hear him downstairs in his office. He usually closed and locked the door behind him when he went in there and I never disturbed him. Again, a lesson I learned on the fourth day there. The lecture about privacy and how to approach people in order to get what you want was not as long and loud as the 'self-presentation' lecture, but mind-numbing all the same. I sat in the middle of the landing so that I could not be seen. Uncle Cane was not alone. Who would be there with him at this hour? I didn't have to wait long for an answer. It was Bagby. Every now and then over the course of the time I'd been there he would stop by for breakfast, but it was Sunday, he didn't come out on Sundays-for any reason. I couldn't help myself; I had to know what made him break his own rule.

Uncle Cane peered at his long-time friend and shook his head.

"Cane what I'm proposing isn't insane and I know wasn't a part of the deal. I could convince Kim and you take care of Evelyn Rose."

"You say that like it's easy."

"Use some of that charm you have."

"It doesn't work on her. My brother couldn't even use it on her."

"Fine, then I'll talk to her."

"Are you dying? Why would you risk your life like that? Peaches hasn't changed Bagby."

"She likes me."

"She won't after you ask her to do the impossible again. And you need all the friends you can get."

"You, Kim, and Evelyn are more than enough. People are messy."

"Exactly."

I could smell the coffee and brandy all the way up the stairs. I peeked a little at them. They had on the same clothes from yesterday. They couldn't have been up all night discussing me. Bagby had been trying to get Uncle Cane to listen to reason about something concerning me. I couldn't understand why Uncle Cane was so afraid.

"Cane I stayed on because Kim has a gift for numbers and a writing talent that's unique. Everyday we did four hours of reading, writing, mathematics, science, and history. Her comprehension was average. However, any component of those subjects dealing with writing or numbers her scores went through the roof."

"I've always wondered how you were able to get her to study and work."

"I built a music studio in my basement. Monday through Thursday she worked like she owed me money and Friday for four hours I taught her how to produce her own music, trained her voice, and let her record demos. That was her elective. Any time she slacked off a little bit, I canceled the whole day. That punishment was too much for her because we also worked at a table in the studio. It was a visual aid and torture depending on her actions. She came through like a champ."

"That's amazing. I didn't know how you were going to do it."

"Hey, I schooled you and your brother, why not her?"

"You did not school us; we took a couple of your suggestions."

"Hey, whatever version gets you through the day. She's actually a pretty good student. Before I forget, SUNY sent her associates degree. It made more sense for her to take the Regents Exams than her GED. I guess she can hold on to that since you're too chicken-shit to consider the possibilities."

"Hey, hey, hey, now remember who I am got-damn! I'm a dangerous man!"

"So am I. We were there together, remember?"

"Oh, yeah, damn this self-absorption of mine."

The two friends chuckled and clinked mugs. Bagby took a deep breath.

"I love her Cane. She's my Goddaughter. I don't know what Chaz was thinking of when he named me but I'm glad he did. So, if it means that I have to go to New York and see Evelyn Rose, I will."

"You could have just said that hours ago and we could have gone to bed."

"Yes, but that wouldn't give Kim a chance to overhear what we were talking about."

I sat like a statue. I didn't know if I should run up or down or defend myself or stay quiet. While I was deciding, the two men rounded the corner and blocked my path at the bottom of the stairs. They shook their heads at me. I sat with my hands covering my head as if I were preparing to block blows.

"I'm sorry. No excuses. I'm just sorry. Don't you think I need to know what's going on? Please?" Bagby stared at me. Nine months ago, I was full of excuses. He made me recite the quote his father made him recite:

excuses are tools of the incompetent

used to build monuments of nothing

for those who specialize in them

seldom amount to anything

A few weeks of that straightened me right out. He was proud of the non-violent way he disciplined me. He said his father often had a belt that went along with that punishment. He smiled at me and my impatience.

"Your father was my friend too. I was around when you were born. Your father made me your Godfather. I haven't done a very good job of keeping in touch with you, but things were difficult after your father's death...anyway, I want you to go to the Atlanta School of Music. You've already been accepted. I took the liberty of submitting all the necessary documents for admission including the mini sonata you wrote. Your uncle doesn't seem to think that you'd want to go or that your mother will support..."

I jumped up from the seated position I was in, leapt down the stairs and nearly strangled Bagby in the tight embrace.

"ATL? I am so gone! And I knew you liked me a little bit even though you so mean."

"Please stop abusing the English language. Have you learned nothing? Your mother is still an obstacle."

Uncle Cane looked worried for the first time that I could remember. Then I thought about how excited my mother sounded that I was coming home. Now, *I* wasn't too sure about how my mother would react.

After the first few weeks when I got here, I stopped calling home so much because it seemed like my mother was always too busy to speak to me. About five months into my stay, my mother started writing me letters. The first one was just a 'how are you' kind of letter. Every two weeks after that I received a letter like clockwork; I responded the same way. The letters afterwards started to have a personal tone to it. She began to tell me a little about herself and my father.

I was so grateful because she never wanted to talk about her childhood or even her marriage. I needed this knowledge because I was so young when my father passed away. I didn't even know how he died. All I was ever told was that it was an accident. They wouldn't even tell me what kind of an accident.

She told me that I got her talent from her and my father. She wrote about the good times they shared gigging at clubs and singing on the stoop of my grandfather's brownstone. She wrote that my grandfather played in a jazz band when he wasn't working at the post office. In one of my letters, I asked her why did it seem like she hated music and anybody who loved it? And I asked her to tell me more about Uncle Cane. She wrote back and said that she would tell me in person. I decided not to ask her about Bagby because I didn't think she knew him. I didn't mention him by name in my letters.

The mother that wrote me was a different person than the one I had grown up with. This mother joked in her letters, cried a little, said sorry, and loved me. I wanted to see this mother and hug her. I bet she would let me hug her. It was in a letter that I finally told my mother the truth about what happened in Harlem. It took that return letter a little longer to get to me, but this mother didn't judge me. This mother told me that everyone makes mistakes and that she could never hate me. She told me I never had to be afraid to come home.

I hadn't realized I that I *was* afraid until the closer the day came, the more I was running. It was why I was on my way to run this morning when I overheard my uncle and...my Godfather? It sounded so weird. It took Uncle Cane snapping his fingers in my face to bring me back to reality. I blinked at him as I regained focus.

"Where did you go?" he quizzed me.

"Not far. If we're going back to the city, I guess I better go back upstairs and pack for that long-ass...I mean long trip." Bagby gave me a wry look. I swerved my body to keep Uncle Cane from popping me. Cane and Bagby looked at each other. Bagby put his hand on Cane's shoulder.

"We need to have another drink before we go to the airport." Cane put his hand on Bagby's shoulder.

"Who's gonna drive? We've been drinking all night."

"Kim will drive. I taught her. She has her license."

"You've been quite a busy man."

"There is nothing to do out here. What do you think we do when you go to the city?"

"*You* want to move back to the city?"

"Hell no, too many people."

They shared a good hearty laugh and then Bagby left to gather his things. Uncle Cane turned to walk up the stairs to his room one step at a time. I ran past him upstairs to my room.

I sat in my room wondering how I had forgotten that I had already packed. The events of the morning were a lot to take in. Music had been my focus for so long that I never considered anything else as an option. But now, I was going to college for the dream that nearly destroyed me. I was so afraid at one point that I started hating music like my mother. Bagby was the one who reintroduced me to the love of my life. He showed me that I could not just write lyrics but create a sound by writing the music. I almost divorced music. Funny, how things always work out. I heard a knock at my door. It was my uncle.

"Come in."

"Damn, you packed at record speed huh?"

"Ancient Chinese secret."

"Very funny. Okay you're going to drive us to the airport. Are you up for it?"

"Yes sir. Why are we flying instead of driving?"

"Bagby is impatient. Okay, meet me downstairs in about twenty minutes. Bagby should be here by then."

"Twenty minutes? Uncle Cane, I'll see *you* in about forty-five minutes. I know how *you* do."

"You're just a regular Eddie Murphy huh?"

He closed the door and left me to my thoughts. I laid out my outfit and jumped in the shower. I was so anxious. When Uncle Cane descended the steps an hour later, he didn't give me the satisfaction of looking in my direction. Bagby on the other hand looked miffed.

"Cane we're cutting it close. Let's go now!" We had more than enough time but Bagby liked to arrive at his destinations in *more* than enough time for the just in case moments.

I left the house that I had known as home for over three years. I looked back at it like I forgot to tell it something. I felt so torn between staying there with the seclusion and safety and facing my demons in New York. I hadn't seen the girls in so long. They finished college and I was just about to start—in a way. I was older and wiser. I wasn't sure about the Bronx. In fact, going to Harlem was creating more butterflies in my stomach than telling my mother that in a month I would be leaving again. I wondered if Sean would be on the block. I wondered if he had forgiven me; if he was ready to see me.

CHAPTER **26 Still Reinventing**

Sage

I was subleasing the second-floor apartment in beautiful brownstone from Kim's uncle. Ms. Evelyn told me he was looking for a tenant, but I think she told him that I was looking for a place. Either way I was in there. It was slightly more than what I wanted to pay but it was in a safe neighborhood and that's what I needed for August. It had a nice size kitchen a level up off of the living room. It had two bathrooms; one in the master bedroom and one in the hallway. I think the one in the master bedroom was built recently. I didn't know many brownstones to have that in their floor plans. I had two other rooms other than the master. One room was for August, the other room doubled as my office and guest room. Hardwood floors were everywhere so I placed area rugs anywhere I thought August would be spending a lot of time. I loved my place. It had lots of light and it was just mine.

A week ago, I received an envelope from Federal Express at my office. I was just getting around to bringing it home to open. I was juggling my purse, two grocery bags, a diaper bag, and August in my arms because it was raining.

"Hold the envelope for mommy baby," I asked August.

He looked at me sideways, grinned, and grabbed the package. Now I had to race from the mailbox into the house before he decided to open the package that he clearly thought was his. He would saturate it with his saliva first and then easily rip it with his teeth and hands. I made it in the house, dropped everything on the floor including August. He had secured himself by repelling down the side of my body for a soft landing. He giggled rolling around the floor. I had to tug a little to get the envelope out of his hands. I placed it on the counter and scooped him up again. I took him to his room to change his clothes and my own soaked clothes. I ruined a good pair of Nine West black pumps. I would have to replace them; Nine West had great leather shoes. I left August in his room playing with blocks and dancing to a *Barney* cd. I walked into the kitchen to put away the groceries. I put something out for August and me to have dinner. I poured a glass of wine while I cooked and was reminded about the envelope.

I opened it up as I took a sip. What I pulled out looked like a questionnaire. I turned over the envelope and read the sender's address; it was from Bukaii's lawyer. There were about twenty-eight questions asking me things that I couldn't believe. Some of the winners were: 1. How many sexual partners did I have, and did they have contact with August? 2. How many felons have lived with me in the past two years and did they have any contact with August? 3. How often did I use drugs of any kind and did I engage in using them in front of August? 4. Did I permit August to use drugs? 5. Had August ever been hospitalized while in my care or injured?

6. Was I ever convicted of a felony? 7. Why do you think that you would make a better parent than the other? The lawyer also wanted my work schedule, bank records, proof of employment, and...then my phone rang. "Hello."

"Why the hell am I being subpoenaed by that dumb ass?" Isa hollered.

"I didn't know you were subpoenaed," I said calmly.

"I got my own shit going on here. I can't be running to North Carolina behind your bullshit."

"Isa, this is about my kid. This isn't bullshit and I can't believe I have to even go there with you. What's wrong with you? I'm not forcing you to do anything for me or mine. You do what you gotta do." I hung up on her. She called back. I picked up the receiver and hung up. She called back again. I answered.

"What? You said what you had to say," I yelled.

"Stop yelling at me. I'll be there. I'm sorry. I had a little selfishness left over from high school. I can't help it; sometimes it just pops up."

"You get real reckless with our friendship sometimes."

"I know, but if I don't keep shit exciting you might cheat on me," she joked. I did feel a little better going a round with her. I told Isa quickly about the package I received because I knew she had a limited amount of time on the phone. She told me about some of the craziness happening with her. She had to hang up right as she told me that she had seen Rodriguez again. I guess I would have to wait to find out the rest. I went to check on August. He showed me his wonderful creation of which he said was a truck. It looked like a long wall to me. What did I know? I gave him an apple slice, a kiss, and walked back to the kitchen. I called my father and told him about the package while I finished dinner. He understood as usual. I hung up with him and set the table for me and August. He hated his highchair, so I had to stack pillows up on a chair so he could reach the table. The phone rung again; it was Bukaii.

"Let me speak to my son," he demanded.

"He's eating dinner. Call back in an hour," I said calmly. I hung up on him as he began to argue. I turned off the ringer before I went back to the table. I watched my son eat. He was so independent. He wanted to feed himself and he was making such a mess, but I chose my battles. This was his time with me. We were going to eat dinner, he was getting a bath after dinner, and then we would watch a Disney movie together. Bukaii was taking up too much space tonight; I'll deal with him in the morning.

I didn't check my phone messages in morning because I knew all five were from Bukaii. After I dropped August off at daycare, I called Bukaii.

"Why you calling me so early in the morning?" he asked.

"Most people are awake at nine in the morning on their way to work. Ask your mother what that's like. I want to talk to you about this custody hearing?"

"What about it?"

"I want you to stop it. Why are you giving me a hard time?"

"Cause I can. You let that n**** put me in traction! You stole my son from me! You took all the money out the account! You gonna pay for all that shit you did to me," he screeched.

"You want to compare notes? First of all it was my money in the bank. You quit working. You did ecstasy and coke. You did cocaine! Who does cocaine? You left my son all alone so you could stick yourself in the next-door neighbor. Who knows who else you could've had up in my bed? I didn't steal August, I saved him. You are a bum Bukaii! You are irresponsible. I'm not filling out none of that bullshit questionnaire you sent, and you are not getting my son!"

"You gonna lose this case and you never gonna see August again," he said, and the phone went dead. I hate him. It was time for me to pull out the big guns. I spoke to Auntie last night after I put August to sleep. I was meeting her on 57th and Park. She was introducing me to her everything lawyer. That's what she called him. I was hoping he would be my everything lawyer too.

I took the elevator to the fifteenth floor. I walked down the long hallway and entered a suite of offices. Everything was no different than the average lawyer's office. There were rich browns, teal, and golds with overstuffed antique furniture. I walked to the young receptionist. She was plain looking with her hair pulled back in a bun so tight it made her eyes disappear. She had a headset on and was speaking in fluent Chinese—only the young lady was clearly black. She gave me finger to silence me and then ended her call. When she spoke, she had British accent. I was so confused.

"Good morning, may I help you?" she asked.

"I'm here to see Alex Mikkos," I said.

"And you are?"

"Sage Mensa." She put a call in to the office I assumed and directed me with her finger down the hall as she took another call. This time she was speaking fluent Spanish. Guess I wasn't as important as whoever was on the phone. When I got to the door it was opened by another secretary. She had on the same headset as the first one that I saw. In fact, she looked exactly like the first one I saw. The only difference was she was pacing around her desk instead of sitting behind it. Also, her desk was white. She faced me and spoke.

"She's my *older* sister," she said reading my thoughts, "I'm Ms. Mikkos's executive assistant. She is awaiting you in her office along with Mrs. Steney. Please enter." She picked up the conversation she was having with whoever she had online in a language that I didn't recognize at all. I hope this was a good idea because I didn't think that I could afford this lawyer. Plus, I thought *she* was a *he*-Alex Mikkos that is. When I walked in Auntie was seated in a white plush chair with her feet up on a footstool. Everything in the office was white. There were a couple of exceptions like a picture frame, hanging degrees, and the legs of some of the furniture. I was sure I couldn't afford this lawyer. Alex Mikkos was as tall as Auntie which would put her at six feet tall. She added to her height with her three-inch heels. They matched her salmon-colored two-piece pant suit. She had wild, curly, long, brown hair. She wasn't super beautiful, but she wasn't ugly either. She was at least a size sixteen and well tailored. She wore light make-up and light perfume. She walked around her desk and shook my hand.

"Sage, I'm glad you're here. I'm Alexandra Mikkos but everyone calls me Alex. Everything is white because I want to be the center of attention not because I have O.C.D. Your aunt has been telling me so much about you and your situation. I hope you brought the documents with you. Have a seat." She was speaking a mile a minute. She sat at the third chair next to mine. I sat down in the middle chair and said the first thing that came to my mind.

"Nice to meet you, I brought the documents. I'm sorry to waste your time but I can't afford your services." Auntie looked disinterested in my statement and Alex looked amused.

"Sage shut up and let this woman do her job," Auntie said.

"Sage, you're right. You can't afford me. That's why this is called a favor. My normal retainer is three thousand dollars to think about a case. Your retainer is one thousand. I hope you brought that with you. I'm doing you a favor, but this won't be for free. We'll work out a payment schedule and go from there." Auntie sat up and put her shoes back on her feet.

"This is starting to sound like it's going to be boring. I'm leaving. I have money to get and people to do." I leaned over and gave Auntie a kiss on cheek goodbye. Alex jumped up and hugged Auntie and walked her to the door. Auntie whispered something in her ear and then she left. Alex came back to her seat and took my hands.

"I know you want to know how your aunt and I know each other but it's not your business. That was another life. She is a good friend of mine and that's all. Let's see those documents," she said. I handed her the documents and she looked over it in silence for almost ten minutes.

"Do I have to fill out that questionnaire?" I asked.

"Yes, but so will he. Based on what your aunt has told me that would make him an idiot. Not to worry. I'll be in contact with his lawyer this afternoon. First thing I'll do is try to get a continuance. I need to be able to do some research on this idiot. Make your check out to Alex Mikkos Esquire please in the amount of one thousand. In your memo section please write retainer." I did what she told me as she pulled out a spreadsheet and handed it to me.

"This is your payment schedule. Adhere to it please. And Sage, not to worry, I will bury him. Your son will stay with you."

"Thank you," I replied. I got up and left the strangeness of Alex Mikkos. I couldn't read her. The only thing that I felt was assured. I guess that was going to have to be enough.

CHAPTER **27 Still Reinventing**

Isa

I took Rodriguez's hand and stood up. Lanky man was right behind him. I shoulda been surprised to see Rodriguez and jumped on him like it was scene out of *Love Jones*, but I didn't.

"Hi Rodriguez," I said. Then I reached around him and started punching

Lanky man in the stomach like I was Annie. He started to go down and his boys jumped in. Grove jumped in with my teammates. We was throwing punches left and right for a good minute. I saw a flash of Rodriguez trying to break it up. Then he was gone. I let out all my frustration over the past ten years on whoever was throwing it at me. I was sitting on Lanky man's back trying to break his leg when I heard a gun shot. Everybody ducked down and scattered. Lanky man threw me off his back and I kicked him in the side as I rolled over. Before he could do anything, else Rodriguez dragged me up by my arm. Lt. Sallye looked at all of us with her gun still drawn. I thought she might shoot one of us; mainly me. I wiped the blood from my lip since it was busted again. There was blood on the court. There were torn shirts and swollen faces all around. She didn't have to yell because nobody was talking or moving.

"Both teams have clean up duty. You will eat after the entire compound has eaten. Then you will clean every dish. Then you will clean every table. Then you will remove any garbage you find on the grounds. If it takes you all night so be it. You are welcome to decline your consequence by packing your bags and walking home." I was mad as hell.

"This is some bullshit!" I hollered.

"Yes, yes, it is. Steney, you have morning duty too. Or are you going home?" I stared at Lanky man real hard. I wanted to snap his neck. If I had my gun, I think I woulda shot him. I'm still not right in my head. Damn.

"No Lt. Sallye."

"Good. Everyone is dismissed." Everyone moved fast because Lt. Sallye still hadn't holstered her gun. I probably would have moved too but Rodriguez still had my arm, and he was squeezing hard. Lt. Sallye turned to him and holstered her gun.

"I would apologize for their behavior, but I have a feeling you might be used to this since you are acquainted with Steney here. I trust you won't beat up our guest Steney?"

"No Lt. Sallye."

"I will leave you to this short visit. Then I expect you to handle your business."

"Yes Lt. Sallye." She walked away. Rodriguez let my arm go. I had my head down. I didn't want to face him.

"Look at me Isa." I picked my head up. He looked good as hell. His clothes was wrinkled from trying to break up the fight but he didn't have a scratch on him. He grabbed my arm again and walked me to a bench nearby.

"I want to ask you what's wrong with you, but I know you don't know. I want to ask you are you crazy, but I know that you are." I was pulling my lip like I could see the damage without a mirror. He moved my hand away from my mouth and kissed it. I looked at him.

"Say something Isa," he said. I tried but then I started crying.

"I look crazy and I am crazy. I thought being here would help me with my crazy, but it didn't. I'm the same like I was in high school and college. How long does it take for somebody to get right?"

"I don't know," he said.

"What do you mean you don't know? You always know."

"Yeah, but now I don't know. Do you really think you're that bad? I won't be here all the time when you make these stupid decisions. They're stupid Isa. I understand you. I know you're better than you were when you were younger but that doesn't mean anything if you don't know it." I wiped my face and pushed my hair out of my eyes. I breathed out.

"Why are you here Rodriguez? You're supposed to be in South America. And how did you know that girl in D.C.? What's up?" I was tired and I hurt all over, but I might not see him again. He leaned back a little.

"That girl you saw at the station was one of my kids from the Scared Straight program in Southeast D.C. She was tough to break. Her mom took off before she was eight, her dad overdosed on crack by the time she was nine. Her grandmother wasn't interested in being a parent, so she let her run wild. She let Tasha, that's her name, stay in the house as long as she got the SSI from her father being dead. He used to be in the service. Tasha ran the street and slept around. She wound up locked up in juvenile hall and she still was getting into trouble. I worked with her for almost seven months. She had eidetic memory. She passed any test you gave her. It took a lot of letter writing and researching for scholarships before she started to believe that her life could change. She's still rough around the edges but so were you. I was interviewing at the United Nations consulate in D.C. when you saw me. I was trying to grab something to eat after walking from the Monument. When I saw you standing together, I saw what Tasha could become. That's when I realized that's what I wanted to do with my life. I want to be a counselor for kids like Tasha. I started my master's program at Columbia the following week. My father was pissed to say the least, but I have a title with the Scared Straight program here in New York, so he has something to brag about to his friends."

"Yeah, you over here helping the n***** and crackho's," I said. I know I was wrong for saying that.

"Isa."

"Sorry."

"You have about thirty minutes left before you need to get to the cafeteria and clean up. I won't be here. Isa I gotta tell you that I will always love you. Just like you are. You are more amazing than you realize. You don't have to do anything but sit at home and be my wife. I'll take care of you. I can't believe you're really going to be a police officer but then again that's what I like about you. You always keep me guessing. You think a woman can be a good cop? What happens when you're ready to get married or have a kid? What happens when one of these guys harass you? You can't run and tell, and you can't keep trying to kill them." I leaned back and looked at him like he had seven heads.

"Have you lost your fucking mind?! You think I just want to sit at home with some kids doing nothing? Just to be your wife? Like you all that. I'm going to be a great cop! I didn't do this to prove a point or work through no issues. I believe in protecting people who can't protect themselves. I believe in making the world a better and safer place. I believe that the hood needs cops like me. I understand what's going on there better than anybody. Maybe I can keep some of these young kids from getting killed and change how people think about cops; black, female, or otherwise. I'm damn good at this baby!" He was smiling but looking up at the sky. I couldn't stand him. He was the only one who could make me look at my life and make the right decisions. But I'm making the decision to believe in myself by myself. I didn't tell him about the offer I got from Commander Brown. I doubt if he knew about it, but I could see some light at the end of the tunnel.

"You still love me?" he asked.

"Yeah, I still love you." He put his arm around me.

"So, is it okay if I ask out that hot cheerleader? Since I'm not all that and you don't want to marry me," he asked.

"Sure. If you want to play stupid go right ahead and get both of you killed." He pulled me up to my feet and hugged me so tight I couldn't breathe. He kissed me, smoothed my hair back, and walked to the exit gate. I went to take responsibilities for my actions, life, and future.

CHAPTER 28 Still Reinventing

Kim

We left the car at the daily parking garage. Bagby would be on the first thing smoking after he spoke to my mother and loaded up on cannolis. We boarded the plane and took off without incident.

Maneuvering through LaGuardia airport was second nature to us three native New Yorkers. Visualizing a path through the masses and not touching a soul was like an unspoken game between everyone who chose to dance to the music. The random 'I'm so sorry' alerted others to tourists to the city. In an hour or so we too would be in a syncopated rhythm.

We *would* arrive on a sweltering day. I pulled the shades from the top of my head to shield my eyes. Bagby had already loosened his tie and soaked his handkerchief mopping his brow. Uncle Cane leaned on a *No Parking* pole as a black tinted town car stopped in front of us. A leggy blond in a chauffeur's skirt outfit hopped out of the driver's side, moved swiftly to the passenger side, and held the door open for us. I shook my head in disbelief; always some female jumping to it for my uncle. Uncle Cane got in first as the blonde placed the bags in the trunk. I got in followed by Bagby. The blonde closed the door behind him, glided back to the driver's side, and pulled out into the airport traffic. The partition between us was down. The blonde was staring at Bagby but spoke to Uncle Cane.

"Mr. Rose has there been any changes made to the itinerary?"

"No Natasha. We are on the same schedule."

Bagby rolled his eyes and pressed the button to close the partition.

"I would like to keep my face, so I'll just close this."

Uncle Cane looked at Bagby in disbelief.

"Why do you treat her like that?"

"You never say anything to *her*. I'm always the bad guy."

"She makes you a dangerous man Bagby. She did the right thing to put distance between you."

"I wouldn't be dangerous if she would date respectable men. Hell, if she would just date men. One good man. No, not her, she likes women. So, when men approach her, she has a whole other world of problems when she tells them no *and* that she prefers women. Do you know how many jaws and arms I've broken?"

"Nevermind Bagby. Just let it go. She's your sister. You'd have broken those legs and arms just the same. I will tell you this, you're going to lose her. No body is going to willingly put up with that kind of abuse."

Bagby turned his body away from Uncle Cane to quietly fume. I held my head down to keep from moving back and forth between them. I could not even imagine Bagby raising his hand to kill a gnat much less breaking someone's bones. I also couldn't believe that Bagby was so close-minded to being gay; not that I understood it myself, but Natasha was his sister…younger I guessed. She seemed to be much younger than Bagby but older than me. I put her maybe in her twenties. If I could see her eyes, which were covered with hot Gucci shades, then I could make a better guess.

The Major Deegan appeared out of nowhere. We were exiting off of 138th and the Grand Concourse faster than I expected. The car sped past Cardinal Hayes, the all-boy's school, and then down the block past the closed down C-Town supermarket which was now a traditional African church.

P.S. 156 stood on the corner as a proud testimony that Black children still loved school, even if it was summer school. The kids were pouring out of the building like they had battery packs on their backs. They rushed the ice-cream truck and the cherry-coco man on the corner. The crossing guard made our car stop to allow the slow-moving elementary students across the street. No doubt they were heading up the block to the Sweet Shop to buy penny candies and play video games. When we turned the corner and pulled into the Concourse Village driveway, I felt myself pull into a tight ball. Natasha stopped the car in front of the entry wall. She lowered the partition to address Uncle Cane. She didn't turn around.

"Shall I bring your bags upstairs Mr. Rose?"

"No Natasha. We'll carry Kim's things upstairs. You take a lunch break, and we'll page you when we're ready to leave."

"Okay."

Raising the partition again she popped the trunk open. Bagby hopped out of one side and Uncle Cane slid out of the other. I tapped on the partition. Natasha lowered it. I hadn't planned on what I would say to Natasha, but I felt bad for her and was suddenly very interested in her.

"Do you drive for my uncle all the time?"

"Is there something that you need?"

I understood I had asked the wrong question. No one discusses Cane Rose with anyone.

"Um...when you come back to take Bagby to the airport and my uncle to Harlem, can you take me somewhere?"

"You can't afford me," she said.

"Actually, I want you to come with me. You can park this car if you want and change into some jeans or something. I don't know when you get off or whatever, but I don't know where my peeps at and for real I don't want to see them yet. But I got something I got to take care of and..." She cut me off.

"People saw them come in with this car. They won't be leaving the same way; especially not Bagby. Call me on the car phone. I'll be in a black Benz with tinted windows when you come down."

Natasha handed me a card with her number on it and rolled the partition back up and I stared the darkened glass for a moment. I didn't know what to think or say so I got out of the car clutching my oversized Louis Vuitton handbag. Natasha pulled off. Bagby and Uncle Cane were nearly to the building. I walked with quick strides to meet them in the lobby. I saw some people outside that I recognized and others I didn't. They stared at me as I passed them by without speaking. My shades gave me the courage I needed to keep moving. People had always talked about me and I saw no reason to be phony now. They didn't like me then and would have only tried to get in my business now. I heard one of the older ladies make a comment to her friend that I must have gone on some kind of diet after I had my baby. The other one replied that she heard I gave up the baby to an aunt who couldn't have children. It amazed me how people could continue to lie on me. I never been pregnant before and these old hags had me giving up a child. I'ma tell my mother. That was my thought as we entered the elevator and then fear gripped me as Uncle Cane pressed the tenth floor. He squeezed my hand as the light let it be known that the next stop would be ours. Bagby stepped off the elevator first but stopped short. Uncle Cane half pulled me out of the elevator. He let my hand go and turned to face us.

"Now look, we have to stick together on this. Eve is not a monster."

Bagby grunted, "Speak for yourself. Do you remember '74?"

"Yeah, but Eve's not that person anymore."

"What are you talking about Uncle Cane?"

"None of your business," he said.

"It seem like this family got more secrets than a little bit," I said.

Bagby pulled me along. "Let's just get this over with," he said.

We turned to the right and went down the hallway toward the *K* apartment. Then, all three of us took a deep breath and the door flew open. My mother stood there beaming at me. Apparently, I was all that she could see. She squeezed me with all of her might. Then she pulled away and spun me around. She checked to see how different I looked. My hair was longer, my body was leaner, my face was fresh, and my eyes were healthy. Upstate had been so good to me. I felt happy.

I looked at my mother. She looked overjoyed. Her face was bright and soft. Her hair was pulled back into a ponytail and she had on a pink warm-up suit with matching Reeboks. I couldn't ever remember my mother looking this relaxed. She looked happy.

"I missed you so much Ma."

"I missed you too and...oh my God...Brendon?"

I looked confused. My mother was looking at Bagby.

"Brendon?" My ignored me and stepped around me.

"Brendon Bagby. Why are you here? Who's dead now?"

"Evelyn Rose, that isn't fair," Bagby said.

"No, it isn't, but too often it's true." I noticed there was no anger in her voice the way it was when Uncle Cane reappeared in our lives.

"I'm sorry Evelyn Rose. There isn't more I can or will say. Let's talk inside."

Bagby pushed past my mother with the same confidence that Uncle Cane did years ago and sat in the living room. She stepped aside and made a gesture with her arm for me and Uncle Cane to enter. I only go by Steney instead of Rose-Steney. I noticed that my mother and Bagby used their full names to address each other. I figured there was a story behind that as well, but I might have to try to overhear that too. My mother sighed and locked the door. She entered the living room and sat in the upright overstuffed chair. Me and Bagby sat on the edge of the sofa ready to take flight. Uncle Cane, cool as a summer breeze, lounged in the loveseat like he was waiting on a tropical drink. My mother looked at all three of us not sure of where to focus her evil eye to evoke the truth. She went with the one most susceptible to it: me.

"You're still alive and looking well so what's this all about?" she asked.

"I've learned so much Ma and Uncle Cane and Bagby have been good to me. They taught me so much and I think that when you hear what we have to say that you won't be that angry because you know it's still a college education--" she cut me off.

"Wait, wait, wait. You're going to college? Oh my goodness! Why would I be mad about that? That is a blessing! Where? NYU? City College?"

"No Ma, the Atlanta School of Music. Bagby taught me how to read and write music and how to play the jazz piano and little guitar and how to produce music and I want this more than anything. I think I want it more than just singing. I don't know what else to say Ma. Can I go?" I said all of that with my eyes half closed. My mother took a second to take it all in. "Can you go? I couldn't really stop you." She stood up and paced in front of the three people who were throwing her for a loop. I thought she needed time to process what she was hearing.

"This isn't my dream or nightmare. This is your future. You doing it better than I did; than your father did. If I learned nothing over my lifetime, I learned the hard lesson of letting go. What kind of parent denies her child happiness? I'm not that person anymore. Who knows where you could go with this? Maybe you can go further than me or your father did. As a matter of fact, you've already gone further; you're alive and happy doing the thing that makes you happy." She stopped pacing and looked at me. She sat down in the chair. I didn't know if she was done talking or not. Then she started up again.

"Can I go with you? I mean see the campus and help you register? I need to see where you'll be this time. I want to see what surrounds you. I want to see what kinds of people you gonna be around. I want to see where you'll rest your head at night and where you'll study and where you'll eat. As a mother, you can never understand how hard it is to send your child somewhere sight unseen and have to imagine the answers to all the ramblings in your head. I need to see."

I found myself kneeling in front of my mother and resting my head in her lap. She stroked my hair.

"I'm so proud of you. I just want to share in your happiness."

"Ma thank you. And you have to come with me. I want you to see where I'll be and who I see and what I'm doing. Remember daddy said you had to keep your good eye on me." My mother wiped my tears and she fell into a fit of laughter.

"He said that because you was in my make-up; always in something! Okay get off of me. When do you start school?"

"School begins August 8th for underclassmen, but they are allowing new students to come in the last week of July to do financial aid, schedule classes, and get room assignments."

"Okay, that's good. C.J. will still be in Barbados with his other grandmother. But I wrote you that already. We can go shopping for everything you need before we leave."

My mother looked over at Bagby who looked like he wanted to escape and Uncle Cane who looked like a permanent fixture in the couch.

"Kim, I'm sure some of your friends would like to see you. Why don't you give them a call?" She was trying to get rid of me. I took the hint.

"I'm gonna put--" Bagby frowned at me for using slang, "I'm going to put my stuff away and call a friend or two."

I walked toward the back of the apartment to unpack. I would call Natasha and keep unpacking until Natasha called me to meet her downstairs.

CHAPTER 29 Still Reinventing

Sage

Isa and I were sitting at the airport waiting for Sienna to pick us up from RDU, Raleigh Durham International Airport. When we first got together at LaGuardia airport, she ran down everything that happened with her and Rodriguez and the academy in full detail until an hour into our flight. I spent the next hour and our wait time telling her everything about me, Bukaii, and work. We both were looking at each other not sure what else to say. Life got in our way and had missed out on the trauma in each other's lives. I put her hand in mine and squeezed.

"Girl this ain't shit. We been through worse and we came out alright," she said. I nodded my head. I wanted to believe that. The night before I watched August for hours after he fell asleep wondering what I would do without him. He was my whole world. At two and a half, he was almost potty trained, he ate by himself, he didn't fight me when it was time for a bath or bed, and my name was Mommy. Of all the names I had been called, that was my favorite name. No matter how he said it, all I heard was: I love you forever. I started crying.

"It's really going to be okay Sage," Isa consoled me. I stopped mid-sniffle and shot Isa a look.

"What happened to 'stop that crying shit'?" I asked.

"You should stop before we see that lying sack of shit, but right now it's okay," she reasoned.

"Who are you? Should I start calling you Isabelle now? I'm not sure how to be friends with you. What am I supposed to do with a *nice* Isa?"

"I don't know but you better take advantage because I had to do extra hours at the academy because of this trial. They didn't care that I was subpoenaed. So, make sure you're there on Thursday for my ceremony" she said and without any attitude I might add.

"Sorry about the hours but I'll be there."

"Don't worry. I'm going to curse Bukaii out when I see him. That will make me feel better." We laughed and Sienna pulled up in a Ford Explorer. She blew the horn and yelled out of the window.

"How much for both you ho's? I got three quarters." We rolled our eyes and got in the truck. By the time we got to the courthouse in downtown Raleigh, Sienna was ready to kill Bukaii too.

"He better hope they have armed guards in here," Sienna said.

"We're going to act like we have sense for once," Isa said.

"Who are you?" Sienna asked. I chuckled.

Alex Mikkos was already walking toward us when we entered the floor where our case was taking place. She flew down the day before. She said she needed to get the lay of the land. I didn't have to look back to see Sienna or Isa's face. I knew Alex was a lot to take in. She had big hair, big body, big voice—she was just everywhere at once.

"Sage, glad you're here. Are these the character witnesses? Of course, they are. I'm Alex Mikkos. You have a seat on one of those benches. I'll be right back," she speed spoke.

We walked to the nearby benches and sat down. I heard a loud commotion coming down the hall and saw Bukaii, his mother and two sisters.

They were so loud; naturally loud. His mother stepped up in front of Bukaii when she saw me.

"This is what you want to do to my son? He done everything for you, and you take his child, our grandchild away? You not supposed to separate a boy from his father. What kind of mother are you? This ain't back in the day young lady. Just 'cause you the mother don't mean you automatically gonna get custody. You ain't never at home anyway. You out all times of the night and all over the country. You go off and any and everybody watching him. You need to just leave him here with me. Where is my grandchild?"

I was wondering when she would notice. She was three hundred pounds easy. Her ankles were threatening to snap with every step. Flowers were her favorite pattern to wear and she had magnolias all over her skirt and blouse set. She wore pearls, miraculously, because she had no neck and a hat that had as many flowers on it as her dress. She topped off her outfit with a bright red Dooney & Burke bag. The two sisters had on tight two-piece suits. They weren't as large as their mother but after a hamburger or two that goal was attainable. One of them had a gold, not blond, gold weave that reached the middle of her back. The other had purple and black micro braids in her head and she was popping her gum. She checked out her multi-colored nails while she spoke to somebody named Pookie on the phone. I had to poke Sienna in the side when she started laughing. Isa was still standing there with her mouth open. Bukaii's stepfather stepped around his wife and hugged me.

"Ignore her," he said. Then he whispered in my ear, "I'm proud of you. I'm gonna run away too, soon." He smiled at me, I smiled and whispered back, "Just call me and I'll come get you wherever you are."

Bukaii's stepfather was that family's only saving grace. He married into that crazy family. He's the one that brought the money into the family. I guessed after twenty years they beat him down so bad; he lost his manhood. I know that I hurt him most of all when I left. He loved August. A few months after I left, I started sending him pictures and letters to his office. I didn't want Bukaii's mother to have anything and I know she wouldn't give it to him if I sent them to the house. He reluctantly went back to the enemy camp. Bukaii grinned and licked his lips at me. I thought I was going to throw up. I can't believe I let him touch me. The bailiff came out and called our docket number. Bukaii's family rushed in ahead of us. We followed behind shaking our heads. Isa and Sienna sat in the row behind Alex and I separated by a short wooden fence. The judge was already on the bench, so we remained standing until told to do otherwise. Bukaii and his mother were already sitting. I didn't see a lawyer.

"Bailiff since these people are already seated, I suppose we'll get started," said the judge. Bukaii and his mother scrambled to get to their feet.

"Sit down. The damage is done," he said. I didn't laugh because I was embarrassed for him. The judge was a youngish, maybe late forties, early fifties, white guy with a thick southern accent. He was from one of the southern states but I'm not sure which. I was paying attention though. I needed to watch what I said and how I said it. I didn't want to sound like an obnoxious New Yorker. That's what I was but he wouldn't know it. Alex was enough of a show alone. He looked over at us and spoke.

"What do you have for me young lady?" It was a trick to see if Alex would be a feminist or a southern belle. There was no in between—I thought. She stood up. Alex purred, I think.

"Your honor," she smiled, "I'm Alexandra Mikkos. I'm representing Ms. Mensa in this case today," she said softly.

"Your reputation precedes you. Are you going to make magic happen in my courtroom today?" he smiled.

"I'm only here to present the facts your honor and obey the rules of your court." I think I saw her wink at the judge. I looked back at Isa and Sienna. They had smirks on their faces. So, I wasn't imagining this flirting going on. But I still was keeping my face expressionless.

"And are you this young man's attorney?" The judge asked Bukaii's mother. She stood up.

"No," she said as nasty as possible, "I'm his mother. He don't need no lawyer. That heifer stole my grandbaby and she need to give him back," she said rolling her neck. The judge cocked his to the left.

"Bailiff remove this woman from my courtroom," he paused because the bailiff paused, "right now son." The bailiff approached Bukaii's mother. She was stunned.

"You can't just put me out. I pay my taxes and that pays your funky check! I'ma bring Al Sharpton down here and get you kicked out your job! See how you like that Mr. white man!"

"If you don't shut up, he can escort you to a cell on the ground floor. You can make your one phone call to Al if you want to but he's in the middle of a pastor's conference right here in North Carolina. He's not going to like being disturbed by nonsense. I got his number when you're ready."

Unbelievable, Bukaii's mother left the courtroom saying stuff under her breath, but not loud enough for the judge to hear. I snuck a peek at Bukaii. He looked nervous.

"Once again young man, do you have counsel?" The judge asked Bukaii. Bukaii started stuttering.

"I, I, didn't think I needed no lawyer. My mother said we didn't need no lawyer 'cause Sage was gonna be too busy to get one, so we fired our lawyer," Bukaii explained.

"That's unfortunate son because Ms. Mensa brought her lawyer. A damn good one too," the judge said, "the show must go on."

Alex interrupted the judge. "Your honor, if it pleases the court, my client doesn't object to postponing this hearing until Mr. Jenkins can obtain proper counsel."

"That may be good idea. Let me look at my docket." He flipped through some pages. He talked out loud. "No that's no good; that's my birthday. That's too close to my mandatory vacation. That puts us at September 4th. Ms. Mikkos, I believe I can do away with this request for a continuance?"

"Yes, your honor."

"Mr. Jenkins, I imagine this is more than enough time for you to obtain a new attorney or rehire your original one."

Bukaii appeared perplexed, "I, I, don't know. I gotta move some things around and see if I can afford one and do some other things. I mean I gotta live..."

The judge removed his glasses and wiped his eyes. He looked at me.

"And you chose this winner did you?" I grimaced and put my head down. "Let me rephrase Mr. Jenkins. The date is set for September 4th with or without your legal representation. I am also ordering a paternity test be done prior to the next date. Maybe there was a mix-up Ms. Mensa, and we can all be free from this. Upon your return Mr. Jenkins, leave your mother at home along with whomever that is chewing gum like a heifer in the pasture. Now get out of my courtroom."

The judge sighed loudly and asked the bailiff who was next. Both of Bukaii's sisters rolled their eyes at the judge but they didn't speak. Bukaii's stepfather laughed loudly. That was a bold move for him. Maybe he was really thinking of running away. We all filed out of the courtroom. I *thought* I was going to make it out of North Carolina without getting into it with Bukaii. I *thought* I could walk away from that group of hillbillies and not say a word. Everybody had different plans.

A white girl so skinny I could see her next thought was standing at the bottom of the stairs outside the courtroom building. She had on cut-off shorts and a tank top that read *Shake It Fast* across the front which also let the world know that she chose not to wear a bra today. She had really long blond hair that even up in her ponytail went below her behind. She had on way too much black eyeliner, but it matched the color of her inch-long fingernails. She had one hand on what was supposed to be her hip and the other was on a stroller with a lit cigarette between her fingers. She was tapping her foot fast as hell which made a kind of rhythm because her four-inch heels had an inch of platform at the toe area. I probably wouldn't have paid her any mind, but she had the smallest brown baby I had ever seen in a stroller that was meant for maybe a two- or three-year-old; one of the easily collapsible ones that you can get at the dollar store. She *was* a sight, but I would have still walked silently to Sienna's car. And then my karma continued to bottom out.

Sienna, Isa, and Alex were at the bottom of the stairs. Bukaii's entourage was in the middle staring at the girl like she was a ghost. I thought they should be used to that kind of nonsense especially with those sisters looking crazy all of the time. Bukaii and I were at the top of the steps and he grabbed my arm. I yanked my arm away from him. Whatever he was going to say got lost when he heard his name being shrieked from the bottom.

"Booo-kaiiiiiiiii, who is dis bitch wit her hands all over you? You want me to fuck somebody up out here huh? Right here in front dis courthouse? I ain't 'fraid to go jail about mines aiight! You was 'posed to get yo little boy and meet me back at da house. So, I could get ready for work. You need to watch B.J. too. Now, what da fuck is going on here?" I wanted to say something, but I couldn't.

"Wow," Isa and Sienna said simultaneously. Alex looked up at me and asked,

"Is this real? Is she for real? Why does she sound like that? You have to be joking? Oh, I'm going to have the best story at the poker game tonight with the partners." She laughed so hard tears rolled out her eyes. Bukaii stood like someone had shot him. Beads of sweat were forming on his upper lip. His mother grabbed at her heart.

"You know this piece of can't use your comb trailer trash Bukaii? Did she say B.J.? She better not be saying that baby is your junior. I know she better not be saying that!"

Bukaii's sister with the purple micros went to the stroller and picked up the baby. The gold-hair sister pulled a cigarette out of her purse, lit hers with the white girl's cigarette, and faced her mother.

"Stop tripping mama you act like this the eighties or something. Civil Rights been over since the seventies. Cappuccino is cool as hell. We dance over at the Silver Slipper together."

"And Capp you need to stop tripping too. You know Bukaii ain't even studying that fake bitch. He just trying to make sure he don't pay no child support so he can take care of B.J." said purple hair.

"What kind of name is Cappuccino?" Bukaii's mother asked. Of all the things to ask that's what she chose.

"Mama her real name Rachel; Cappuccino is her stage name. Be for real. Don't you no nothing?"

"My Jesus in heaven," she said. Alex was taking notes and saying, 'this is good stuff', Bukaii's stepfather was shaking his head in embarrassment, the sisters and baby mother were smoking over the baby's head and talking about a new pole technique, Bukaii was standing mute and bug-eyed, and Isa and Sienna was laughing their asses off. I walked down the steps grabbed the keys from Sienna and got in the car. I *didn't* say anything. I was too ashamed of myself. I couldn't believe that I was actually angry that Bukaii had another child with that girl. I was actually mad. Unbelievable!

CHAPTER **30 Still Reinventing**

Kim

From the living room window, I could see my mother, uncle, and Bagby smoking and looking off into the haze of the day. I walked onto the terrace unnoticed.

"I'm leaving everybody." They all turned to face me. I smoothed down my tank top and jeans. I shuffled in my wedged sandals.

"What's wrong? I look bad or something?"

My mother smiled at me. "No baby you look just fine. Where are you going?"

"I'm going into Harlem for a little while." They all paused and struggled to speak.

"I'll be alright. I have to go there sometime," I said.

Bagby and Uncle Cane reached into their pockets and pulled out money for me.

"No that's alright I have some money," I said.

Bagby and Cane looked at me in silence.

"But I'll take it just in case, you know, I see something I might want like a book bag or something."

Bagby turned his head. Uncle Cane grinned at me and my mother laughed openly.

"I see these two have grown to know you very well," she said. I smiled and headed toward the door.

When I got outside, more eyes followed my movements while I jumped into the car with Natasha. Before I left the neighborhood, I was always jumping into some shiny new car, so this was no exception. The eyes however, were just as hungry to know where I was going, who I was with, and why I always was chosen for the ride? I know how they satisfied their curiosity—with an envious justification: I must be fucking somebody. Once upon a time, they would have been right. I leaned back in the coolness of the car. The camel-colored leather seats were room temperature defying the soft gust of air coming from the coolant system. The tinted windows allowed me to observe my changing neighborhood and city without looking like a tourist. So much had changed. I picked up the daily newspaper that Natasha had on the back seat. I alternated flipping through it and looking out of the window.

Billboards showed coming or current attractions of *He Got Game, I Got the Hook-up, Player's Club,* and *Rush Hour.* That was some movie with Chris Tucker and Jackie Chan—doubt if that makes any money. Arsenio Hall just went off the air and Martin Lawrence was still saying, '*You go girl*!' In hip hop Biggie and Tupac was making the rap game insane with their East-West Coast beef. On the front cover of every newspaper and the top story of all news channels was the O.J. Simpson chase. The *Free O.J.* t-shirts would be in fashion in about two days. Meanwhile in a one-paragraph article on page 23, there was a little blurb about a small, unfortunate country in Africa called Rwanda. There was something called genocide going on there, but I couldn't wrap my mind around how no one in the world was helping them so I just closed the paper and looked outside with full focus.

The guys and girls were wearing Tims despite the summer heat. Guys were wearing baggy pants and hoodies. Girls were still wearing the New York City uniform: tight—tight jeans, tight tops. People with a little money though, had on Jordans and Hilfiger and Versace and FUBU. Unfortunately, they were mixing all the name brands together trying to floss. They wound up looking ridiculous. My sense of style remained casual, but after being upstate for so long I didn't feel pressed to impress anyone but myself. People would either take me as I was or leave me alone.

I was so deep in my thoughts I almost forgot Natasha was there until she spoke.

"Which bridge? 145th or 135th?"

I was in no rush to meet with destiny, so I chose the 145th street Bridge. That would give me an opportunity to see my second home and what it had become. I was overjoyed to see people heading to the Pologrounds for basketball games and the coco-cherry man selling his flavored ice. I could see the corner bodegas chasing out little kids trying to stay cool because the cops were on the other block turning off the hydrant. I smiled at the hustlers getting paid and recognized a few who apparently made their come-up faster than I anticipated. I also spied a few who fell off and now they were customers. Turning off of Lenox and heading down toward 8th on the side streets, I also saw what AIDS was doing to people. It was sobering thought that no one was exempt from AIDS, no one.

"Where exactly are we going?" Natasha asked breaking into my thoughts.

"122nd and Morningside," I answered.

"Do you need me to come inside with you?"

"No."

"Good I'll just wait in the car."

When we got near Sean's apartment, I asked Natasha to pull up in front of the building and let me out.

I rode the elevator to the fourth floor. I was trying to mentally prepare for whatever I would find behind that door. I stood in front of the door for a full five minutes before I rang the doorbell. I heard shuffling behind the door and then a pause. Then there was the unlocking of several locks and the door swung open. Jokk stood there handsome as ever and anger was coming from his whole body. He was in clean dark blue jeans, green polo shirt and white Jordans. A pair of gold praying hands hung from his Cuban Link.

"Fuck you want?" I shuddered and took his gruffness like a champ.

"I don't want any problems. I wanted to see you and Sean. I wanted to say sorry even if you both don't forgive me. I woulda...I should have said something before I left. I know how tight you and Sean are."

He looked me up and down. I didn't know what he was looking for. I had a little scarring on my arm and on my jaw line from the glass, but only if he looked hard enough. I turned a little showing I was self-conscience about it.

"He ain't here," he said dryly. I dropped my head. I know he was waiting for me to get loud and animated like he knew me to be, but I didn't.

"Okay. Well, I just want to say again to you that I'm sorry for everything. Could you tell him for me that I'm sorry and that if he ever wants to hear it from me, he can call, and I'll come by or whatever he thinks is fair. You look good Jokk. Take care of yourself."

He watched me turn around and get on the waiting elevator. I didn't press him for information. I didn't try to push past him to get in. I put my sunglasses on and stepped out into blazing sun. It was fighting to stay on stage and keep night away for a few more hours. I saw Natasha's car and was heading there when my arm was jerked back. I swung around to land my punch on whoever was attacking me. Jokk caught my fist in midair.

"You trying to get yourself killed?!" I screamed.

"By who? You?" he chuckled.

I glared at him. He smiled at me.

"I taught you that move. I'm flattered that you remembered."

"You're *flattered*? You know the English language?" I asked.

"Look who's talking. I went to class. My pops ain't play those games with me and I ain't play around with him."

"Well, I just learned. What's up?"

"Something's different about you and I can't put my finger on what it is. I ain't used to people changing. People are always one way, they never change. He asks about you sometimes—Sean. Personally, I don't know what he saw in you, but I think he might need to see you now. I thought you might want to ride with me to the airport to pick him up." I gave him a skeptical look.

"I don't know why you changed your mind. But I don't think it would be a good idea. He might not want to see me. I could barely handle the way you came at me...even though I deserved it. I just don't know if at the airport is the best place for a reunion or to catch an assault charge."

Jokk nodded his understanding. "However, it goes down, you need to let that man decide. I ain't gonna let him hurt you."

"Yeah, you was real successful last time."

"Don't knock the skills shorty. We was all caught off-guard. Let's get this cab before we're late. You know how he gets when people are late."

"I know...I remember." Natasha got out of the car. She approached us. Jokk moved me to stand behind him. He was always weary of white people in the 'hood. They either wanted money or death. I stepped back in front of Jokk. I put a calming hand on his shoulder while facing him.

"This is my friend Natasha," I gestured toward the tall blonde woman, "Natasha, this is Jokk."

They looked each other up and down like two battling lions.

"Are you ready to leave?" she asked me.

"Yes and no. Sean's not here. He's flying in today. Jokk asked me to go to the airport with him. If you have plans, you can go ahead, and we'll take cab."

She thought for a moment. "I didn't have any plans other than picking up some Thai food and watching the game. I can tolerate this friend of yours.

I'll take you both. Make sure you don't have shit on your shoes. I just detailed my car."

Jokk snorted, "You mean you had it detailed." We headed toward the car.

"No, I mean I detailed it. I own a detailing and car service."

"Bullshit!" he said.

"I shit you not. I'm the best in the city."

"Get by on your pretty face?"

"I hook them with my pretty face. I reel them in with my skill...business skills that is." On the way to LaGuardia Airport, Jokk and Natasha talked business, cars, sports, politics, race relations, and economics. I was glad I chose to sit the back seat. Their debates would get heated and then turn into riotous laughter. They even exchanged numbers and made plans to do something the next day. Meanwhile, I was shitting bricks. I looked regular. I started worrying that I didn't look my best. I was worried most of all, that Sean wouldn't speak to me at all. I could deal with anything but that. Natasha waited in the car. Jokk got out with me walking slightly behind.

"He said he would be waiting by the baggage claim, but he's probably at the bar since we're seven minutes late." Jokk said. No need for me to answer. I followed him to the bar. Sean's back was to us. Jokk noted that Sean was slipping. At least that's what he thought until he noticed the bar length mirror behind the bartender.

Sean swung around on his barstool and jumped down. He hugged Jokk tightly.

"Wished you woulda came to N.C. You could've taken some of the pressure off of me after my grandfather got in my ass. I'm glad to get back to the city; missed the griminess of it," said Sean. When Sean stepped back from hugging Jokk he noticed me. He backed away from Jokk and placed his hands at his sides. I walked toward Sean slowly. I was wringing my hands together.

"Still wring your hands when you nervous huh? I was with you for a whole year. I thought I knew everything about you until I saw the video tape. Yo, what you did just drove me to insanity. I knew how much you wanted to sing. I didn't know you would do *anything* to get there. You can leave," his words hurt more than the slap. I stepped up closer and took a deep breath.

"I'm leaving. I just wanted to tell you how sorry I was for everything. For what I did with Butter, for how I hurt you and the position I put you in. I'm not here for your forgiveness. At least, I don't expect it. I just wanted you to know that I was really sorry."

"Glad you not expecting me to forgive you because I don't." I nodded my head, took another deep breath, and put my glasses back on

"Thank you Jokk for letting me come with you. Sean...I...you won't see me again."

I turned around and disappeared into the crowd. This was the second time I had done that today and I was grateful for all the people that stuffed themselves onto the swelling peninsula. The burst of heat was met with a little resistance from the air behind me. Natasha had driven around the airport twice. She was on her third run when I stepped out. She pulled the car over and the door popped open. I stepped inside and closed the door. I was surprised that I wasn't falling apart. I didn't know if I felt like crying or not. I didn't feel like anything. I just sat there and stared ahead as Natasha drove onto FDR. I didn't even care where we were going, I just wanted a lot of space between me and the airport. Sean wouldn't have to worry about ever seeing me again. He was the only reason that I went to Harlem. We pulled off the highway via the 33rd street exit. I still couldn't pull myself out of my daydream to follow where we were going. Natasha veered the car into a downtown parking garage and paid the ticket in advance. Natasha turned to face me before we stepped out of the parking garage.

"You don't have to talk about it if you don't want to. But you do have to shop. This is yours," Natasha handed a credit card to me, "Cane said try not to max it out. But we need to shop and release some of this tension. Things that you need for school, your mom wants to do that with you. So, we're going to shop frivolously."

I smiled slightly at the card. Free money always did make me feel good. I needed something to take my mind off of Sean. Shopping would do that. We placed the last of our bags in the back seat of the car since the trunk was full. Natasha announced that she was hungry. I walked as if in a fog and was turning myself into Gray's Papaya when Natasha swiveled me around.

"Darling I don't eat red meat or pork so you can forget about your hotdog dreams. We can eat at Applebee's. I need to sit down anyway my feet are killing me." I looked down at the three-inch heels Natasha had on.

"Serves you right; you knew we were going shopping. Who shops in downtown New York with three-inch heels on? It doesn't make any sense."

"This is New York so there are a high percentage of women walking around shopping in three-inch heels. It's one of the fashion and model capitals of the world. Look around you."

I stopped and looked around. Natasha was right. I was about to be drawn into the allure of it when a sound so wonderful drifted to my ears from corner of 42nd St. Three guys were beating on large buckets; the kind that industrial laundry detergent comes in. I was trying to work out the beat in my head when it came to me. They were sounding out "*Top Billin'*" by MC Milk. But that same beat was used for Mary J. Blige's "*Real Love*". The young men had a nice sized crowd around them. There was a smaller bucket beside them with some change and a few dollars in it. I couldn't help myself. Before Natasha could put together what I was about to do, I was already singing the first notes to "*Real Love*".

The crowd was swelling, and Natasha had to hold her ground to keep me in her sights. I moved through the crowd like we were all old friends.

When I finished the song, I could see that the small bucket next to the three guys was half-way full. The crowd erupted in applause. I took a bow and gestured toward the amazing accompaniment beside me. They stood and took a bow. I smiled and hugged Natasha.

"I hope I didn't embarrass you," I said. Natasha shook her head with a stern look on her face.

"I just don't see why you think you can sing. I really don't see what all the fuss is about." I stepped back from her and Natasha broke into a large smile. I playfully punched her arm. The first guy tried to get me to do another number.

"Hey, you want to do another one? We'll give you five dollars," he said. I chuckled humbly.

"Thank you, but nah. You earned that money. I was just playing around. You should find somebody who wants to be a singer to sing with you. This was a lot of fun, but I have to go. Come on Natasha." The guy jumped up and caught me by the elbow.

"Wait, we're not street kids. We have a chance to be in the line up for Harlem Week in August. All we have to do is audition. If they pick us the winning group can get a scholarship."

"What no record deal? Just joking. I sure could use that scholarship money."

"We play drums out here, but Antonio plays the guitar and Genesis plays any kind of percussion there is."

I took a good look at the person speaking to me. It had just occurred to me that he towered over me. He was probably a year or two older than me. His rich smooth skin was drenched with the sweat of diligent drumming. He was some kind of handsome. I smiled at him and then took a step back. I didn't have the time to fall in love. I had to keep on working to make sure my life stayed on track. Being selfish and using men did me no good. My smile faded.

"Did I say something wrong?" he asked. The crowd was busy bopping their heads to the new beat that Genesis and Antonio were sharing.

"No, you didn't. What's your name?"

"Nazareth."

"You're kidding right? What's your real name?"

"I'm not kidding. It's Nazareth. I've heard all the jokes so keep them to yourself." I smiled again.

"I like your name. So, what other instrument do you play?"

"I play the piano. So, what about the audition? Are you interested?"

"Piano huh? Don't you need to run that past your boys?"

"They sent me over here."

"Oh. Well, even if I wanted to I couldn't. I leave for school later this month."

"So, do we, the audition is next week. If we don't make it, no problem. We go our separate ways. If we do, we can raise the money for you to get back here. The show is on a Saturday so we won't be missing class or anything."

I was lost for a moment in his eyes. I had to shake loose my thoughts in order to give him an answer.

"Okay, say we make it. How are we going to practice?" A grin broke out over his face.

"Well, we can practice starting tomorrow until the audition and when we make it, we can practice that Friday before the show. I mean, we're damn near perfect together." I was struggling to regain control of my mind, but I lost.

"I'll do it. Give me your number and I'll call you in the morning to find out what time and where rehearsal is going to be." I thought for a second,

"I need to bring Natasha with me." Natasha cocked her head in surprise. Nazareth didn't realize Natasha was with me.

"Fine with me; what's your name?" he asked.

"Kim," I said. Nazareth stood there grinning at me. I cleared my throat and held out my hand.

"I need your number if you want me to call you," I said.

"Oh yeah," Nazareth reached in his back pocket and pulled out a pen and the wrapper from a stick of Doublemint gum. He wrote down his pager number. My code was the number one.

"My code is number one? Am I that special already?"

"Number one is the code for everyone in the group." I smirked sheepishly. I held up the number and placed it in my pocketbook. I backed away from him and disappeared into the crowd. Nazareth turned and rejoined his group.

I squeezed Natasha's arm in excitement as we continued our way to Applebee's. Natasha was worried I was heading down the same path.

"Kim are you sure about him?"

"Hell no! That's why you're going with me. I didn't always make the best decisions. But I don't want to live my life not taking any chances. There's no record deal involved so I don't have to worry about label execs and all that other bullshit. I could just sing to be singing. Plus, I'll be helping them out; he said there was a scholarship involved."

"Yes, but Kim, they think you need it too."

"I know. But if they don't think I need it, they won't understand why I would be working so hard. Sometimes I don't think anybody understands how much I love music. If we win, I'll tell them that my family came through and they don't have to share the scholarship with me. I'm trying to change Natasha. I get to do something nice for somebody and they don't have to worry about giving me something in return."

"You sound like you made up your mind already."

"I did."

"It doesn't hurt that he's sexy as hell."

"No, it doesn't!" We slapped each other five as we entered Applebee's.

CHAPTER 31 Still Reinventing

Isa

It hurt a little bit less every time Rodriguez came and left. By now I had it made up in my mind that he wasn't supposed to be my man or anything. He was kind of like my fairy godboyfriend. He came around when I was about to make a change in my life, and I wasn't sure what to do. Because of him, it was easy for me to make a list of things that I was good at and that I liked doing. I wasn't the person I was when I was a kid in New York but that didn't mean that I couldn't check people when they needed it. I just had to learn to stop short of killing them or doing or saying something that would hurt me.

Juarez said something else to me when I had the clean-up duty and of course, I snapped on her and wound up with more two more days of consequences. I shut up because I didn't want anything to stop me from helping Sage during her court date and I was getting tired. If I kept running my mouth and getting into fights, I would never be a police officer or get into that Special Forces program Commander Brown invited me to. I don't lie to myself anymore. I didn't think I was good enough to get into the program. Nobody from the outside would know it, but every time I looked in the mirror all I saw was Isa from the hood. I thought somebody would call me on all the mistakes I made before I came to the academy. I know it's not rational but it's how I was feeling.

I don't know if Rodriguez really wanted to marry me or if I wanted to *be* married or have kids. I didn't know if I wanted a lifelong career as an officer, but I *did* know that it was my choice. For the first time in my life, I started feeling like I *could* do anything. Just because I grew up running the street didn't mean that I had to live like that for the rest of my life. I'm going to be better than I was. I'm not perfect so I'm sure I'm going to mess up again, but it won't be the same mistake that I made before.

When I got back from North Carolina, I went to see Lt. Sallye. I don't know when I went from hating her to respecting her and wanting her to respect me. I never cared what another female thought about me other than Nana. Lt. Sallye taught me things without making me hate myself or hate the academy. She found a way to make me want this more than I wanted to be right or slap Juarez or be fly. This was big for me. Lt. Sallye's receptionist told me Lt. Sallye was expecting me but I still knocked on the door and waited for her to give me permission to enter. I stood by a chair and waited for her to finish whatever she was doing. She looked up at me and went back to writing. I waited. Her phone rang and she began a short conversation. I waited. She hung up and looked at me. She went back to writing. I waited. After about fifteen minutes she acknowledged me.

"Sit down Steney."

"Thank you Lt. Sallye," I said.

"No attitude, humility, and grace. Patience and tolerance. Perseverance and teamwork. All these things I have named I never thought you would embrace. I thought you were the worst kind of rookie. You're college educated and from your language and attire when you first arrived educated in the street as well. It's a deadly combination; like having only a little bit of knowledge and then teaching someone else your limited curriculum. I thought you had too many ingrained bad habits and I would have to break you and deprogram you to reach you. I was wrong. I don't say that lightly and it doesn't happen often. You forced me to change my plans. I used what you had and enhanced it to make you a better officer. You are who you are, but you get tired. You're no good after 9pm. All I had to do was run you into the night."

She looked at me like I was going to interrupt or if I was going to make a face. I didn't have to; I figured out what she was trying to do to me, but it was too late when I had put it together. It was easier to go along with the program. Plus, if I wanted to do Special Forces, I was going to need Lt. Sallye and if I didn't, I still was going to need her as a reference because I wasn't leaving the criminal justice field.

"Very good—no reaction, you're not my favorite rookie, but I don't hate you. You are one of the best that's come through here in a long time. In fact, it's been ten years since I've recommended anyone to Commander Brown, but you've got talent. You're a leader and you take the initiative. I'm hoping that you're here to accept her offer." She stopped talking and folded her hands. I was coming in here with a whole speech ready with a little begging thrown in, but her speech threw me. If I was understanding her right, she didn't like me, but she was still recommending me. She separated her feelings about me from my abilities. This was the greatest lesson I learned from her.

"I came to accept the offer. When would I have to start?"

"Officially—October 19th."

"With all due respect, what do I do for money? It's July. I have student loans to repay and..."

"You'll be assigned to a local precinct. You will be partnered with veteran officers. It'll be like a paid internship. Doctors do rounds with different specialist and you will do your tours with officers in different divisions until it's time for you to leave. Don't do anything stupid like die before you are fully trained." Wow.

"Okay. What do I do now?"

"Be on time for your swearing in and get out of my office."

The day of swearing in came and I had my uniform. It felt like I had on pure Persian silk, like Chanel made the cut just for me, the cap was made for my head alone. I was...happy. I had my degree, I was a police officer, and I was happy. I looked out over the crowd and saw my family, my mother, and my friends. Jewel, Sienna and Sage with August; he was calling my name from the crowd. I could not believe he was three years old.

My name was called, and I crossed the stage with a big smile. I shook the hands of Sgt. Snow, Lt. Sallye, the mayor, and the chief of police. In the back of the room, I saw Commander Brown. I turned to take my picture. I did not look back to where she was because I knew she would be gone. At the reception, I caught up with my friends and got hugs from everybody. My mother grabbed August and told us to go out and celebrate.

"Wait guys I have to change. Ma, wait for me to come back. I need you to take my uniform with you. I'll pick it up tomorrow." I ran to change.

In the changing room the mayor's office set up for us, Juarez walked in while I was walking out.

"Steney, hey, no hard feelings?" I looked at her like she was crazy.

"No feelings at all," I said and walked away. I never could be phony.

Me and the girls went to the Shark Bar in Harlem and shut it down. The Shark Bar was a hole in the wall bar with zero room for a dance floor. That didn't stop us from putting on a floor show when Lil' Kim's *Big Mama Thing* came on over the speakers. We got lots of claps and more free drinks. By the time we left we were three sheets to the wind and hungry. We stopped at Willie Burger on 145th and got meals to go. The line was a little long but so worth it. We were at Jewel's house. She was letting me live with her until I left in a few months. We shared the rent and utilities. It was a cute two-bedroom one bath on 138th Lenox. Jewel was an actress. She did parts on soaps, off-Broadway, commercials, and movies. She had an agent too. She got pretty regular work, so she was doing good. Sienna was passed out on the couch. She left her husband with her two kids and hopped a plane for my ceremony. I think she wanted to get away for a little while. Sage was on the fire escape on the phone. I don't know how she handled business at all times of night. If I was her, I would shut everybody down at 8pm. People never respect her time. Jewel was doing that thing where she looks at me and knows everything that goes on inside.

"What's wrong Isa? You gonna bust Sage?" She laughed.

"I should but you will always be my family. Nothing changes that unless you kill somebody. But you know it was like that whether I was a cop or not baby! I do not rock with jail."

"Ha, for real, what's up?"

"I was thinking that Sage needs to hang up that phone 'cause it's late. Who could she be talking to? It's not a man."

"I don't know. Maybe it's a new interview or something. Guess what?"

"What?"

"I just got a part in *Macbeth* in Shakespeare in the Park," she said excitedly.

"Really? What's the part? And what about *Days of Our Lives*?"

"I play Lady Macbeth's nurse and I'm in a coma for the next three weeks on *Days* so I'm free."

"That's what's up Jewel. We'll come see you when you start."

"Yeah right, you don't even like Shakespeare."

"Yeah but I like you...a little bit. So, I'll deal with it." She rolled her eyes at me. We heard the base from the loud music of an approaching car. That wasn't a big deal; cars always came through this block like that. This car sounded like it was right in front of the building. *It's All About the Benjamins* was blasting out of somebody's speakers. Somebody was hollering from the street. I could see Sage jump up and look over the fire escape. She was yelling too. The music stopped, car doors slammed, and then--

"Oh shit, oh shit, 3L!" Sage said and then she hung up on whoever she was talking to. She gave out our apartment number. She rushed in the window and ran to the door and opened it. Jewel and I were moving a little slow because of the food and liquor but not that slow. I grabbed my gun and Jewel reached for hers. I raised my eyebrows up at her. I was going to ask her about that later. Sage never turned around to us. I yelled at her.

"What the hell is going on?"

"You'll see in one minute!" She was dancing around the door. I could hear click, click, click, click of heels. Next thing I know Billie was standing in the doorway screaming. She and Sage started hugging, screaming, and talking fast. Sienna jumped up when she heard the screaming and then fell off of the couch when she saw the guns. Jewel put her gun back in its hiding place and I put mine back in my pocketbook before Billie collided into us. She was all smiles. I was hoping we didn't wake up the neighbors. Funny I never would have cared about that before I became a cop. Oh brother. Sage closed the door and Billie started talking a mile a minute.

"Ladies, I don't know what you're doing October 1st this year, but you better cancel it," she said.

"Hell no, I have plans with Joshua. He owes me from last year for getting me pregnant." Sienna's husband was a caterer, and she was an event planner in North Carolina when she wasn't having babies. They had a good business too. Billie tried her luck in Atlanta as a physical therapist.

"Well, that's too bad because you don't have a choice; just like I didn't have a choice when it was your turn," she said. Sienna focused her eyes on Billie's ring finger.

"You gotta be shitting me! Ow! I am so happy for you!" Jewel yelled.

"Girl, say you getting married here in New York, please. Joshua owes me big and I could really cash in," Sienna said.

"You know it! That's why missed your ceremony Isa. He just asked me today and I got on the earliest flight I could get on, but the flight was delayed because it was raining in Georgia." I was happy for her, but I had some questions.

"Honey, who are you marrying? We don't know him. You haven't mentioned him at all."

"I have so! I'm marrying Mills."

"Mills?" We all said together. He went to Jewel and Billie's school. He was a guy who chased her freshman and sophomore year before he transferred to another school. He gave her hell and she ignored him.

"I need you to explain this shit to me like I'm four because I don't understand," I said.

"I was contracted to be the physical therapist for Georgia State University when they went to the Combines—that's like NFL tryout qualifiers. Anyway, while I'm there right, the coaches are all talking and doing they thing but I never pay them any attention not like to get at them because this is business, right? The players try me but once I check them, they stay in their lane. Okay, okay, but there's other coaches from other schools there and some of them know each other from playing in the NFL or college or going to the same school or golf or whatever."

"This is so exciting," Sienna said.

"I know right," Sage said.

"It's taking too long," I said.

"Be quiet and let her finish then," Jewel said. Billie took a deep breath and picked it up.

"Okay so I see them looking at me and talking. So, I look at myself. I have on khakis and a white polo shirt and a baseball cap with my company logo on it. I advertise only business. Nothing too tight. I have all my medical supplies and that's it. But they keep staring and it starts bothering me, so I ask them what's up. Ladies, Mills steps up, but I swear to God I didn't know it was him. He asked me my name and about my business. He asked me for a business card, and he gave me his. He's the defensive coach for the Navy football team. I went into my pitch immediately because I'm all about making my business grow right?" Jewel interrupted.

"Didn't you recognize his name on the card?" she asked.

"No. It said Victor Miller. We always called him Mills. He looked familiar but I thought I saw him on TV or something like that. He's young to be on a coaching team, which is what I said to him. He told me he played for Navy his junior and senior year. He helped the coach develop plays because he was a quarterback. He tore his ACL during his Combine. He wasn't going to the NFL, so they offered him a job."

"Billie wrap this up. Some of us want to do other things before the new millennium, damn!" I said.

"Alright I'm almost done. He's talking to me and he's all in my space. I step back, he steps in. Finally, he asks me do I recognize him, and I say no. He tells me I'm prettier than ever and I'm nicer now. I tell him thank you and ask him where he knows me from because you know I wasn't for no bullshit. He tells me he's Mills, and I almost passed the fuck out." I gave her a hard look.

"He laughed at me when I tried to back pedal. I told him that what happened back then was me being a kid and this was my legitimate business and if he was going to give me a hard time just rip up my card and we can go our separate ways. But damn ya'll, he was looking good as hell, do you hear me? He doesn't look nothing like he did when he was at State. He got contacts, muscles, facial hair, a haircut...whoo. I'm getting hot thinking about him." I gave her one more look.

"Okay, okay, well we started dating and I got to know him and then I fell in love and then he asked me to marry him and now I'm going to marry him and we're going to live in Annapolis. The end."

"Wow, don't you wish you would have given him a chance in college? I told you he was a nice person," Jewel said.

"Hell no! I would've eaten him alive. I treated him like I did everybody else who worried my nerves. I dated a couple of guys who didn't look all that hot and a couple of them even got a little of this na-na. But men who sweat me, never get me. He didn't have any confidence. But now he's got it everywhere!" I love my girls. They're crazy. I was tired and the sun was coming up. I left them in the living room and crawled into my bed. I had to be fresh for work tomorrow—I was one of New York's Finest.

CHAPTER 32 Still Reinventing

Kim

Natasha picked me up for the rehearsal at nine a.m. We drove up in the Bronx to a two-story house in Mount Vernon. Nazareth lived about two blocks from Sydney and 4th. It was a nice neighborhood. It was busy with people leaving out of their homes headed toward a bustling strip of Mount Vernon where mom and pop stores were still a viable part of the community. Some gave Natasha who was a strikingly blond, white woman a third glance, but gave me even dirtier looks for being with her. The darts from the strange eyes couldn't penetrate through my nervousness; I was wringing my hands.

"You're going to rub all the skin off of your hands," Natasha said. I jammed my hands into the front pockets of my short jean skirt. I had on a pair of red and white Jordans and a tight white tee shirt that read *Just Do It* in bold red print. I changed my clothes at least four times before I decided that I would wear whatever made me feel comfortable, but I still had butterflies in my stomach at the thought of being close to Nazareth. He wasn't anything I was used to, and he was broke. I was a get money chic; at least I used to be.

I still wasn't ready to see my friends. I wasn't sure if we were still friends anyway. My mother told me they asked about me, but they were probably being nice. I heard that Sage had a kid and was a writer for an underground hip hop magazine. She was even on the radio a couple of months ago. Sienna got married, had two kids and lived in North Carolina. Jewel was on *Days of Our Lives*. Billie had a private practice as a physical therapist. Isa, I wasn't too sure about. I knew Isa didn't care really if we ever spoke again, but all that stuff between us when we were younger didn't matter. It wasn't like I was angry with her. I fell out of touch with her like I did with everyone else. Their lives were coming together with school and everything when my life was falling apart. But it is what it is. My thoughts came to a quick end as I rang the doorbell. I could hear shouts from behind the door: a woman's voice.

"I seen her through the window. She can't use your comb! Send her white ass home! What the hell make you think it's alright to be bringing her stringy-hair ass up in this house? The house that a Black Panther built!" Nazareth could be heard yelling back at the woman.

"Girl be quiet! Only time you seen a Black Panther was on that Janet Jackson video! I don't care what color she is, she's welcome in this house if she's my friend. Plus, you got a lot balls to be talking. You looked at yourself lately?" With that, Nazareth opened the door. He saw Natasha first and understood what the woman talking about. He was blushing when he saw that we had heard what was said.

"Is it safe to come in or do I need to show her my Klan card?" Natasha said. Nazareth frowned.

"Please don't get her started. I'm sorry if you heard what she said."

"But not about what she said," shot back.

"No, because that's her apology to make. That's her hang up with white people not mine. You can still come in, but you have to deal with her just like the rest of us." Nazareth stood aside and allowed us to walk in; the woman stepped out of a side room and walked all around me and Natasha.

"So, uh, Naz your band turned into the United Colors of Benetton?" The woman was lighter than me. Her hair was the same texture as Natasha's. She held no physical or facial feature which indicated that could hope to be Black. She wore full Muslim garb. She stopped in front of us. Natasha took a deep breath before speaking.

"I don't feel like answering for all the crimes my race has committed against the world. You're going to have to be angry by yourself. Nazareth is this the door to the basement?" Nazareth looked at her with confusion. "How did you know we were in the basement?" he asked.

"It's my job to know." Nazareth pointed to a door adjacent to where we were all gathered. Natasha pushed the door open and went down the lit staircase.

"This is still my house Naz and I will not be disrespected. You were raised as a Black king. How could you stand there and let the devil talk to me that way?"

The woman was confrontational, loud, and in search of her identity.

"Kim this is my sister Sylvia, but she calls herself Africa. Africa this is the great singer I was telling you about Kim."

"Oh, my beautiful Black sister, do you know who you are? Or have you subscribed and bought into the propaganda that the man has spoon fed us through the miseducation of *his*-story?" I wasn't sure how to answer. I didn't want or need a lecture about myself. So, I answered honestly.

"I'm still searching." I turned toward the door and walked down. Africa touched her brother on his arm.

"I think I could learn to like her." Nazareth looked at his sister.

"Girl, you strange," He walked downstairs after me.

The basement of the house had been renovated into a rehearsal studio. The walls were padded to reduce the noise level and there was an isolated, padded booth for recording. Antonio and Genesis were already tuning up their instruments. Me and Natasha sat in a loveseat in one corner of the basement. Nazareth made the introductions, and everyone shook hands.

"Natasha I'm sorry. My sister is going through her own thing. That stuff upstairs doesn't have anything to do with you."

"Don't worry about it. We're not here to solve the world's problems just make a little music." I let a sigh of relief escape my lips. Africa was a lot to take in and I knew that Natasha was not a pushover period. Nazareth clapped his hands together and looked around the room. His eyes landed on his piano and he went over to it. He opened the piano bench and pulled out four pages of sheet music. He handed them to me.

"These are the songs that we chose to sing for the audition. We have to do a popular song and an original piece."

I looked at the music. The cover song we were going to do was the remix to "*Love No Limit*". The original piece had no title and was incomplete. I bit down on my lip and looked at Nazareth.

"Okay, I love this song. I don't have any problem with it...if I have any say about it. But what's up with the original piece? You don't have a title and it's not finished. The audition is in a few days right?" Genesis smirked at Nazareth.

"Yeah Naz, where's the title and the rest of the lyrics? Isn't the audition in a few days?" Antonio chimed in.

"Yeah, that sounds like the same questions we been asking you for two weeks. Maybe Kim can inspire him to give up some answers or lyrics? Either one is fine with me." Nazareth twisted his lips while giving each of them the evil eye.

"Anytime you want to write the lyrics and the score you're welcome to it. We're a band remember?" I circled the room while holding the lyrics. I hummed a little to myself to develop the melody in my head. There was a pencil on the piano bench, and I picked it up. I began to make notes, literally, on the sheet music. There was a glass door in the basement which led to the back of the house. I held the sheet music and pencil in one hand and went to the couch where Natasha was seated and grabbed a pillow. I walked over to the door and dropped the pillow on the floor next to it. I lowered myself onto the floor and began writing notes and lyrics. Every now and then I would look out of the door as if expecting a visitor and then continued writing. Genesis, Antonio, and Nazareth continued to tune their instruments and then run through a series of warm-ups. They were music majors for real and took their music seriously. Natasha pulled out her phone and an appointment book.

By the time Natasha had finished her conversation, I had written the notes and lyrics to the end of the song. I stood up and rolled the sheet music in my hand. I took the pencil and used it as a pin to pull up my hair. Antonio noticed me first.

"Let's see what you got there." I shook my head.

"No sir, I need to warm up my voice. Can we do the Mary song first?" Genesis and Nazareth spoke up at once.

"No!" Antonio eased an arm around me. Antonio was an old soul and spoke in the same manner.

"Don't listen to them. You take your time baby." They looked at Antonio. He would take in a stray from anywhere. They relented and began the introduction to "*Love No Limit*". The vibe was an immediate synchronicity. We heard Africa open the door separating the kitchen and the stairs to the basement; she didn't come down. When we finished with a satisfied drum exit, we smiled in appreciation to each other.

"That was incredible!" I said. I was really looking at Nazareth, but they all accepted the compliment. I unrolled the sheet music and they gathered around me.

"This is what I added to the end. The melody stays the same up to this point right here and then I thought a melody change to take it up another octave would give it like a haunting feeling and then end with the piano drifting out with that haunting beat. It kind of makes me feel like...I don't know sad as hell but in like a Sade kind of way. Know what I mean?" Antonio nodded his head and then took another pencil from his music stand.

"What about softening the melody right here and then building the crescendo in a loop through to the end of the song? That way it slices open your heart over and over again like a sore." Genesis screwed his face.

"Why you gotta be so graphic all the time?"

"I'm a tortured soul."

"That ain't the point." Nazareth stood between them.

"Kids...just make the changes. It all sounds good to me," I said. They agreed. We ran through the end changes a cappella with the guys singing background to my lead. At some points we made more changes where we harmonized to blend the sound better. When we were satisfied with the finished product a little more than an hour had passed before we performed it. Africa had taken that opportunity to make brunch; we could smell it. Natasha ventured upstairs to make an attempt at being civil toward Africa. She said she had cracked harder nuts and Africa was definitely nuts.

There was still a tension between them, but they worked together for the sake of the brunch. It was at completion of the brunch that they heard the opening notes to our original song. They were setting the table in the kitchen area when they began to process the lyrics of the haunting song. It told of a love so true and evasive that the person was dying of a broken heart.

At the end of the song, Natasha walked downstairs in time to see the each of us leaning on instruments or the microphone in my case. We looked spent.

"You guys okay?" Natasha asked. I wiped my face and looked up.

"Yeah...we're good." The guys held up. They didn't cry, but clearly the song was disturbing to them.

"We need to copyright that song now...before we perform it. That's a winner," Antonio said.

We all nodded. Nazareth and Genesis still had knots in their throats. Natasha tried to lighten the mood.

"We have happy food upstairs." We all chuckled a little and followed her upstairs. Nazareth pulled me back while everyone went up the stairs.

"You made the difference in that song. It's amazing now. I'll make sure you get your credit as a songwriter." He held my forearm as he spoke to me. I could feel him breathing hard.

"I just was feeling a way lately and what you wrote down was just like what I was feeling. I just added a little bit to it," I said shrugging my shoulders.

"You have any ideas for a title?"

"What about 'Forgot'?

"What about 'Forgot on Purpose'?

"I think I like that better." I was nervous standing so close to him. I could smell that he used Ivory soap. He smelled clean to me. He smelled new. He smelled like...I had better get away from him. So, I backed away.

"Let's go eat. Genesis looks like he might not leave us anything," he said releasing my arm.

"As skinny as he is?"

"Don't let skinny people fool you. Both of my brothers are skinny, and they eat more than a little bit." He smiled at me and turned away to go upstairs. I followed behind quietly.

We ate with compliments to the chefs and made scheduled times for the rest of the week. Natasha and I said goodbye to everyone. I locked eyes with Nazareth and sent him a silent goodbye. He winked at me.

"Where are we headed to?" I asked when we were outside.

"We're going to a friend's. You have a date?" she asked.

"I wish," I mumbled and looked back at Nazareth's closed door.

"What?"

"Nothing let's go."

What can I say? We made it into the line up. I was proud of myself. I kept my hands off of Nazareth. I liked him definitely, but I was going to do things differently this time. He didn't know the 'get money' Kim; he didn't know the 'video' Kim; he didn't know the scheming Kim; he knew the Kim that I was now, and I wanted to keep it like that. Naz, Antonio, and Genesis went to NYU's The New School. They were right behind each other in school; Naz was a junior. I went on to Atlanta for school. When we met back up in August for Harlem Week, we came in second place with the prize being one thousand dollars. We split it four ways. Naz rode with me to the airport on Sunday and waited until my plane took off. He was holding my hand; he was sweating. I had an hour before the plane took off.

"Kim, I know you go to school in Atlanta and I'm here in New York, but I want to get to know you better," he said. I raised my eyebrows in shock, which was okay because he wasn't looking at me—but his fingers mixed with mine.

"Umm, I was talking to a couple of people before I met you, but nothing serious for real. I like how calm you are. You chill out with my family or my friends and you don't judge anything I say or do. You listen to me. I don't know any females like you."

He had that right! I started biting my lip. He was wringing my hands for me. I was enjoying him. Before I left my mother's house, she showed me her invitation to Billie's wedding. Billie sent me card asking me to be a bridesmaid. I called her and told her that I would. I had to face them sometime and I had until October. I had a daydream of Naz going with me to the wedding. When I told him about it, he said he didn't mind going with me. That dream busted as soon as he asked to get to know me better. He made me want to tell him the truth. I knew he wasn't going to like it and I needed to see how guys would react to my past and get used to it. I won't lie right about now, I was glad I went to school in Georgia. I wouldn't have to see him anymore; that would take a little bit of the hurt out of it. I pulled my hand away, wiped my hands on my jeans, and made him look at me. I told him word for word what happened in Harlem. I told him in more words than I told my mother. When I was finished, he was looking at me with his hand covering his mouth. He stood up and walked away from me. I puffed up my cheeks and blew my breath out. Well, at least I know that I told the truth. I wanted to cry. Since this isn't a movie, he didn't come back. I got on the plane and cried quietly with my shades on facing the window.

CHAPTER **33 Still Reinventing**

Sage

And so, here I was again in North Carolina. In the same court room with Alex beside me, Isa and Sienna behind me, Bukaii and his lawyer were across from me. There were only two people missing that worried me. Bukaii's stepfather—he made a break for the boarder last month. He called me and stopped by to see August before going to the Bahamas. That's where he was originally from. I don't think he divorced Bukaii's mother, but I know he wasn't going back to her. The other person was the judge—the original one. We all stood as a new female judge entered. She had brown and white hair—more white than brown. She had on pearl earrings, necklace, eyeglasses rimmed with pearls. She sat, we sat, and she started in on Alex.

"Ms. Mikkos, your reputation precedes you. I'm sure you hear that a lot. However, you pull any of your shenanigans in my courtroom and I will hold you in contempt. I am not as easily charmed as Judge Patterson. He will no longer oversee this case insofar as he has been called into a federal case. Upon reading these notes, I see that Mr. Jenkins was unable to retain counsel the last time you all met. I can see that issue has been resolved. Yes Mr. Jenkins?" Bukaii was elbowed by his lawyer to answer the judge.

"Yes, your honor," he said softly. His lawyer cleared his throat.

"Your honor, I just want to say..."

"I didn't ask you to speak," the judge cut off Bukaii's lawyer. She was looking through a bunch of papers and looked up at all of us. I don't understand why we are here. Did no one from Judge Patterson's office contact either attorney?" Both of the lawyers waited to be told to speak. She nodded at Alex.

"My office was unsuccessful in reaching the judge's offices concerning any aspect of the case including the paternity testing."

"Again, he was pulled onto a federal case, so you weren't that important," Wow, this judge was unbelievable, "Beyond that Mr. Jenkins here, didn't submit his sample until late last week. There would have been no results until now anyway." Bukaii's lawyer attempted to speak again.

"Your honor, I say we drop this whole thing then and everybody go home." We all whipped our heads and looked at him. Bukaii looked straight ahead like he didn't hear anything. The judge leaned over her bench as far as she could.

"Counselor, what law school are you disgracing at this moment? Did you pass the bar?" she asked.

"I ain't go to no law school and I did not pass the bar. It's too early to be drinking your honor."

"Young man, are you serious?" I took a good look at Bukaii's lawyer. Nothing on him matched—not his suit to tie to shoes. He wasn't polished enough to be a public defender. I could see into his briefcase and it was filled with loose leaf paper. This was unreal. I know that Bukaii didn't try to scam the court.

"Yeah, I'm serious!" Then Bukaii spoke up.

"I told that other judge I couldn't afford no lawyer, so I got somebody to look like my lawyer. He's on my side and he been in court more times with his four baby mamas than anybody I know. He know more than probably you your honor." The judge looked over at me.

"And you chose him huh?" I was so tired of being asked that question.

"Unfortunately," I said. She shook her head. She read the papers in front of her one more time and looked up.

"Ms. Mensa, aside from your relationship with Mr. Jenkins, you have made good decisions where your life and that of your son are concerned. I commend you for removing him from and dangerous situation where most women who find themselves in environments where drugs are prevalent remain in that environment. I understand this came at a great hardship for you, but I believe there is a lesson in everything we do. Therefore, I offer you this gift: there is no way possible that Mr. Jenkins is the father of your child. So, it is my profound pleasure to dismiss the case against you due to the fact that he has no legal right to your child. This case is dismissed! Bailiff...I need my special tea please."

Because this was the perfect time to give God the praises, that's what I did. I went and sat down in between Sienna and Isa, held their hands and prayed a prayer of thanks to God for the miracles I never ask for. I thanked him for the experience that I had with Bukaii because how could I ever understand that this kind of joy was possible if I hadn't gone through the desert with Bukaii. What I should have known all along was that He had always been there with me. So, I wasn't angry at myself or Bukaii or regretful of these past years—I felt nothing but pure joy—unbelievable joy—pure joy—indescribable joy! I let the tears run down my face freely. Alex put her hands on ours as I finished the prayer. We all hugged and left the courtroom.

We all walked arm in arm and were greeted by Bukaii's mother, sisters, and mother of his child. They all had their hands on their hips like they were read to start some nonsense. I felt a little bad because August did know these people as his family. I was thinking for a split second that I would work something out with them; then his mother opened her mouth.

"Where is my grandson? You can't keep him from us forever. You know Labor Day coming up. You shoulda just brought him with you."

"Please stop talking to me. You might want to go inside and get your son. He in there crying." I got in the car smiling. There wasn't anything else to say. I was going home to squeeze my son and be grateful for God's grace. It didn't occur to me for one second that I had another problem. It would rise to my consciousness with the gracelessness of a heart attack.

CHAPTER 34 Still Reinventing

Isa

I take your man right out the box and put him under my padlock... That's how my theme song used to start. Now I hear reggae beats and I'm singing: *Bad boys, bad boys, whatcha gonna do, whatcha gonna do when dey come for you* or *Baaaaad booooooyys come out and plaaaa-yeeee!* I loved being a cop. I thought I was going to catch a lot of bullshit because I was a female, but the men treated me like I better know what I'm doing. I found out quick that, at least at my precinct, they were more concerned about me knowing what the hell I was doing so I didn't kill anybody or get myself killed. That's when I realized I was watching too much TV. My mentor officers trained me well. They taught me how to take in each situation and not to hesitate. I had to understand that when a perp had a weapon especially—it was either me or them. I could risk shooting him in the leg and then he would shoot me to kill. I had to make a judgment call for each situation but know that sometimes the situation would turn out fatal.

I made friends with a lot of the vets fast. I was myself and happy in my skin. I didn't act like I knew it all because I didn't. I kept my mouth shut when they were teaching me something and I wasn't scared to ask questions. I think though, they probably liked me because I was one of the best shots in the precinct. I loved guns but I respected them too. I liked looking for evidence too. I learned how to read people and know when they're lying and when they were telling the truth. In the first two weeks I had picked up my own informant. I was scared sometimes but not scary.

I thought that polyester/cotton blend uniform and I were going to have issues, but it became my favorite thing to wear next to my Azzure jeans. Every now and then I would bug out that I was a cop. I used my degree. What I learned in college did help when I was out in the field. I didn't entrap anyone, and I didn't contaminate evidence by touching it. I made mistakes sometimes, but I didn't end my day with it on my mind. I learned from it and kept it moving.

Toward the middle of the month, after that craziness with Sage and Bukaii, it was time for me to meet with Commander Brown. I was told to meet her at One Police Plaza the following week and make sure that I wore sweats, socks, and sneakers. I was glad because it would be before Billie's wedding and I could get back to my schedule at the precinct. When I got there, I didn't see Commander Brown. I looked at the desk sergeant and asked for her. He didn't look at me. He just pointed to an empty desk, so I walked to it. There was an unsealed envelope on the desk with my name on it.

It had seven simple instructions:

1. Fill out the application and writing sample on the desk
2. Put the completed app in the envelope and seal it.
3. Report to TEAM leader #1 for psych test
4. Report to TEAM leader #2 for physical
5. Report to TEAM leader #3 for substance test
6. Report to TEAM leader #4 for fit test
7. Report to TEAM leader #5 for human resources

I thought this was going to take an hour at the most, but it looked like I was going to be here all day. At least now I know why I had to be here at seven in the morning. It took me that first hour to complete the application and the essay. I went in order for the rest of the list. The psych test was crazy. I walked into a lime green room with two metal chairs and one metal desk. No windows. The door was my only way out. I took the empty seat across from my proctor. It was one guy—a plain looking white guy with gold rimmed glasses. He asked me the same questions over and over but in different ways. I think he was trying to make me crazy. He was monotone and dry so by the time he got to the last question I had my head on the desk and I was staring at the ceiling answering with whatever came to my mind. When he told me to go to my next test I answered, 'Blue zebras break dancing to Mozart'. I felt him looking at me before I registered what he said to me. I ran out of that room.

There was a Sgt. Snow look-alike who handed me a cup for a urine sample and then pointed to another room down the hall. I knocked and went in. It was set up like a doctor's office. I put the cup down. A nurse walked in. She wrote some things down on a chart, took my blood, gave me gown, and told me to get undressed for the doctor. Five minutes later the doctor walked in and ran a regular physical on me. I was glad it was a female doctor. I've never had a male doctor and I wanted to keep it that way. She told me that I was fine, get dressed, go in the bathroom in the hallway, fill the cup and give it to the Sgt. Snow look-alike. I didn't know that the look-alike would be in the bathroom with me making sure that I didn't do anything to my urine. I was behind a paper curtain that showed a shadow of everything I was doing. I was not alright with that. Guess that was my substance test.

The fit test was the most fun and easiest. I could run, jump, and do push-ups with the best of them. If I didn't mention it, I started out with five people. By the time I came out of human resources, there was only one other person sitting outside. He was the guy I played ball with at the academy. I hadn't seen him since graduated from the academy. I sat in the seat next to him.

"What are you doing here? Still body slamming people?" I asked him.

"They recruit fighting supermodels mami," he said. He was Dominican.

"Really?" I asked sarcastically.

"Yeah, they heard my body was *perfecto* and had to put me on the team," I looked at him, "I know you want me, but I can't mami. We played ball and fought together. I don't date my teammates. You'll just have to find a way to get over me."

"Oh brother, nice to see you again man. What happened to the other three? I didn't even see you come in."

"I came in after you. The other three crashed and burned. One cursed out the white dude for the psych exam and he got put out. The other female beside you failed the drug test. She gave some excuse but they wasn't hearing it. And the last guy made it all the way through like us but when they told him what the job detail was, he said he couldn't leave his wife alone because their baby was almost due. We're the only ones who made it."

"How do you know what happened with everybody?" He winked at me.

"That's why they hired me love. I can get information." I punched him in the arm.

"Now what?" I was anxious.

"How about we introduce ourselves? I'm Israel Colon, but I'm Izzy."

"Isabelle Steney, but call me Isa." He nodded his head like he approved my name. We exchanged numbers and then the look-alike came out.

"You two can leave. You'll receive paperwork prior to the 19th indicating your new assignment." She turned on her heel and walked away. I walked out with Izzy to the nearest cop bar. Me, I was going to a cop bar and Izzy was cute, but he wasn't Rodriguez. One day I would be ready for Rodriguez. He was the one...I knew Billie's wedding was going to make me start thinking about him. It's been years and I'm not even his girlfriend. He doesn't return calls, emails, or anything. I'm going to start doing me. I'm going to enjoy letting Izzy buy me drinks and the interesting way my career is going. At least I have something good to look at. His body is wonderful.

"I see you looking mami."

"Liking what I see papi."

3

Book Three: Getting Up

CHAPTER **35 Something Like Breathing**

Sage

My first year at *Shine Magazine* had been spent going back and forth to North Carolina fighting for sensible visitation rights of my son. I had full custody alright but because I moved out of state without Bukaii's *permission*, I had to fly my son down to North Carolina *every other* major holiday and long weekend so that Bukaii could visit with him. Truth be told, his family were the ones watching him, but as long as I couldn't prove it, I was in a battle.

It had been affecting my go-getter spirit in scoring interviews, but since I had brought in three big names that first year I was somewhere between untouchable as far as the owner of the magazine was concerned and lucky to have a job as far as my editor, Anya, was concerned. My editor had a leg to stand on. Nowadays, I worked from home, so Anya felt I had more autonomy and time to move around than those who reported to the office. I was a contracted freelance writer. Therefore, I was at the hottest parties, opening nights of anything, and fashion who's who from New York to Europe. It sounded glamorous but I was working. Going back and forth to North Carolina used to eat money out of my pockets and drained me physically and mentally. Bukaii tried to break me; there were times when I felt like he was winning; the judge made it clear that if I missed even one visit, I would be in jeopardy of losing custody.

Every grimy instinct in my body told me to just not go anymore. What was he going to do? Report me? Good luck finding me in the Big Apple. I had run the fantasy of leaving New York and moving to Africa permanently through my mind several times. But who was I punishing? And my subconscious was telling me that it might be Karma for the way I treated Joon. But I couldn't let my mind delve into that dark cave again. It still sounds awful, but there was a time when I felt like I would be able to handle letting Bukaii have August, pay the child support and go about my business the way that Bukaii did. I was the only one who heard it since it was in my head but still...he was the only father my son knew.

August was almost four and I was no longer vacillating between continuing the fight and letting Bukaii have sole custody. The paternity test brought to light something I had been suspecting about for some time now. This frees me from Bukaii's tyranny for good, but harms August. For a long time, I was called all manner of bitches by him and his family. Not to mention the threatening phone calls and emails. Their craziness was at a trickle now. While I still despised Bukaii, I know that he loved August. I wouldn't wish that kind of pain on anyone but that whole family was a bad influence. I prayed that I had made the right decision and that both of them would recover.

CHAPTER **36 Something Like Breathing**

Isa

Being a cop is like a new kind of drug. I'm addicted to it so fast. It's nothing like the movies and everything like the movies. I work a regular shift from seven to five. I woke up early and worked out before I went to work. Sometimes I would run in Riverside Park. It wasn't Central Park but don't knock Harlem. Every other day I would wake up thinking about Rodriguez. A couple of times I dropped by the academy to see if I could catch him around, but he was never there. I started feeling like he was ducking me. I thought we were better than that. He's a good guy but he's not a good guy to me. So why did it hurt so much that he wouldn't contact me at all? He said he loved me, and I told him that I loved him...I know he loved but...but what? He's not showing it.

Izzy was cool, but he was my brother. I played ball with him sometimes when our schedules matched up. I was learning Spanish from him—not just the curses. Growing up in the Bronx surrounded by Spanish speaking people turned out to be really helpful. I was picking it up faster than I thought. Maybe by next year I would be fluent. I was meeting the girls later at Sage's house. Everybody was in town including Kim. I hadn't seen her in years. I wonder what she was like now. Billie said she looked good and was different. Billie was still in Georgia and I heard Kim was in a music school there now. This was going to be a long two days. I worked a double yesterday so I could have today off. Saturday and Sunday were my regular days off—I was getting special treatment because I was leaving soon. I got some dirty looks behind that, but I could care less—they couldn't beat me.

New York was having a good Indian summer; I was going to take advantage of it and go run in the park. I was running for about an hour or so when somebody bumped into me. It's the park, it happens. I tossed a sorry over my shoulder and kept it moving. Then I felt the back of my sweatshirt being pulled back. I stopped, pulled the earphones out of my ears, and took step forward so I could have a little more room between me and the person before I turned around. I was facing Grove. I was so surprised to see her. She had on a nice cream dress with a matching leather jacket, brown boots, a Louis V bag and matching shades. I hugged her before I took in that she was looking at me funny.

"Steney girl how you doing?" she asked me. She was giving me a funny smile.

"Grove? I'm fine. What precinct are you at?"

"No precinct! I told you what I was doing there. I learned to fight and surrounded myself around New York's finest...men that is." I don't know if it was the cop in me or b-girl instincts, but something wasn't right with this meeting. I felt like I was being set up.

"Grove, what are you doing here?" I asked.

"I'm meeting my husband for lunch," she said.

"You got married already?" She nodded showing me her ring. Her rock was ridiculous.

"Not yet, engaged but you know it's me shawty, so this is just a formality. The wedding's in three weeks—he's giving up his college homecoming for me."

"You're meeting him here, in the park?" I couldn't shake this feeling I was having. Grove was one of my peoples, but she was giving me a bad vibe.

"Yes, in the park. He likes something about park. He's here almost two or three times a week. I can't really figure out why since it's so far from Queens," she was looking at me through her shades like she was waiting for my reaction, "he's picking me up from here and we're going to Sylvia's. You want to join us?"

"No, I'm good, but I'll walk you to the street," I offered. I was trying to get rid of this feeling. She locked arms with me and talked about her wedding plans and the house they were renovating in Queens. I nodded and smiled.

"So, you are a po-lice officer for real huh?" she asked.

"Yes I am. And you look like you married a lot of money."

"Oh, bay-bee, my family been had money, but my Paw Paw said I couldn't have none of it until I showed him, I was serious about getting married and having a family." I raised my eyebrows.

"You're pregnant?"

"Yes, only a few weeks though I want to look hot in my wedding dress, so I told my honey we had to get married now." Again, it felt like she was waiting for my reaction. My cell phone rang when we walked out of the park. It was my captain.

"I have to take this," I said to her. I turned my back and listened to what the captain was saying but I got sidetracked. Grove's voice squealed. I guess her fiancé showed up. I turned around to sneak a peek. I wanted to see what chump got mixed up with her. My heart stopped. Grove was wrapped up in Rodriguez's arms. She was smiling so hard. When he saw me staring, he looked like someone had kicked him in the stomach. I hung up on my captain and reached for my gun and realized that it wasn't on my hip.

"Isa..." he said and stopped. I held my hand up. I knew my tears were coming and if I put my hands on him and Grove, I would have to kill them. I probably would never see him again, so I said what was in my heart.

"I loved you more than anyone and now I hate you more than anyone. There is nothing you can ever say or do. I will never forgive you. You are a fucking coward." There was so much more that I wanted to say but not that I needed to say. I stood there dialed my captain back and told him it was a bad connection. I walked away talking to him so that they both could see that they couldn't kill me. I hung up the phone, put my earplugs back in my ears and jogged home.

When I got to the house, Jewel left me note saying she went to Sage's house already. I laid out my outfit, stripped out of my clothes, jumped in the shower and sank to the bottom of the tub and cried my eyes out. I was feeling like I wanted to die. After thirty minutes, I finished my shower, got out, got dressed and made a hair appointment at the Dominicans. The shower destroyed my hair. I looked in the mirror. I survived the greatest heartbreak ever from a man I loved for my whole life—my father. There was no way I was going to destroy my life over somebody I knew for a few years. I didn't have time for a breakdown. It would have to keep until after the wedding. Me and these fucked up men ain't no new situation. I'm sick of it myself.

CHAPTER 37 Something Like Breathing

Kim

I know I did the right thing, but it seems like I keep telling these guys the truth and they keep shitting on me. My mother said it's the consequence of a clear conscious. You can't predict people's reaction. Naz was different from the guys I was with. He didn't try to rush me into anything. He opened doors for me and talked to me not at me and he was nice. I didn't know guys could be nice if you weren't having sex with them, but Naz was nice. I feel bad that he walked away from me. I thought he would call or write me after he thought about it a little while, but nothing.

I loved school. I was doing well. Uncle Cane, Bagby, and my mother came for parents' week last month. They were satisfied that I was okay, and no one was picking on me and I was doing the right thing. They heard about Freaknik and thought I might get tempted by all the partying, but I had school on my mind. I was already a year behind where I would have been if I had taken high school seriously. Atlanta was cool but it wasn't New York. I missed home and I was glad to be back even though it was only for the weekend. Billie was getting married tomorrow. Me, Sage, and Sienna were doing the decorations and favors for her Bachelorette party tonight. Jewel was keeping Billie busy, so she didn't bother us.

Isa and I did a fake kind of hug when we saw each other and waited for instructions. Everybody had a job, so we got busy. I kept stealing looks at Isa. She looked good but sad. Her eyes were so bloodshot. It looked like she was crying, but she could've been drinking for all I know. We were all talking but Isa and I didn't say anything directly to each other. I found out that she was like supercop or something. I was surprised they put a gun in her hand. They all looked surprised when I told them that I was in New York this summer and didn't see them. They lost their minds when I told them that I performed during Harlem Week. They said they would have come to see me. They still looked like we did in high school and I still felt that I had to protect myself from what they weren't saying. My cell phone rang saving me from having to answer them. I answered it without looking to see who it was.

"Hello," I said and walked away from the table.

"Ummm...hi...Kim. It's Nazareth."

"What's up?" I didn't know how to be.

"Did you make it back up here? You said your friend was getting married this weekend," he said.

"Um, yeah, I'm here. What's up?" I tried to sound like I was easy, but my heart was beating so fast. I should be mad at him...I think.

"I know you're busy with the wedding and all, but could I see you for a little while before you leave? I just want to talk to you."

"Oh, so you know how to talk now?" I couldn't help it. He sighed.

"Aiight, I get it, but can you make some time please? I want to talk about that day and explain if you let me," he asked me.

"Um, yeah, okay what about tomorrow after the wedding reception?" He was quiet for a minute

"Okay, were should we meet?"

"In the hotel lobby; we could go to Central Park and talk. This way I won't look stupid when you walk away from me," I said. He sighed again. "Which hotel?"

"The Waldorf-Astoria, around five," I said.

"Aiight see you then." I hung up before I said something stupid. I don't know why I was so excited; I should be mad. Something in me told me that I should see him and see what's up with him for real.

CHAPTER **38 Something Like Breathing**

Sage

Javon Johnson and I had a mutual dislike for each other. We were probably too much alike; very ambitious. Right now, she had something that I wanted. She was John Wayne's publicist. He was the newest, hottest, underground rapper out. He didn't even have a contract with a major label, but his voice was on the hook of everyone who *had* a contract. All the right money people were looking for him and no one could pin him down. Javon lied initially about even knowing him. But I had done my homework and called in more than enough favors to find myself right back where I began with Javon.

"Javon you know me. This interview will keep his street cred up. Everyone who's anyone reads *Shine Magazine.* It's not that little underground mag it was when we first started. And I don't usually ask artists for an interview they come for me. What, your man thinks he's that hot?" I questioned.

"It's not that Sage. He's really gun-shy about reporters. He doesn't want to be misquoted or any of the other bullshit that comes when people read into editorials like yours." I was beyond angry as Javon started rattling off a list of excuses. I all but guaranteed my editor that I would score the interview with John Wayne and Javon was trying my patience and my integrity. She was trying to protect her connection with John Wayne, and I got that, but Javon had already lied to me and who knew what she was telling John Wayne about me. I could be the first person to get him to sign his name to *anything*, but Javon wasn't risking it; not even for me who helped to make her famous and quite a few of her clients. She was New York's most sought after publicist thanks in part to me. She knew that she owed me, but something was holding her back.

I was toggling with the idea of using my plan B on her—writing an article about him indicating that he declined to an interview as I watched Isa's agitated face. I could talk a supermodel out of his pants in the middle of winter in Antarctica. I knew how to talk to people and how to get them to talk to me. I moved to my dining room table and sat down next to Isa. She, Kim, and Sienna were tying little ribbons on miniature penises that read: *Thanks for the memories—Billie's Bachelorette Party.* They had a little assembly line going. Kim was popping the milk chocolate and white chocolate penises out of the mold. Sienna was wrapping them in the clear cellophane; I was snipping the long roll of ribbon into the right proportions so Isa could tie them on. However, when I started to get upset with Javon I stood up, walked away from the large mahogany table on the second floor of my brownstone and started flipping through my date book.

I was supposed to be off this week helping everybody who was sitting at my table plan Billie's bridal shower. I decided in a split second that yelling or threatening Javon would not be the right choice. It almost never was. So, I remained silent for a moment and then spoke softly to Javon.

"Javon, I'm sorry. Don't worry about it. He doesn't want to meet with me, that's fine. It's not worth going over the edge about. Give me a call whenever you need me, and we'll get together." There was such a long silence that I thought Javon had hung up.

"Hello, Javon?" There was a lot of movement and then Javon came on the line.

"I'm here. I had to move to a quiet place. Listen Sage, I want you to do the interview. John Wayne wants to do the interview, but somebody is standing in the way."

"I don't pay for interviews Javon. You know that."

"No, it's not that," Javon insisted. "I'm having a party tonight at the *Muse* to celebrate John Wayne signing with my company. Come out tonight. Of course, you're on the guest list and you have a limit of five you can bring with you. You *need* to be there tonight. If you want that interview you need to see what's standing in your way. That's all I can say."

I was intrigued by the mystery. I hope it wasn't some baby mama drama or his real mama. I didn't feel like working anyone's ego tonight, but my editor made it quite clear that without this interview some changes would have to be made.

"Are you still there Sage?" I returned my thoughts to Javon.

"I'll see you tonight." With that I hung up. I eyed my life-long friends. Isa concentrated on what she was doing while the words slipped effortlessly from her lips.

"Bitch you miss Billie's bridal shower you better notify your next of kin."

"I'm not missing the bridal shower," I said as I re-established myself at the table.

"And you better not show up late," Sienna added.

"I'm not."

"And you can't leave early," continued Isa.

Kim looked back and forth; dying to know how I was going to slither out of this one. I got paid to get out of jams.

"Look the shower is over around ten or eleven. No club is going to be jumping before midnight, so I have plenty of time to celebrate with my friends before going to work." Sienna was shaking her head no.

"Don't do it Sage. I have a feeling about this. You're going to be looking tired tomorrow and Billie is going to have a heart attack."

"First of all, I'm grown. Second of all I always do what I say I'm going to do. So, I will be there tonight at the shower and then I am going to the *Muse* because at the end of the day, I have to feed my son and myself. I have some passes; do you want to come?"

"No, we don't." Isa was not going to let me ease the tension with my star-studded olive branch.

Kim spoke up quickly although her words were garbled with the chocolate penis she just popped in her mouth.

"Yes, we do! Or rather I do," Kim said excitedly, "I haven't been to a club in who knows how long."

We all questioned Sienna with our eyes.

"Stop staring at me. I can't go. I have to make sure everything is right for that wedding tomorrow. I don't know what made Billie think that if I was catering the wedding that I would want to be in it."

"Come on you got that already in place and you know it. Come out tonight. Have a drink. Meet a man. Get your back blown out." I sang.

"Don't play with me, I am happily married." I laughed knowing that would get a rise out of her.

Kim

I was astonished.

"Sienna, I knew you could cook, but how you gonna cook all that food for all those people out of your kitchen?" I slipped back into my street vernacular out of Bagby's reach. By the way they were ogling me, I had the uneasy familiar feeling that I had said something that wasn't too bright. But it was an honest question.

"Do anybody live in there? She has her own catering business with twenty people working under her." Isa said as she pointed to my head while everyone laughed. A lifetime ago I would have been oblivious to Isa's slight. Half a lifetime ago me and Isa would be going round for verbal round. It was time for Isa to meet the reinvented me. I reached for the vocabulary Bagby had armed me with.

"If these changes had occurred in her life or your life, how would I know about it? We stopped talking a long time before I went upstate. As a matter of fact, I'm just finding out about everybody's life this week. Okay, so I did things differently than everybody else. I made some mistakes because I wasn't paying attention. But I pay attention now and I learned how to treat people so much better; especially the ones I love." No one was laughing anymore. I began evenly and softly, but my voice was cracking.

"Everybody gets to change except me? Do you see the same Kim? You all seem different to me. Sienna you're married with kids. You don't look like you've even had one. Sage you're this hot writer and your son did wonders for your body. Jewel is on TV! I watch her everyday on my soaps. She's somebody we grew up with! Isa you protect and serve; a police officer. And Billie, wild-ass Billie, is getting married tomorrow! What makes you think that I didn't change or learn anything or grow?"

I paused to wipe the tears that had long since cascaded down my face. The others sat in stunned silence. I hoped that the tears threatening to spill from their eyes obeyed and remained in their starting gate.

"And no matter what you think, no matter what anyone thinks, I am not dumb!"

Isa jumped up from the table letting loose of her anger.

"Who the hell said you was dumb huh?!"

"You did! You always did! All of you!" Isa paced around the table.

"I never called you dumb! Some of the shit you did was dumb! Like that shit in Harlem Kim. Did you think we didn't know? You think we just let people talk shit about you and didn't say anything? All kinds of bullshit was floating out here about you. They said you was pregnant and that's why you went upstate. They said you got chased home by some girls. They said you was messing with the *wrong* bitch's man. They said you had the fucking *package*! Who do you think was cleaning all that shit up?"

Sienna got up to pull Isa into a seat to bring some of the threat out of her words.

"Get off me Sienna! She needs to know! Do you know how many hours we had to sit with your mother and convince her that the shit that nosey Ms. White told her was a lie? She told your mother that you had the package Kim! AIDS! She told her that you gave it to a few people in Harlem and that's the real reason you begged her to leave town. She said people was looking for you. And people *was* looking for you Kim. The police in particular. They came and asked everybody about you, and you know some people told them lies. They was asking about Sean and Butter but nobody knew about that and then out of nowhere they never came around again. We did what we always did for you Kim, we protected you." Isa sat down spent. Sienna grabbed her hand on the table and grabbed my hand before speaking.

"Kim it should've been you who told us. We never should've heard it on the street," she said.

"What did you want me to say? Hey y'all I fucked up again? I did something dumb again? We wasn't even speaking like that anymore. I just wanted to get away and start all over again." Isa looked at me directly.

"I know what that's like Kim, after Murder, yeah...I know what that's like. I'm somebody you could've talked to." I nodded.

"Did you feel like talking at the time?" I asked. Isa smirked.

"Not one fucking bit."

"Okay then."

We all burst out into laughter and dried our faces.

"You gonna turn me in Isa?" I asked.

"For what?" she said. I looked at my lifelong friends. Then I remembered Natasha and thought she might like to go to the club tonight.

"Sage, can I invite a friend to the club?" I asked.

In chorus they asked, "Who is he?" They giggled and I shook my head.

"It's a she," I said. Sienna's eyes went big.

"What?"

"It's not like that. I mean she *is*, but I'm not," I explained.

"Oh, I was about to say...you for real changed." They slap five laughing.

"Yeah, it's fine with me. Isa you going?" Sage asked.

"Fine, I'll go. This could've only been more drama filled if Jewel was here." And on cue, Jewel walked through the door.

"Okay your boring lives can now be illuminated I am here!" Jewel threw her arm up and struck a Diana Ross pose of adoration. Sienna threw her a wry look.

"Your majesty you can take over my stack," Sienna said.

"Where are you going?" Jewel asked.

Sienna kissed Isa, Sage, and me goodbye on the cheek. She did air kisses with Jewel as hello and goodbye.

"I'm on kid duty until my husband gets back from his fraternity's annual baseball game. And between my youngest and Sage's son, my poor daughter Zoe is losing her mind. So, I better get over to Ms. Evelyn's house and pick them up."

"Tell Zoe we love her and not forget next summer she and I have a date in Paris," Jewel said. Sienna rolled her eyes.

"Sure, I will. See you guys tonight at the shower." After the door closed, Jewel pulled her sunglasses on top of her head, smoothed out her form fitted strapless sundress, and sat down before giving us her million-dollar smile.

"Okay what'd I miss?" Isa popped a vanilla penis into Jewel's mouth.

CHAPTER **39 Something Like Breathing**

Isa
****

I kept getting this passing sadness whenever I thought about Rodriguez but how would I look? Having a meltdown about Rodriguez when Billie was so happy? I just have to get through these two days and Sunday would be all mine to think about what went wrong. The bridal shower went off without a hitch. The decorations were done in every shade of green per the bride's request. That request was honored on the condition that the bridesmaid's dresses *not* be that color. Sage had threatened to wear the monstrosity when Billie least expected it if Billie did not choose better bridesmaid colors and styles. We all knew Sage did whatever she said she would do. Billie saw to reason and chose a soft coral color for the bridesmaid's dresses. It was a nice style too.

Kim

Billie's mother's contribution to the wedding was the booking and payment of a suite at the Waldorf Astoria Hotel. So that was where Sage, Isa, and I changed for the club when the shower was over. Jewel had cut out early to redo a scene so that she would be able to have the entire day to celebrate Billie's wedding. Billie had been none too pleased that all of her bridesmaids were leaving her alone and she wanted to go too. However after her eleventh or twelfth glass of champagne, four blunts, two male strippers, the erotic fantasy lady, a room full of bridal gifts-some still unopened, an impassioned plea for her husband to come and 'give her some'-which he couldn't because he was at his own party and tied to a chair in a full length fur so that he could sweat but not cheat on his wife-to-be while the stripper gave him a lap dance, Billie passed out. Just like old times.

Sage

People were pissed as they often were when I walked up to the front of the long line at the club. But usually they let it go because I was usually alone. Trailing me was Isa, Natasha, and Kim. People grumbled loudly. The dark club with the velvety black walls was illuminated by the black light which cast an eerie purple luminosity on any article of clothing that was white. And if it wasn't white, it would be quite embarrassing if your white wasn't glowing with the purplish haze.

The Muse had two bars on the first floor and three on the second; but only one of the bars on the second floor was off limits to the average person. That transparent glass bar sat on an elevated platform. There were several tables, chairs, and violet plush velvet couches quadrant off by a velvet rope, also on the elevated platform. The second floor could be viewed from the bottom due to the open area above the dance floor where a ceiling should have been. The top floor looked like a large indoor track in construction including the ornate banisters above waist length to avoid any accidental or purposeful falls. The stairs which led to the second floor lit up as one stepped on it; like the Michael Jackson video. It was there that several movers and shakers accosted me after making insincere and swift small talk with Isa, Kim, and Natasha before whisking me away.

Isa

Kim and Natasha were seduced to the dance floor by some club song. I decided to walk over to the bar and get a drink. As soon as I sat down a swarm of men surrounded me. I ignored them like I always did when I went out. This was a fallback from the old days. Lately, I had turned myself into a workaholic. The men I had encountered always seemed to need me to be something that I wasn't. I wasn't interested in changing for anyone. The men each tried to order a drink for me, and I dismissed each one. However, one was insistent—there is always one who doesn't get the hint. He was average height with the average looks and intelligence to match. I tried to ignore him, but he would not be ignored. I tried nicely to tell him that I wasn't really interested. But again, he persisted.

"Oh, I get it. You one of them get-money hoes. Well, I got money!" He pulled out an average wad of money and flashed it in my face. My eyes grew large. He thought it was from the wad, but it was from him annoying me. I felt the outline of my gun in my purse. That made me feel better. "Yo, listen son, don't even start liking me 'cause I'm not for you okay?" With a flick of my wrist, I pulled a wad twice the size of his out of my purse. "You come see me when you working with something like this. You can put your milk money back in your pocket before I beat you up and take it from you." People sitting close enough to us and could hear over the music, laughed harder than they normally would have due to the alcohol intake including the bartender.

"Bitch!" he hollered.

I jumped up and threw my drink in his face. He jumped up to redeem himself physically when a strong hand sent a piercing pain through his shoulder blade. He screamed out in agony. It wasn't me.

"You seem tired to me. Maybe you should go home and sleep it off my man." It was a strong suggestion sent with the hint of the promise of more pain if he had not complied. He nodded his head and turned to face his aggressor. The man behind him stood with his hands by his sides. He was taller than him by a foot and a half. He was of an average build, but it was his calm demeanor and the finality of his words that chilled him to his soul. His handler stepped to one side and allowed an even bigger man to escort him out of the club. I think I just profiled this whole situation.

I watched in anticipation of my next move. I didn't know who this man was and in New York, there was zero tolerance when it came to disturbing the groove. I was supposed to have been thrown out too. I locked wills with this man and his dark skin that was calling to me and fell back on the only thing I could rely on, myself.

"Thank you," I said with a smile. He nodded and wiped the smile from his face.

"Yeah, well don't start liking me," he said and turned his back on me. I decided that I'd rather have a drink than to go back and forth with him.

"Whatever." I tried to order another drink when my arm was pulled back with a little too much force. Now I was going to get kicked out because I'm not going to be handled like this all night long. I turned to face a distressed looking Kim.

"We need to get over to VIP where Sage is quick."

"What for?" I regretted not staying at home.

"I'll explain when we get there but we have to hurry. He just walked in, but if we get to her first it won't be so bad," Kim said. I allowed myself to be pulled by Kim. I was looking around for who might want beef with my girl. We were steps away from Sage in the VIP section when I saw Natasha downstairs holding court unsuccessfully with a man that was too familiar. I didn't know if I was grateful, I didn't have a drink to choke on or if I was upset, I didn't have a drink to dull the creeping migraine.

Sage was in full sell mode leaning on the bar with John Wayne. I hated to break it up, but we had to go. I gave Sage the silent raised eyebrow and head tilt signal to indicate that I needed to speak to her now. Sage returned the look along with an annoyed jut of the mouth. John Wayne noticed the exchange.

"I think your peoples need to speak with you." He gave her a sly smirk.

"She understands that this is business. She'll wait a minute," Sage said as calmly as possible. She didn't like to be handled by anyone.

I didn't take kindly to being pushed aside for any reason. I maneuvered my way between John Wayne and Sage. Sage's back was to the staircase. Javon saw the storm from her seat and moved swiftly to intervene. I'm sure she didn't want her client caught in the crossfire.

Javon interrupted, "I knew that John Wayne would want to do the interview even more after he met you Sage. I hoped that meeting you, it would make him convince his manager to let him do the interview. But more importantly I don't want to lose my newest acquisition. But honey I cannot and will not let him have a moment of bad press." She whispered into John Wayne's ear. John Wayne focused too late thanks to too much Dom P. He, Javon, Kim, and I wore the same look of horror as Sage gave her winning line.

"If you don't give me the interview then who are you going to give it to?" She flashed her winning smile, and it broke into thousand pieces when she heard the reply come from much too close to her ear.

"Anybody but *you*," said a familiar voice. A visible shiver went through Sage. She looked like she was trapped, and the club was closing in on her. She placed her untouched glass of champagne on the bar. Her hand was shaking so badly some of it slipped out. Javon had to tug on John Wayne's arm to pull him away from his mentor and manager. The man he had known his whole life.

"What's up partner? See you in a minute. You know how these females be, always pulling on my...." Javon slapped his arm and John closed his mouth.

"Fool, let's go!" Javon hissed. John Wayne stumbled alongside Javon. I stood my ground in front of Sage. Kim and Natasha fell back after I gave them a nod of my head. I found my voice first.

"We don't have to do this here Joon. We're leaving."

"I ain't got no beef with you Isa. I just came here to see my boy and make sure he shakes the snakes that slide up to him," he said trying to make eye contact with Sage.

Sage

I closed my eyes tighter as if that would make him disappear. He was standing so close to me I could smell his cologne and the peppermint he was sucking on. I felt three years reverse and saw traces of pain in Joon's face as much as I could hear it in his voice. He hated me. What could I say? I'm sorry? Again? For the first time in my life, I decided that I was going to be quiet and let God take care of the situation. I turned to face him. I slowly let my eyes meet his starting from his chest area. A chill went through me once more. I saw no light in his eyes. I had done that. There would be no redemption for me that night and maybe never where he was concerned. I nodded my head yes as if he had said the words himself. I side stepped him and walked away from them all. The crowd erupted when they heard the opening melody for *Before I Let Go* by Frankie Beverly and Maze. I was moving in a drug-like stupor, but my mind was already calculating my next move.

"You ain't got to leave baby!" Joon was calling after me. I turned once more and saw the sinister smile on his face. He was expecting me to turn around and get the argument started. I was tired. I was sorry. I closed my eyes again and walked away.

Isa followed me but I placed a hand on my friend's arm and gave her a sad smile.

"It's okay Isa. I was bound to run into him somewhere someday. I'm going home. I'll see you guys in the morning. Besides, somebody trying to take the skin off your face." Isa turned toward the direction I was looking.

Kim couldn't see over the crowd to see who Isa was looking at. In the VIP section Isa could see the same guy from the bar staring her down; the one who came to her rescue. Kim and Natasha came up beside us. Kim looked so concerned.

"You okay Sage? We'll go back to the hotel," Kim said.

"Um, no I want to go home. You guys stay as my guests," I said.

Natasha was tired of the scene and being groped but she knew that Kim was having fun, "I'll take you home. Kim can stay with Isa," she said. I began to protest. Isa and Kim looked at each other and shrugged.

"They'll be fine Sage. Right ladies?" They nodded their heads. I hugged them both and held the banister to aid me down the stairs. My walk had lost a lot of its model swagger as I made my way through the club. I turned once more to wave my friends on reassuring them that I was okay. Then I walked out of the club.

Natasha leaned into me, "I don't know the story, but it must have been something deep. The woman I met just a few hours ago was vibrant and optimistic. This one that was leaving with me appears beaten down by life in a matter of minutes and it had something to do with the man upstairs." The warm wind outside greeted us like a soft pillow. The driver saw Natasha and signaled to her. He u-turned swiftly and parked the car. He jumped out and opened the door for us. We jumped in and he closed the door behind us.

Isa

Kim and I shared a knowing moment between us.

"Sage is strong Isa. DDT for life remember?" I smiled. I looked over in VIP to see if the stranger was there, but he disappeared again. But Joon hadn't. I had a few words I wanted to share with him. I didn't care how big he had blown up. I remembered him when he was just trying to make it like everybody else. Even if Sage was dead wrong, she was my girl, and we rode or died for each other the way we always did. Kim recognized the look in my eyes and started shaking her head no.

"Isa, please don't. You gonna make a scene."

"You damn right! Come on you know how I do."

"Well why you ain't just tell them to wait outside? You know we gonna get thrown out."

"Yeah...fuck it. Let's see what's really up with Joon."

I turned so fast that Kim had to double time to keep up with me. Me and Kim were always 'it' girls so getting in VIP was nothing. I strolled right up to Joon and tapped his back. He moved to the side thinking someone was trying to get past.

"Motherfucker who you think you are?" I yelled.

Joon pivoted slowly and met me face to face.

"Oh, I thought for a second that all of y'all lost y'all balls. You fighting her battles now?"

"We fight them together. You didn't have to stop her money. You taking food out her child's mouth. She *had* to get that interview. Her job was on the line."

"That's not my problem and you know I don't give a fuck about no kid that's not mine! I decide what's best for my client. She's not the best. She too low class and hoodratish for him. I'm trying to elevate his game. But I tell you what, maybe if she begs me or suck my dick maybe I let him answer a couple of questions for his *second* interview. He already did one with the *Source* this morning." Where laughter should have been was silence. Everyone knew Sage and she was far from ghetto. Beyond that if word got back that they backed what Joon was saying, she could ruin the careers of everyone there and those trying to get on. A couple of artists had accused her of tanking their careers not for something she wrote, but because she refused their interview. They didn't care if she was really getting fired or not. Her power was far reaching. I stepped in close to him and whispered in his ear.

"I got a secret Joon. He looks just like you. She made a mistake. She tried to tell your family when they wouldn't tell her where you were," I moved away from him to soak in his stupid look, "However much you think you hate her, ain't shit compared to how much she hates herself and the shit Bukaii been putting her through. Stupid." I pushed him away when he reached for me.

"Get the fuck off me!" I yelled.

"Wait, you owe me! You knew what she did, and you didn't say shit! I'm supposed to believe you now? Come the fuck on!"

"You don't have to believe me. I made my peace with this shit baby so think what you want."

I walked down the steps giving Joon the middle finger. Kim followed behind me down the stairs shaking her head. Joon watched as we wound ourselves throughout the swelling crowd. Joon upturned Sage's forgotten glass of champagne on the bar and walked over to John Wayne. I guess he needed something harder to wash away the uneasy feeling in his stomach. We exited the club into the warm air. We decided to hail a cab to the hotel. A figure came up on the side of me. Kim turned around. She gave a soft smile toward the dark man. I frowned.

"You two know each other Kim?" I asked.

"Yeah," Kim said. I checked my disappointment and stepped closer to the curb to hail the cab.

"Don't let me stop you," I said.

"Me and him? Hell no! This is Sean's best friend Jokk," Kim explained.

I kept my head turned to hide my smile. Jokk leaned around me.

"You can stop being evil now. At least turn around," he said. I whipped around to face Jokk.

"You're the one who told me not to start liking you," I said.

"Oh, so you like me? I *am* every woman's dream. Damn I'm good. I wasn't even trying with you. I need to make copies of myself and sell me in a pretty bottle," his arrogant ass bragged.

Kim snickered, "We could call it conceited." I laughed. Jokk shook his head.

"No ladies, convinced would be a better name." Jokk placed a handout to me.

"They call me Jokk." I looked him the eye but kept my hands at my sides. "I don't do nicknames," I said.

"My name is Jacques Bertrand. I'm Haitian. I just changed the spelling for...business purposes." I shook his hand and smiled.

"Isa. You can get a last name when you call me," I flirted with him.

"Sounds good. Can we have lunch tomorrow?"

"Sorry, I'm in a wedding tomorrow." Jokk slapped his head.

"Oh yeah, Natasha mentioned that. I spoke to her when she was leaving." My face fell again, and I looked from Kim back to Jokk.

"Hold on, Natasha and I are just friends. We met through Kim and we go to basketball games together. Besides, she'd rather be with someone like you than someone like me, na'mean?" Jokk slipped into the native New York ending of every statement. I remembered that Kim said Natasha played for the other team.

"Sorry. I just try to stop the drama before it begins."

"I understand that. So back to lunch...the next day then?"

"No. Why don't you meet me at the reception? You can be my guest," I offered. Jokk pretended to think about the invitation for a moment.

"Sounds good. I can get someone to cover here for the night." We exchanged numbers and glances.

"Oh, are you the manager or something?" I asked.

"Or something. We can talk about it tomorrow," he said. Jokk waved over a nearby cab for us and slipped the driver a hundred-dollar bill.

"My man, take them where they want to go, and you can come back for me around four same as always." The cab driver tipped his hat at Jokk and said to himself: only in America.

****

Joon

Sage had the nastiest mouth I had ever run across. She had learned fluent Spanish so she could match me word for word. It was that nastiness ironically that drew me to her. We used to debate street affairs as if the topics were being presented at the world summit. Then discuss world affairs as if they could be solved by each country sending a representative to fight in a ring for a title bout. But what she put me through...I could never forgive. My heart ached so much. I didn't know that I could love somebody that much. I had spent a few days in the hospital. I really stayed to keep from killing her. And I wasn't in a state of mind to stop anyone else from killing her either. I had enough presence of mind to only tell my family that I would handle it. I refused to eat or talk. When the doctors threatened to place a feeding tube in my arm on the fourth day, I decided I would go home. I ate breakfast. I asked to speak to my family. I flirted with some of the nurses and doctors—female. They wouldn't let me leave until I spoke with a psychiatrist at the hospital. I spoke with her and charmed the pants off of her; even got her number.

They released me and I hopped the next flight to Puerto Rico. I spent the first two weeks in a drunken stupor. Each day was the same. My grandmother would force me to eat a large breakfast whenever I woke up. My cousins would kidnap me until the wee hours of the night and leave me in a heap on the floor in kitchen; it was as far as they would go into the house to ensure my safety and theirs from abuela's, (my grandmother) wrath. My grandfather, abuelito, would literally take a pail of water and throw it on me to clean the vomit from my face and clothes. Then guide me to my room and drop me on the bed. When the fifteenth day arrived, I just wanted to swim on the beach, visit other family members, and then got back on my grind. Before I left New York, I was an artist development man at Jive Records. That was my main source of income. They basically told me that I had lost my job when they sent me my severance pay. I hadn't lost my contacts though.

I was working on John Wayne before I left. I flew him down to Puerto Rico and started working on some demos at the recording studio I had built there the year before. I always knew that the job at Jive wouldn't last and I would have to have a backup plan. Howard University taught me to always keep one in the chamber and hustle. Success wasn't an option; it was a state of mind. That's when the studio idea came to me after that first year with them. I reformed a couple of big name acts for Jive and they thanked me very well. I used that money to build the studio. When artists found out about the state-of-the-art studio on the beach, they wanted to record there. I made quite of bit of money from it. It continues to be my money maker. John Wayne was going to put me over the top.

My dark side couldn't be so bothered to give Sage a second thought. But

the third and fourth thought came with my drinks as the night went on...they danced around with Isa's words...*I got a secret...*
****

CHAPTER **40 Something Like Breathing**

Isa

7am: When I came out of the bathroom, Kim was already dressed in running gear. I didn't know she ran. She looked at me strangely too.

"I picked up running while I was upstate. It helps me stay in shape and clears my mind," she said.

"Hunh, me too. Want to run together? Central Park cool?" I asked.

"Lead the way." We came out of the hotel with people staring at us. It was unusual to see regular Black people in the Waldorf-Astoria. They wanted us to be celebrities or something. That would make them feel better about us being there. So, Kim and I in Nike warm-ups, sneakers, and fashionable shades made them believe we were incognito stars because Black people don't exercise, and we don't stay in the Waldorf. I shared my thoughts with Kim when we left the hotel.

"Yeah, I noticed too, but wait till Billie wakes up and starts acting like a diva and goes on a rampage. They gonna swear we're stars."

"Billie will be fine; I'm worried about Sage. You think she'll do something crazy? She probably doesn't have a job anymore and now that Joon is back—I'm just saying I know what it's like to be at the edge."

"Um hmm. I was thinking about her too. But Sage is not going to do anything crazy because she's not *that* crazy and she loves August too much to do anything crazy."

"Yeah, you're right," I agreed.

"Okay, well what about you? Yesterday you looked like you was crying before you came to Sage's house. What happened?" she asked.

"Someone tried to kill me, but I ran away." I stopped still.

"Really? Omigosh!" She looked at me without smiling.

"No, not really, but that's what it felt like," I said as a wave of sadness went through me.

We entered in the park and sat on a bench to stretch. I told Kim about Rodriguez and Grove and how my life had changed. She sat quietly and listened to every word I said. When I was finished, she told me about Nazareth—hot name. She offered to tell her uncle and Godfather about Rodriguez; she said he made an impression on everyone he met. I told her no. Rodriguez didn't exist anymore. I didn't need a fairygodboyfriend. I needed someone who was real. She told me Jokk was a good man. I told her to call Nazareth and speak to him before the wedding; people make mistakes. We finished our run and headed back to the hotel. I think Kim will be alright. I think I will be alright. I think me and Kim will be alright.

Kim

I took Isa's advice; I called Naz. I met him at a Spanish diner on 150th and Broadway for breakfast. The wedding wasn't until six, so I had plenty of time to eat, talk, and get back before Billie lost her mind. Jeans, riding boots, leather jacket, sweater, bag, hair in a ponytail. I was wringing my hands again, nervous as shit. I was there before him. I wanted to watch him walk in. That way I could catch my breath without him seeing me. That was the plan, but my breath was still stuck when he walked in. Avirex leather jacket, Yankee fitted, white t-shirt, white Air Force Ones and a gold watch—clean shaven. He sat down across from me and my stomach growled.

"Hungry?" he asked.

"Guess so," I said. The waitress had come over when I first got there. She put down two menus and I ordered coffee for myself. I didn't know what Naz would want or if he would stay that long but all of a sudden, I had a lot I wanted to say to him. The coffee was helping.

"Did you order already?" he asked.

"No and you might not want to stay after I say what I'm going to say," I rushed out.

"You trying to be funny again?" he asked with a slight smile.

"No, just keeping it real. You hurt me Naz. I told you the truth because I don't ever tell the truth to guys. I liked you. I didn't want to keep something like that from you because I never know when it might come up and bite me in the ass. And just so you know, I used to be able to lie with the best of them. You never would've found out, but I'm different now. I wanted you to know what kind of person I was and why I took things real easy with you. And you said nothing, just walked away." He leaned back in the booth.

"What did you want me to say? I ain't like these other guys out here. I don't deal drugs or do them. I don't have sex with a whole bunch of girls or brag about the ones I been with. I don't hang out in the street and I don't call women bitches and hoes. I'm a different cat altogether. I'm a man Kim. The kind of mess you got yourself into was dangerous. If it was me, I don't know if I would have killed that man or not and that is a lot for me to deal with. That I would trade in my life like that for anyone fucked me up. I didn't know you that long." I leaned back in the booth.

"Okay...I see that. Do you see where I'm coming from? I haven't heard from you in months! You looked at me like I was trash or something."

"That's something you going to have to learn to deal with Kim. Everybody not gonna embrace what you did like a childhood mistake. Somebody is going to be turned off by that shit."

"I know I have to deal with it. I don't need you to tell me that. And I did deal with it. I gave you your space. But what I did, I didn't do to you. You wasn't the one who got hurt. You don't have to understand, but you didn't even try. You judged me on somebody I used to be and that wasn't fair."

"I know; that's why I called you. I'm not trying to rub this in your face and I didn't think I did before, but we're saying the same thing. See, baby, it's all about perception."

"Explain."

"You saw what was in the past, I saw what you could do if you're that ambitious again. You are so talented Kim and beautiful and smart. And that was all I could see. Then I had a different perception. I saw what life was like without you and if you didn't get a chance to be with someone who accepted you like you was—what would life be like for you then?"

"So?" I said. He chuckled.

"So? You don't get it do you? If I care about what would happen to you then that means I care about you. I'm dumb sometimes and judgmental sometimes and hard on people sometimes, but you check me on all that and I like it. Life is fun with you."

"What? We getting married? I'm not ready for all that," I said.

He laughed out loud.

"Me either. But me and you work together. We fit together. If you could forgive me for waiting so long to tell you...maybe, we could...be."

"Be?"

"Be." Be. I didn't understand what that meant but I did know what it meant to give someone forgiveness since I didn't get much of it. The waitress returned and my stomach growled again.

"Mami, I see you ready to order. Whatchu want chica?" I gave her my order and asked for more coffee.

"Okay papi, whatchu need?" Naz looked at me, "mijo from the menu. Ay, every day with this love shit..." We laughed and he ordered. He slid my coffee cup on his side and sipped it. He grabbed my hand and pulled me closer to him. He put his hands on my face and kissed me so softly. Breathing is overrated.

Sage

I pushed the sheets off and let the breeze from the ceiling fan dry the perspiration that layered my skin. I awoke to the nightmare that was my career. The sun burst through the summer curtains and reminded me that God was real, and everything would be okay. Then I felt a sharp kick in my side. My son smiled up at me. August was squeezing his eyes tight but giggling as he continued to wedge his toes in my side.

"Boy, I don't know how you always manage to get in my bed. How did you know I was home?" I said in a sing song voice while nuzzling my nose into my son's neck.

August squealed and strangled me with his embrace. He was chubby only in his cheeks and toes. I was so in love with him. With that in my mind, I decided I didn't want to work for the magazine anymore. I didn't like being away from my son; it wasn't worth it. Therefore, it was alright that I would be "officially" fired on Monday during a meeting. Anya had a sent me a scathing email about being scooped for the John Wayne interview. I knew what that meant: they already had my replacement. Although the owner of *Shine* had all but secured my job, I knew he and Anya were longtime friends and that would have some merit along with me losing the John Wayne interview—on top the days missed and I *had* been distracted.

I still had quite a few contacts; I could reach out. But did I want to be forced more into the limelight than I wanted to be? I'm lying; I don't mind the limelight—it's being away from August I can't deal with. But there *was* an offer that had been on the table for a long time. The pay was comparable to what I made at *Shine* and the hours were better. I could watch my son grow and there was a reputable daycare in the building. The people at *Kiss* FM were making the offer so lucrative to my lifestyle I didn't know how I could say no.

After receiving the email yesterday or rather this morning, when I came home from that humiliating night, I called the owner of *Shine* on his private line. He was not pleased at being disturbed. He was a playboy and not necessarily sleeping. I didn't care. After the way Anya had all but unceremoniously fired me...he listened rather than deal with human resources. I asked for only one thing, besides my last pay and that was not to be black balled by him or anyone at his company. He agreed not to black ball me but couldn't guarantee that I wouldn't be written up in the magazine after I took my new job. I would be a local celebrity and therefore fair game. I acquiesced as long as there would always be space for my rebuttal. When I was in college and interning, interviews happened in an office Monday through Friday. As an adult with a career in media, interviews and hires and fires were rarely done in a traditional fashion. In a few hours I would meet one of the radio execs for brunch at Tavern on the Green. The restaurant was more upscale than I was used to or needed. But it was his money, and I was not turning down good free food. Joshua said he would be here at nine. I still had enough time to get August ready so that Joshua could drop all the kids off at my father's house and he could still make it to the church on time. Billie insisted that he be at the wedding and then he could run to oversee the reception. Thank goodness Billie's wedding was at night. I gave August another hug and kiss and yet another hug and kiss. I was warmed by the idea of being able to do that every day. I scooped him up and carried him to his room. Sienna and Josh's kids were already there watching cartoons and eating cereal. I must have been sleeping hard. I didn't hear anyone come in the door. August wanted to stay and play but bathing was non-negotiable. After bathing him and pulling out a play outfit for him to wear, I walked down the hall to one of the guest rooms. Sienna loved the room at the end of the hall because it gathered the most early morning sunlight. I barged in the room hollering. "Okay, y'all stop being fresh in here," I joked. I received the surprise of my life. Sienna and Joshua were completely naked. Sienna was seated on the floor at the foot of the bed with both feet planted on the side of the bed pulling Joshua's arms. Joshua was laying face up screaming into a pillow. His legs were lodged into the spaces between each rail in the headboard. It looked as if his leg muscles had swollen or something to that effect because he was definitely stuck.

Joshua snatched his hands away from Sienna and covered his private area with the pillow. When he saw me, he placed the pillow back over his face. He quickly realized that he was exposed again and covered his private area. Sienna calmly stood and placed her hands on her hips. She was always very uninhibited about her body. While placing a sheet over her husband's entire body-so that he resembled a mummified pharaoh, she wrapped the fitted sheet around herself and turned to face me.

"Sage please get me some Crisco or oil or something," she ordered. I was much too stunned to move. I had to be pushed out of the door by Sienna. I stumbled down the hall and turned the corner toward the kitchen with my directive in mind. I passed by the kids who were happily watching some colorful dinosaur on the television set. Something in my mind told me that it was a good thing that they were occupied. I grabbed the Crisco and walked intently back toward the guest room. I paused once more to check in on the kids. They were still enraptured with the talking tyrannosaurus. I knocked on the guest room door, opened it slightly, and rolled the canister of Crisco through the opening.

"Here you guys go. Um...I have to get to a meeting. Not to sound insensitive but do you need me to drop the kids off at my dad's for you?"

Sienna stepped out. She dragged me until we reached my room. She slammed the door in order to block the guffaw that erupted from her belly.

"Oh my God my husband is a fool!" I didn't know if it was alright to laugh just yet.

"This is funny? His legs are stuck in the bars. I saw you and your husband naked. Gross by the way-my retinas are burning. How the hell did that happen?" I asked with humor in my voice.

"Girl that husband of mine decided we would come back here and cheer you up...Isa called and told us what happened. We know how August makes you light up, so it was my idea to bring him home. My mother had a date, so we brought the kids too."

"I want to be like her when I grow up," I said.

"Hanging out at bars with pimps and hustlers?"

"Hey, don't knock the hustle."

"And you *know* this *man*." We broke out in laughter so loud that we jumped out of our skins when the door opened, and Joshua was standing there. The scream made August and their youngest child run down the hallway screaming and pushing past Joshua before they climbed up on Sienna and I. We calmed them down, put them out of the room and then Sienna pulled Joshua out of the room.

"I just want to know what's so funny?" he asked. "I ain't shamed 'cause I wanna keep the spice in my marriage," he continued out of the door. I shook my head.

"You both are so very special. Pull those sheets off the bed before y'all leave!" I called after them.

CHAPTER **41 Something Like Breathing** or *Til We Meet Again...*

A random guest catches the bouquet at the reception. After the garter toss, Billie heads for the honeymoon suite to change while her husband and his frat brothers go into a rousing chorus of their fraternity song. The wedding was a success. It started and ended on time without any drama which was all Billie asked God for *and* that her husband would be waiting for her at the end of the aisle.

She got on the elevator and headed up to the room on her own. Anyone who had been watching closely would have seen the rest of her crew inconspicuously disappear one by one. However, everyone was way too tipsy to play inspector gadget, so they all made a clean get away.

She couldn't wait to get out of her wedding dress. The Vera Wang original that Jewel secured for her was a dream dress and she knew that her wedding pictures were going to be phenomenal because of it. But she was tired and wanted to put on her tight Chanel dress that she was wearing on her honeymoon flight to Paris. She fished the pass card out of the breast area of her dress and opened the door. She was greeted with the wonderful aroma of frankincense. She knew that it was doing an insufficient job of covering up the cannabis which wafted through the air.

"Alright ladies, it's my wedding day, pass the dutch!" Billie yelled to her bridesmaids and longtime friends. They had all changed into jeans and cute t-shirts that read '*bridesmaid on the edge*'. She had ordered the shirts along with other personal gifts for her close friends. Jewel, Sienna, Sage, Kim, and Isa waved her over so she could take her turn smoking before she changed.

Billie, a veteran smoker was able to smoke and disrobe at the same time. When her turn was over, she passed it to the left. Billie stepped out of her wedding dress and carried it with her to the bedroom. After hanging it up neatly in its garment bag so that her grandmother could pick it up later, she changed into a robe. She didn't want to smell like smoke when she said her goodbyes to everyone. She came back into the living room suite and plopped in between Sienna and Isa.

"I love y'all so much for everything you did for me today and last night.

This was the best day I have ever had in my life!" Billie said holding the blunt in her hand.

"Girl, can we smoke with you? Damn, pass it!" Jewel said.

Billie passed it to her and kept on talking.

"We have been through some shit together over the years girls. I'm going to miss y'all so much."

"Are we dying or something?" Sienna asked.

"Yeah, you only going to Paris for a few days," said Sage.

"I know because Mills has to get back to work," Billie lamented, "but you know I'll be living in Annapolis from now on. I'm not going to be coming back and forth. I have to keep up with my business and my man. Shit, I can't believe I got married," she marveled.

"But you love him, right?" Sage asked.

"It's too late now Belinda Mills," said Sienna, who believed in marriage whole-heartedly.

"It ain't never too late!" Jewel and Sage stated simultaneously. Love was still on probation with them. Sage long since closed the door on love. The only one who seemed to be campaigning for love was Kim.

"I say you never know..." Kim smiled and thought about Nazareth's soft kiss after they met for breakfast earlier in the day. Isa grinned as well. Jokk was picking her up soon and for the first time in a long time she was looking forward to giving someone a chance.

Fifteen minutes later, all of the ladies had their carry-on bags and headed out of the hotel room. The elevator stopped at the mezzanine for Billie to exit. She was the only one who needed to say her goodbyes and of course collect her husband from his frat brothers. Jokk was there in the lobby area to pick up Isa. They all nodded approval in the looks department to Isa. She generally didn't care one way or another about looks. She cared more about what kind of man she was dealing with. So, they knew that Jokk must be the worst kind of man to cross because he was gorgeous.

Jewel, Sienna, and Kim jumped in the limo that took them uptown. Sage rode in a limo which took her to Harlem. She had plenty to smile about. She got the morning slot at the radio station, which meant she would be in direct competition with *Star and Buckwild*, the radio personalities on the new station, but she was up for it. Her son was happy and healthy. One of her best friends just got married to a great guy and was on to a wonderful future. In fact, all of her friends were doing pretty good and it had been years since any one of them could say that.

She was so lost in her thoughts that the driver had to tap on the partition to alert her to her arrival at home. She tried to offer him a tip which he turned down.

"Sorry miss, my boss would have coronary," said the gentle old man.

"He won't know if you don't tell him," Sage offered.

"*She* would know in a heartbeat. Ms. Natasha is never to be crossed." Sage conceded. In the brief time she had known Natasha her mysterious air alone made a believer out of Sage. She was quietly strange which probably made her a no-nonsense boss. The driver opened the passenger door for her but blocked her exit.

"You want I should walk you inside?" he asked. Sage was confused by his question. He moved slightly to one side to show the man sitting on her step. Sage breathed in deeply. She handed her carry-on bag to the driver and stepped out of the vehicle.

"It's alright. He's someone I used to know." Sage relieved him of her carry-on again and patted the driver on his arm. He tipped his hat toward her.

"Okay then, miss, goodnight."

"Goodnight." The driver jumped into the car and drove off looking in his rearview the whole way. Sage stood at the edge of the sidewalk watching him drive away. She wondered if she should have stayed in the car. She turned to face her visitor. He looked grim.

"How did you know where to find me?" she asked.

"Ask me a question you don't know the answer to," he said.

"You have your ways. Who told you?"

"Ask me a question you don't know the answer to," he repeated.

Sage walked over and sat on the step next to him; Isa had to have told him.

"It's late Joon. You didn't know that I would come home tonight. Why are you here? You gonna try to take my son from me?" she asked pointedly.

"I would have waited here 'til the next morning Sage, if I had to. I've been here since you left this morning. You looked nice. Job interview?"

"You have no right to ask. Why are you here Joon?"

"Sienna got married huh? She looked happy," he stated avoiding her question.

"You spoke to Sienna?"

"Nah...I was about to, but there were kids around her, and she was tying this little kid's shoe that her husband was holding. I was stuck yo. He looks *just* like me. I didn't need to speak to her."

Tears rolled down Sage's face, scared of the battle that she feared was coming. She was just at peace and she felt raped of it all at once.

"Joon, please, what do you want? I am so sorry. I don't have any other way of expressing how sorry I am. I don't ever expect you to forgive me. But I can't just give you my son Joon. I have fought long and hard for him. I have fought to accept that I am a good mother and can provide for him everything he needs even if he doesn't...didn't have a father."

Joon's jaw tightened.

"What's his name?" he asked.

"August."

"Yeah? After that man that wrote that play, we went to see?"

"Yeah, you liked the play so much after you swore that you were going to hate it."

"You know, I seen couple of plays since then," he shared.

"Really?" Sage nodded her head and wiped her eyes although the tears kept coming.

"Yeah..."

"Joon...what do you want?" she asked again.

"No matter what I ask for, you would think that you would be in a rush to give it to me the way you fucked me over."

"That's where you're wrong. I'm not about to give you whatever you want," Sage said quietly, "So if you came to let me know that you want to fight, then fine we can do this."

"I'm mad as hell Sage. I don't know when I'm not gonna be mad. I'm not...I don't want to take August away from you, but I do want to be in his life. I want to know everything," he explained.

"Like what?"

"Start from the beginning and stop when we get to where we are now," he directed.

"Okay, I can do that. Let's go upstairs," she offered. Joon shook his head.

"I'm mad, but not crazy. Upstairs with you is a bad idea," he said. Sage chuckled. She thought to herself he wasn't that safe on the steps but if it made him happy fine. Joon wiped the remaining tears from her eyes and held her hand. Sage looked down at their fingers intertwined, took a deep breath for the second time that night, and began where they left off.